Redrawing the Global Economy

Also by Alice Landau

BARGAINING ON POWER, BARGAINING ON POLICY: The CAP Reform and the Negotiations on Agriculture in the Uruguay Round

CONFLITS ET COOPERATION DANS LES RELATIONS ECONOMIQUES INTERNATIONALES: L'Uruguay Round

RETHINKING THE EUROPEAN UNION: Institutions, Interests and Identities (*with Richard Whitman*)

THE ENLARGEMENT OF THE EUROPEAN UNION: Issues and Strategies (*with Victoria Curzon-Price and Richard Whitman*)

Redrawing the Global Economy

Elements of Integration and Fragmentation

Alice Landau
Assistant Professor
University of Geneva
Switzerland

First published 2001 by
PALGRAVE
Houndmills, Basingstoke, Hampshire RG21 6XS and
175 Fifth Avenue, New York, N.Y. 10010
Companies and representatives throughout the world

PALGRAVE is the new global academic imprint of
St. Martin's Press LLC Scholarly and Reference Division and
Palgrave Publishers Ltd (formerly Macmillan Press Ltd).

ISBN 0–333–80240–3

This book is printed on paper suitable for recycling and made from fully managed and sustained forest sources.

A catalogue record for this book is available from the British Library.

Library of Congress Cataloging-in-Publication Data
Landau, Alice.
    Redrawing the global economy : elements of integration and fragmentation / Alice Landau.
        p. cm.
    Includes bibliographical references and index.
    ISBN 0–333–80240–3
    1. International economic integration. 2. Regional economics. 3. Globalization. I. Title.

HF1418.5 .L36 2000
337—dc21
                                                                    00–053043

10   9   8   7   6   5   4   3   2   1
10   09   08   07   06   05   04   03   02   01

Printed and bound in Great Britain by
Antony Rowe Ltd, Chippenham, Wiltshire

For Lea, Herbert, Yaël
and David Harris

Contents

List of Tables

List of Graphs

List of Abbreviations

ALADI	Latin American Integration Association
APEC	Asia-Pacific Economic Co-operation
ASEAN	Association of East Asian States
BIRD	Bank of International Reconstruction and Development
BIT	Bureau International du Tavail
CET	Common External Tariff
CFSP	Common Foreign and Security Policy
CITES	Convention of International Trade in Endangered Species
COMESA	Common Market of Eastern and Southern Africa
COREPER	Committee of Permanent Representative
CUFTA	Canada–United States Free Trade Agreement
ECOSOC	Economic and Social Committee
ECOWAS	Economic Community of West African States
EMU	European Monetary Union
EPU	European Payment Union
EPC	European Political Co-operation
FDI	Foreign Direct Investment
FTA	Free Trade Agreement
GATS	General Agreement on Trade in Services
GATT	General Agreement for Trade and Tariffs
IGO	Inter-Governmental Organization
ITT	International Telephone and Telecommunications
LDC	Least Developed Countries
M&A	Mergers and Acquisitions
MERCOSUR	Mercado Commun do Cone Sul
MFN	Most Favored Nation Clause
MTN	Multilateral Trade Negotiation
NAALC	North American Labor Commision
NAFTA	North American Free Trade Agreement
NATO	North Atlantic Treaty Organization
NGO	Non Governmental Organization
NIC	New Industrialized Countries
NIEO	New International Economic Order
OECD	Organization of Economic Co-operation and Development

OSCE	Organization for Security and Co-operation in Europe
PCTD	Pacific Conference on Trade and Development
PEEC	Pacific Economic Co-operation Council
PREC	Pacific Rim Economic Council
RIA	Regional Integration Scheme
SACU	South African Customs Union
SADC	South African Development Community
SAFTA	South African Free Trade Agreement
SPS	Sanitary and Phytosanitary Measures
TBT	Technical Barriers to Trade
TNC	Transnational Corporation
TRIPS	Trade-related Intellectual Property Rights
UDEAC	Union Douanière des Etats de I'Afrique Centrale
UNCED	United Nations Conference on Environment and Development
UNCTAD	United Nations Conference on Trade and Development
USTR	United States Trade Representative
VER	Volontary Export Restraint
WEU	West European Union
WIPO	World Intellectual Property Organization
WTO	World Trade Organization

1
Portraying Integration and Fragmentation in the World Economy Today: an Introduction

The overall character of the contemporary international system has been dramatically altered over the last decades. On the one hand, globalization has become a widely-used label to characterize some current features and best illustrates the increasing integration and the homogenization of the world economy. However, it has also been increasingly criticized by a large reservoir of groups and individuals. Globalization may contribute to an increasing number of problems and iniquity. If globalization entails elements of both integration and fragmentation, what is globalization? On the other hand, there is a similar trend towards regionalization. The world economy is being split into regions. How can we reconcile this trend with the vision of a globalized world?

The other face of Janus

Globalization is a conjuncture of economic components, supported by powerful players and a web of institutions. As coined by Cerny (1999: 11) globalization translates as

> internationalization of markets where products are widely traded, capital is mobile, not particularly site-specific, and will move to different locations should profits be higher (and secure); consumption patterns in different countries are not mutually exclusive, or at least can be catered to by extending the product range, and prices are sensitive across borders and predominantly set in world (cross border) markets.

Globalization is not simply a product of one of these components, but of all of them. They are inextricably intertwined with each other, and

1

it is difficult to establish priority among them. It is their confluence at all levels, their magnitude, and their dynamics, which explain globalization, and why it both captures the imagination and, at the same time, irritates so many among society.

This book contends that globalization has added a new line of divide in the world economy, and identifies the winners and the losers. The winners are increasingly integrated in the world economy. They benefit from trade flows, investments, and capital, and transnational corporations are located in these countries. The losers are detached from this process. Rather than participating in the interconnectedness of globalization, they are left aside. Globalization encompasses elements of integration, but also elements of fragmentation in dividing the world between countries, and within countries.

Regionalization is not exempt from this duality. The 1990s witnessed an explosion of interest in regional integration, which was due not least to its spectacular development. It is innovative in the diversity of its forms and functions and has affected all continents. Virtually all members of the World Trade Organization (WTO) belong to some form of Regional Integration Agreement (RIA). The WTO Secretariat inventory notes that 59 free trade areas are currently in force.

For many, such as Lawrence (1991), or Bergsten (1997), regionalization is a potent force of globalization and an element of integration. It is a chapter of globalization, fostering the establishment of global strategies and policies and operating as building blocks. RIAs force the creation of instruments that would not have been sufficiently envisioned or implemented by the General Agreement on Trade and Tariffs (GATT)/WTO. Some of the RIAs have been innovated by introducing new topics and have provided food for thought for the multilateral trade negotiations.

Moreover, regional integration has had a domino effect, and a growing number of countries are involved in RIAs. Regionalization is a response to domestic forces. Policy makers may sidestep opposition and protectionist segments of society by locking in economic reforms. Mexico's decision to establish the North American Free Trade Agreement (NAFTA) followed those lines. Developing countries may use regional integration as a strategy for increasing the international competitiveness of their economies.

For others, such as Krugman (1991), or Bhagwati (1995: 1–11), it may be regarded as a reaction to the challenge of globalization, ultimately splitting up the international economy, hence marginalizing countries and invalidating the rules that once ensured and governed economic stability. Proliferation of free trade arrangements creates 'a spaghetti bowl' which clutters up trade with discrimination rules. Regional blocs compete among themselves to get bigger shares of the world trade. The most feasible way to lead to liberalization is to move to fully multilateral free trade at the WTO. Indeed, the WTO has been instrumental in promoting trade liberalization and globalization. Where does regionalization stand between these two visions? This book contends that regionalization is compatible with globalization. However, like globalizaton, regionalization divides the world. Some parts of the world have flourishing regional schemes, while some are experiencing only problems in building theirs.

Globalization and regionalization: new incarnation?

The debate over globalization and regionalization stems from past experience. Some venture to argue that globalization is only a new expression of a long-term historical process, which began five centuries ago. However, globalization is not the reproduction of past patterns. Current globalization is distinguished by the magnitude of its process, and the congruence of its components.

Concerning regionalization, in the interwar period, many states retreated to the safety of limited economic agreements, because states were unable to arrive at multilateral solutions to economic problems, and because political rivalries between major powers and emerging powers left small states with few alternatives (Mansfield and Milner, 1999: 597). There was a revival of regionalization in the 1960s in the aftermath of the creation of the European Economic Community. The EEC was a model of integration that managed to ensure the economic prosperity of countries which were, at the time of their accession, still weakened by the effects of the war. This model naturally inspired countries that found themselves in economic difficulties once they had achieved independence.

Contemporary regionalization is distinguished by the strategic moves from regions towards other regions, or from member countries to other countries: the EU has made moves towards NAFTA and MER-COSUR, as has ASEAN towards the EU, and NAFTA towards MERCO-SUR. Mexico has made moves towards some Latin American countries; Singapore – an ASEAN and APEC member country – is holding talks with Japan. The regionalization landscape is becoming peopled with a jungle of regional agreements.

Regionalization unleashes its own dynamism, but is also interrelated to globalization. Regionalization schemes are market-led, and subscribe to the same neo-liberal credo. RIAs take measures that will guarantee the multilateralization and liberalization of trade, and the maintenance of a loyal and competitive framework. They are even front-runners. Globalization and regionalization provide evidence that the same phenomenon can have multiple contradictory effects, and that both entail tensions.

Integration and fragmentation: twin processes

Globalization has been reinforced by democracy, which has largely become a common standard. The end of the Cold War has concluded decades of hostility between the Soviet Union and the USA, and had a deep impact on the global order as it terminated a series of tacit understandings about the conduct of international relations. It put an end to the conflictive international environment. Is this world a better world if it is only composed of allies, free to trade with each other?

As argued by Agnew (1995: 93):

> There is a confusion between democracy and economic liberalization. This confusion was characteristic of a certain American position during the Cold War in which the terms capitalism and democracy were used synonymously. Although the conduct of open elections was a necessary part of this definitional conflation, open markets were much more central to the calculus. Democracy was essentially redefined as a market-access regime in which the free factors of production was the central attribute.

Competitiveness has nested nicely in a democratic environment, and has become a standard of efficiency, free trade, and performing state: an example that should be duplicated elsewhere, including developing countries. The choice is judiciously channeled by the international organizations that map out the international system, and propel the same credo.

Agnew's argument is similar to Fukuyama's claim (1992: 43) on the ultimate return to the unchallenged and universal liberal democracy. According to Fukuyama, there are no serious ideological competitors with pretensions of universality left to liberal democracies. Choices faced by countries in determining the way in which they will organize themselves both from political and economic angles have diminished. Authoritarianism and central planning models have failed, leaving liberal democracy as the only valid and universal ideology and form of government. Conflicts between industrialized countries have diminished. Immanuel Kant stated that democracies do not conduct wars among themselves. They can devote themselves to globalization.

Past foes have become new allies aiming at the same goal, and willing to reap the same benefits. Shared values of free trade and market economy set the limits of the playing field. Cerny (1999: 6) argues that conceptions of democracy such as pluralism and/or individual independence are favorable to the potentialities of globalization. Many countries want to lock in political commitment to democracy in unilaterally liberalizing their economy to attract foreign investment. A growing number of developing countries have abandoned the common belief that *import-substituting industrialization* was the best development strategy. All have opened up to international competition. FDI is a very attractive candidate for inclusion, since it represents a bundle of assets every state wants to possess: entrepreneurship, technology, and managerial and marketing skills. However, FDI cannot replace everything and still rely on good governance, sound macroeconomic policies, and a responsive society.

Globalization has developed in the shadow of society, which is somehow paradoxical if democracy and globalization go hand in hand. Hence, the resentment of groups and citizens during the WTO Ministerial meeting in Seattle, or during the UNCTAD X in Bangkok. Globalization must be rooted in society. It may be difficult to achieve, but the trust and consensus underpinning globalization and market forces are important enough. Globalization must be built at different levels within the social institutions (Mittelman 1996b: 112).

Regionalization suffers from the same flaws. Most regional schemes in developing countries do not articulate on those in the burgeoning society who are left aside – women, peasants, indigenous peoples – the 'bearers of change', in the words of Mittelman (1996b). There is a parallel between the reaction of society today and the developing countries in the 1970s. Then as now, voices were raised against the winners of the unequal trade and the Multinationals' activity in developing countries: the transmanagerial class, the governmental agencies and bureaucracies. Workers, small businesses, the self-employed and the unemployed were the losers (Cox 1982: 53). In the 1970s, society was more restricted and had less voice than today. Regionalization, like globalization, is a building-down process; in no way is it a building-up process.

States in a changing global context: stresses and challenges

Globalization has blurred traditional lines of national boundaries and reduced some of the states' attributes. It constitutes constraints and imposes limits on the state as the sole agent determining its own future (Held, 1995: 99). The core of the Westphalian system – territorially fixed states with a single authority governing the territory and representing it outside its borders and with no authority above the states – which has dominated world politics since 1648, is disintegrating.

On the integration side, new post-Westphalian structures of power and social organization are emerging less centered on national territories or models of production. The national market is an illustrative example: economic flows are beyond state control. The national space is being replaced by the global space (Petrella, 1996: 67). The concept of the end of geography (O'Brien, 1992: 1) best captures the state where location no longer matters. Transnational companies straddle state boundaries and exploit the opportunities of a deregulated international environment (Cox, 1992: 144). Social movements, organizations, communities, and coalitions beyond and above the state pursue their own agenda independent of national decisions (Risse-Kappen, 1995: 9). They increasingly seek to influence policies and shape decisions according to their interests.

The changes in state roles engendered by globalization, shrinking distances due to communication technologies, and transnational issues (Rosenau, 1992: 3) provide increased opportunities for nationalities to claim their sovereignty or autonomy, and more opportunities for fragmentation and conflict. Among the 134 conflicts recorded by the Heidelberg Conflict barometer (1999), many have been initiated by minorities claiming autonomy: in the Russian North Caucasian Republic of Karachay-Cherkessia, the Cherkess minority is striving for autonomy; so are the national minorities in Abkhazia, Ajaria, and South Ossetia, or the Hungarian minorities in Romania. Nationalities that have no states of their own, or do not fit in a territory, challenge the state as a pillar of social cohesion. In Europe, the Middle East, Africa, or Asia, ethnic or religious groups have expressed their identities. The end of the Cold War engendered an avalanche of ethnic and territorial conflicts that were obscured by bipolarity.

New modes of regulation for new issues

Globalization has exacerbated new sources of conflict. The environment, migration, and ethnicity are issues to which global and regional ramifications have given greater significance than national issues. They cannot be dealt with nationally, thus requiring global co-operation. AIDS does not fall within the authority of one nation-state. It cannot be stopped in one country if it is not stopped in all countries, exemplifying an issue that spans global and local levels (Jönsson and Söderholm, 1995: 460). International organizations have emanated from states as a means of achieving collective objectives that could not be performed by acting individually (Werksman, 1996: xii).

A web of national, transnational, and intergovernmental forces map out the international system, which has given rise to an environment of continuous negotiations. International negotiations have become more complex with an increasing number of countries and a differentiated nexus of demands. Yet, neither is the era of nation-states exhausted (Held, 1995: 92) nor is the era of purposes, values, and interests over. As argued by Dani Rodrik (1997), most states 'retain substantial autonomy in regulating their economies, in designing their social policies, and in maintaining institutions that differ from those of their trading partners'. Moreover, the increased role of governments by the mid-1990s was particularly striking. Globalization increased the demand for social insurance while simultaneously constraining the ability of governments to respond effectively to that demand. Thus, it is paradoxical that dramatic pressures were exerted on states to increase the scope of social action, whereas their capacity to achieve those aims has been reduced.

States that will be more effective to face globalization will be those that solve their problems on the basis of complex organizational and governance pluralism. Although the nation state is losing its autonomy of action to shape policy in a globalized world, national actors still expect effective and efficient government, providing a stable political, institutional, and economic environment (Messner 1997).

The book ahead

The book is structured as follows: Chapter 2 explores globalization. Indeed, globalization is an encompassing concept, and its implications are not merely economic. It has been interpreted differently according to different schools of thought, which deserved to be investigated. Chapter 2 contends that it is accurate to distinguish two lines of thought about globalization according to a moral divide. Relying on this distinction, the *optimists* and the *pessimists* have different views about globalization as a process and as to its effects on the world economy. Chapter 3 deals with the states. Understandably, the role of the state in a globalizing economy is perceived differently by optimists or pessimists. However, all states do not have the same control over their activities. Many weaker states like the Sub-Saharan countries have never been allowed any control. South Asian and African countries offer two opposite patterns. Policies and institutions have to complement economic strategies to incorporate the global economy.

Chapters 4 and 5 look at the stratification of global trade and at the role of the WTO in promoting globalization. The GATT/WTO have been main instruments of globalization, by eradicating barriers to trade, and by pushing liberalization ahead. But they also entail imbalances and inequalities in the treatment of developed and developing countries. Far from correcting the imbalances of trade, the Uruguay Round has resulted in a modestly favorable treatment for developing countries as regards market access. Agreements in services, intellectual property rights, and textiles are also full of loopholes; developed countries are taken advantage of. Special provisions are restricted to periods of transition or technical co-operation.

Many of the findings of Chapter 4 concerning stratification of global trade will be confirmed in Chapters 6, 7, and 8 dealing respectively with FDI, transnational corporations, and capital: all the nerves and nodes of globalization. There is a cumulative and fragmentationist phenomenon taking place, and a widening gap between countries that succeeded in reaping the benefits of globalization and the less advanced developing countries, bypassed by globalization.

Chapters 9 and 10 deal with regionalization with its strong contrast between integration and fragmentation. Chapter 9 is devoted to a comparison between the regions, and focuses on the variance in regional arrangements. There is likely to be a wide range of factors that explain the variance of regional arrangements. Chapter 10 explores the inter-regional trade flows, and the compatibility between the GATT trade regime and the RIAs.

Part I
Globalization

2
Exploring Globalization

Globalization is multifaceted, multidimensional, and intermingles economics, politics, and culture. It refers to people, to issues, to organizations, and to companies which act on a global scale across national boundaries. Few words have given way to such harsh debates. Writers, economists, and political scientists give their own meaning of globalization. They all debate about its causation, conceptual explanation, its origin, its implication for state and governance, or its social effects. Many argue that globalization is irreversible, and that the only option is to navigate its current and give a blanket acquiescence. There is no alternative to it. The only solution is to convert the challenges of globalization into opportunities. It could improve the prospects for developing countries to catch up economically with industrialized countries, bringing in capital and technology flows. Globalization is the absolute objective. Conversely, others adopt rather harsh solutions, and refuse to bend to its Utopian portrayal of the best of the world, unprecedented benefits, and positive-sum game. Globalization is the juggernaut of which people are scared, a term used to lump together all sorts of evils.

Therefore, globalization has generated both hopes and fears. Even more so as globalization has an impact on day-to-day life, and from a topic to be discussed among economists, commercial lawyers, or business leaders, it has spilled out into the public streets and private life. Globalization is not only 'out there' but also 'in here' as put by Giddens (1990: 22). For some, globalization is a spooky phenomenon.

Globalization, free trade, and the WTO

Some associate globalization with free trade, which creates economic innovation, product variety, more efficiency, more gains, and more wealth for countries and for global players (Burtless *et al.*, 1998). Indeed, some players benefit from globalization more than others: business managers (Ruigrok and van Tulder, 1995: 132), stockholders, executives, and employees of exporting firms (Burtless *et al.*, 1998: 10) espouse the spirit of globalization. For others – lagging regions, an unskilled labor force, women, or indigenous people – globalization leads to their exclusion, and exacerbates existing inequalities. Free trade is blamed for causing or contributing to problems ranging from pollution, to global warming, from destruction of rain forests to human rights abuse, and for exacerbating inequality between countries and players, for suppressing jobs and creating wage inequality. According to the supporters of globalization, the argument of hurting employment does not survive evidence: if some workers do lose jobs, many others find them whether in industries or services (Burtless *et al.*, 1998).

The WTO is the focal point in this debate about globalization and free trade. The demonstrations in Seattle in December 1999 crystallized mixed feelings and increasing unease about globalization and free trade. Critics originated from trade unions, environmentalists, human rights activists, and consumers. The mobilization of various groups and tendencies was facilitated by this international *'triggering event'* as observed for other waves of protest by della Porta and Krieisi (1999: 8). These groups accused the WTO of striking down environmental, health, and safety standards in the name of free trade. Too often, they argued, the WTO views national environmental standards as trade barriers that need to be weakened. The WTO is accused of encouraging a global trading system that allows transnational corporations to slash jobs at home, and relocate facilities to countries where environment standards and workers' rights are lax or non-existent.

It is difficult to extirpate the sentimentality of the debate over globalization. What is true is that the 'fear of globalization taps into a large reservoir of public anxiety about slow income growth, potential job loss, rising inequality, and a loss of control of our economic destiny' (Burtless *et al.*, 1998: 128).

Indeed, globalization is a challenge for all the markers that have explained the international system so far: state-power, territoriality, sovereignty. Globalization transcends traditional distinction between local, national, and global, between domestic and international. It has compressed time and space; it has blurred territorial boundaries by propelling transnational relations and structures. Globalization has bypassed states by operating beyond direct state control (McGraw *et al.*, 1992: 7).

Patterns and scope of globalization are unprecedented. Some venture far enough to suggest that we cannot coin the phenomena into adequate vocabulary (Ruggie, 1993: 144; Strange, 1995: 292). Thus, we need to develop a new perspective that:

> should recast the relevance of territoriality, highlight the porosity of boundaries, read the temporal dimensions of governance as no less significant than the spatial dimensions, recognize that networking organizations have become as important as hierarchical ones, and posit shifts of authority to subnational transnational and nongovernmental levels as normal (Rosenau 1997: 29).

Indeed, there are ideological differences over the nature of globalization, and its social impact. Globalization asks fundamental questions of ethics and moral issues, going far beyond its conventional political or economic meanings. Asking the questions does not lead necessarily to finding the answers. Yet, it is important to ask questions as they reveal that there are no general answers about globalization. Nor is there unanimity on its conceptualization. It is an on-going process with some unforeseen consequences.

Although, as asserted by Held (1999: 2), it is difficult to map schools of thought directly onto traditional ideological positions or worldviews, there is a critical perspective which relates to globalization's moral guise. Orthodox neoliberals, conservatives, and Marxists could draw the same conclusion and share the same perspective about the nature of globalization. They capture different aspects of globalization. However, others across these ideological divides denounce its malignant effects and dictatorial rules. Frank Pfetsch (1998: 167) recalls that for neo-liberal economists, wealth gains dominate; for Neo-Marxists or Neo-Keynesians, the results are the loss of steering capacity and the loss of confidence in the democratic state.

Two currents of thought

Held *et al.* (1999: 2–10) distinguish between three currents of thought. The first, the hyperglobalizers, are quite positive about globalization. They praise the new era inaugurated by globalization Within the framework presented by Held, there could be normative differences, but contenders of this thesis share the same set of beliefs that globalization is primarily an economic phenomenon. By contrast, the second, referred as to the skeptics, assert that globalization is a myth that conceals the reality of an international economy segmented into a triad in which national governments remain powerful. Finally, for the transformationalists, such as Rosenau (1997) or Giddens (1990), states and societies try to adapt to the contemporary patterns of globalization, which entail interconnectedness and uncertainty.

However, neither the hyperglobalizers, nor the skeptics and the transformationalists denounce the negative effects of globalization. They acknowledge the changes that have occurred, and give their own accounts of globalization, but they do not put the whole process into a critical perspective. Thus, it is more accurate to distinguish two currents of thought about globalization according to a moral divide, which currents are absent from the classification devised by Held *et al.*, and cut cross the authors' three categories of hyperglobalizers, skeptics, and transformationalists.

The first – *the optimists* – praise the opportunities afforded by globalization, glorify the liberalization and prosperity that it supposedly entailed both for developed and developing countries. For the upholders of this vision, it depends upon countries to seize globalization's rewards. They privilege the economic explanation of globalization and its neoliberal dynamics. They retain only the positive aspects of globalization, celebrating the rationale of global competition and market that motivate enterprizing actors.

The second school of thought, which could be referred to as *the pessimists*, such as Cox (1996) or Strange (1997), denounces globalization's social impairment and increasing polarization between the winners and the losers, and the increased gap between those who are part of the new global work force and those who are left out: 1.3 billion people live with less than $1 a day. The top fifth of the world's people who live in high income countries generated 82 per cent of world exports, the other four-fifths produced 1 per cent (UNDP, 1997). According to an UNCTAD report, since 1971, the number of countries categorized by the United Nations as extremely poor has risen from 25 to 48. During that period only one country, Botswana, has graduated from the list. In the Central and Eastern part of Europe, poverty has increased seven times from 1988 to 1994. Asia is the most sensitive continent: 950 million people are in a state of total poverty, among them 515 million in India. Globalization could indeed lead to more fragmentation.

If free trade is the major unifying force offering opportunity to working and poor people around the world, there is, according to the pessimists, growing evidence that the free trade orthodoxy has devastating results. Francis Fukuyama's (1999) concept of 'great disruption' coins globalization's social perverse effects and discrepancies. Critics warn against the rule of markets and transnational forces, the increasing interdependence between states, which could result in major crises. The Western financial system is rapidly coming to resemble nothing as much as a vast casino, observes Susan Strange (1997: 1). The financial market has sudden, unpredictable shifts which knock over individual lives and governments. Contagion cannot be ruled out. The Stock Exchange crash of 19 October 1987, as well as the Mexican Peso and the South-East Asian crises of 1994 and 1997 raised questions about the extent and dangers of global financial integration. George Soros, a significant player in the financial market, contends that financial markets are supposed to work as a pendulum, and always return to the equilibrium. Instead of acting in this way, 'they act like a wrecking ball, knocking over one economy after another' (Soros, 1999: xvi). More disturbances are likely to occur in the future since international law governing financial flows has evolved less quickly than international law governing trade (Sachs, 1996).

The optimists

For the contenders of the first thesis, globalization leads to a widening of the extent and form of cross-border transactions, production, and financial structures, and of the deepening of the economic interdependence between the actions of entities – be they private or public institutions – located in one country and those of related or independent entities located in other countries (Dunning, 1993: 3).

Globalization is a stretching process. It is a reconfiguration of the world, and a long-term historical process, which began five centuries ago when the 'Conquistadors pressed on, voyage after voyage, league after league, intending to open the way to trade' (Landes, 1998: 45). The widening of markets encouraged technological innovation. People started to move from one place to another. European powers grabbed and exploited colonies. This trend accelerated in the nineteenth century when millions migrated, and trade expanded, and the period before the First World War witnessed many of the current features. Globalization is the result of a long-lasting process punctuated by successive steps.

Petrella (1996: 63–6) made it clear that globalization identifies a process, when he distinguished between internationalization, multinationalization, and globalization. Internationalization took shape through the conquest of colonies and the rise of mercantilism. It refers to the increasing geographical spread of economic activities across national boundaries (Dicken, 1992: 1). Multinationalization is characterized by the transfer of resources, especially capital and labor, from one national economy to another, moving easily thanks to a borderless economy. Globalization is qualitatively different. It is a higher degree of internationalization. Trade, investment, and capital flows generate closer and more intense ties between countries.

Globalization refers to the multiplicity of linkages and interconnections between the states and the society (stretching), and the intensification in the levels of interactions, interconnectedness, or interdependence (deepening). In a globalized economy, 'distinct national economies are subsumed and rearticulated into the system by international processes and transactions' (Hirst, 1995: 3).

Globalization is synonym for a new phase of modernization or westernization (McGrew, Lewis *et al.*, 1992; Giddens, 1990). Anthony Giddens asserts that 'modernity is inherently globalizing' (1990: 63). The old regime in which the aggregate of national economies was linked by trade has been transformed by a number of processes, which includes time-space distanciation and disembedding. Both refer to new networks of social connections which impact upon institutions and economy.

Time–space distanciation entails a new mode of intensified relations between local and distant social forms and events. Distanciation is captured in Giddens' (1994: 177) definition of globalization: 'intensification of world-wide social relations which link distant localities in such a way that local events are shaped by events occurring many miles away and vice-versa has consequences far beyond its specific social context'. Time–space distanciation entails a new mode of intensified relations between local and distant social forms and events.

Disembedding is a related concept since it means the 'lifting out' of social relations from local contexts of interaction and their restructuring across indefinite spans of time–space (Giddens, 1994: 21).

Some notions at the core of globalization, such as 'domestic', 'international', 'multinational', 'cross-border', and 'global' are geographical notions. However, globalization has blurred territorial boundaries as the most significant space. National space is replaced by other levels of interaction and governance. Political, economic, and social activity is becoming interregional or intercontinental in scope as asserted by Held (1999: 13). That is not to say that nation-states do not retain political, military, or security significance. However, national governments are challenged by the proliferation of actors beyond and beneath their jurisdiction. The power of states has been challenged by transnational firms, transnational movements, intergovernmental organizations, and internationalization of issues. There is an overlapping of domestic and international politics. Some domestic policies include an international dimension. States can no longer perform effectively the operations as they did before. These have become more complex. States are not the proper realm of power to devise, control, and implement solutions to the spread of AIDS, to climate change, and to financial crisis spilling over borders as a result of interdependence. Other mechanisms of governance have to be envisaged. Important markers of world politics, such as sovereignty, state power, or territoriality are much more problematic nowadays than they were in the Westphalian era.

Ruggie (1993: 165) places emphasis on the post-modern system of territoriality, or, to be more appropriate, on the 'unbundling territoriality'. The modern system of states may be yielding to a post-modern form of configuring political space. According to Ruggie, the characteristics of the modern system of exclusive territorial rule and demarcation between public and private realms and between internal and external realms are no longer any use. The current international polity ends up in a non-territorial space. The transnational microeconomic links which have increased remarkably over the past thirty years exist as though they were unfolding in some ethereal space (Ruggie, 1993: 149). Trade is made up of intra-firm transactions and most of the goods traded are made up of services. Even if financial transactions are hosted in Tokyo, London, or New York, they are considered to exist in a extranational realm. Realist or liberal paradigms which could master these changes are misplaced. We lack even the adequate vocabulary to explain the changes. The current transformation suggests an epochal threshold.

There is some counter evidence, proving that some markers of the modern international system have remained important. Sovereignty is still a significant engine motion within the EU. Individual Member States are anything but irrelevant in the ever more integrated EU (Ruggie, 1993: 142). They still have the primary role in implementing and enforcing EU rules (Kincaid, 1994: 69). Member States participate in the European collective framework, because it provides them with a negotiating forum for bargaining, linking issues, and enhancing states' preferences, whilst reducing transaction costs (Landau, 1995c: 91). Member States bargain among themselves in an effort to realize their interests, and they are able to determine policy areas where the assertion of national control is considered critical to national sovereignty (Aggestam, 1997: 80). The major national economies such as Germany, the United Kingdom, France, the United States, or Japan also assert how the national economy is important in a context of economic rivalry.

The pessimists

Pessimists echo some of the optimists' concerns on the altered meaning of territoriality, state governance, and the emergence of the non-state forces. However, pessimists contest some of the assumptions about globalization. They go further in recognizing the disruptive effects of globalization, and in denouncing globalization's social impairment and increasing polarization between the winners and the losers. Pessimists as categorized here include some of the authors who are listed as skeptics by Held *et al.* (1999: 5–6), such as Hirst and Thompson.

Differences between optimists and pessimists relate to the starting point of the globalization process. Is globalization really new a phenomenon? Globalization is a myth (Hirst and Thompson, 1996: 2) According to Paul Bairoch (1996: 173), there is a historical parallel to be drawn between the contemporary and pre-first World War eras. The contemporary indicators of globalization are not unprecedented, and the current changes are not unique. David Landes recalls the economic activity and dynamism prevailing in the mid-nineteenth century. The English and the French moved away from high protection to liberalization, and there were abundant international capital flows: 'England invested in French railways; France and Belgium in Prussian ironworks and Austrian banks; Germany in Italian banks and Balkan railways; everybody in Russian mining and industry' (Landes, 1998: 267).

Pessimists contend with the optimists that globalization is a process. As such, they argue, it is never complete, and there is nothing inevitable about its continuation (Cox, 1987; Bairoch and Kozul-Wright, 1996; Clark, 1997). The international economy has characteristics of its own; it is different from previous periods; it is relatively open, more generalized and more institutionalized through different regimes. The trade regime governed by the WTO is a case in point. However, the economy that was prevailing before World War I was also international and open (Hirst and Thompson, 1996: 9).

Pessimists challenge the notion of a truly globalized economy dominated by transnational firms, a system of manufacture and production internationally spread, international capital flows, and financial institutions operating in world markets independently of national boundaries, national political objectives and domestic economic constraints (Bairoch and Kozul-Wright, 1996: 3). Each of these components are contested by the pessimists. They argue that the important aspect of the transnational corporations as global agents does not stand up to reality. Few companies are truly transnational, rather most are multinational, or best retain a clear national home base; they are regulated to the national regulations of their home country (Hirst, 1992: 411). They remain territorially based. What matters most is not their location, but the people who make key decisions on what is to be produced elsewhere (Strange, 1988: 28). Financial flows that are traded daily are delinked from the production and exchange of goods. Patterns of trade and investment are concentrated within the OECD states. Thus, globalization is much more modest than the optimists like to believe.

Far from conceiving globalization as a 'massive shake-out' of societies, economies, institutions of governance, and world order (Giddens, 1990), globalization is depicted as increasing polarization within and among countries, and engendering as the end result social and political conflicts (Cox, 1996: 26). The losers of globalization could as the end result displace their force from individual identities to a unified force of protest (Cox: 1992). Far from unfolding a cover of uniformity of tastes and values, globalization exacerbates tension and fragmentation (Clark, 1997: 27). Fragmentation may be a reaction of too much integration (Holsti, 1990: 54).

On the one hand, there is a tendency to uniformity and integration that mesmerizes peoples all over the world with fast food and drink, clothes, music, sports and entertainment, and technologies, pressing states into one homogeneous world, one 'McDonald's and Kentucky Fried Chicken world' (Barber, 2000: 21). The spread of English as a universal language of communication has facilitated the sharing of more homogeneous tastes, values, and markers. Films, recorded music, news and television, and computers have helped to disseminate ideas, images, and artifacts at global, regional, and local levels (Held *et al.*, 1999: 170). Icons like *Jurassic Park* or *Titanic* draw large audiences in Tokyo and Toronto. Cities and localities and subnational communities are building bridges and linkages with one another across national boundaries. An ever growing area of our lives is getting globalized. A new sort of metropolis-periphery relationship is emerging which is unrelated to or in spite of the state-centric international system. This phenomenon is not uniform; it is not homogeneous, and varies widely in time, extent, intensity.

Yet there are some dividing lines in this world of uniformity. There has been the emergence of different 'social circles'. John Stopford and Susan Strange (1991: 23) observed the emergence of a privileged transnational business civilization. Traders would be the best example of these communities, sharing the same interests, using the same language, and devoted to reaping the full benefits of globalization. They share the same economic and social values about the management of the global economy. They have a territorial geography: local points of control and networks of relations connecting particular places (New York, London, Los Angeles, Hong Kong, or São Paulo). Traders as portrayed here are only one example of those transnational business circles, but there are many others.

On the other hand, there is the antithetical tendency to parochialism. Globalization has also nurtured national cultural fragmentation. Della Porta and Krieisi (1999: 4) note that globalization encourages local movements of resistance which defend their local traditions against the intrusion of foreign ideas and global problems. The activists who demonstrated in December 1999 against the WTO and globalization are an illustrative example of these movements of resistance against globalization.

Globalization may well fuel nationalism, regionalism, and independence movements. In the United Kingdom, the individual flags of the component nations – Scotland, Wales, and Northern Ireland – have enjoyed a revival. For the first time since 1707, the Scots now have their parliament. In France (Corsica), in Spain (the Basque and the Catalonian Movements), in Canada (Quebec), in Italy (Lega Lombarda), or in the United States, groups are struggling to preserve their identity. These distinctive identity groups, converging around specific issues – ethnic, religious, gender, environmentalist – are also one facet of globalization. A 'Jihad world', in Barber's words, is at work, and 'Jihad not only revolts against but abets McWorld, while McWorld not only imperils but re-creates and reinforces Jihad. They produce their contraries and need one another' (Barber, 2000: 229).

In every case, the authority of the state is challenged. Regions call for the EU to get greater autonomy from the sovereign states; Quebec and Catalonia have delegations to the EU. These regional authorities are seeking voices in the decision-making of national and international institutions that shape the rules of economic integration. All these movements are nurture by the diffusion effect of globalization. Diffusion is central to globalization.

There is an emerging free market of regional and local governments. These governments are becoming more entrepreneurial, and are entering the global marketplace directly to recruit investors and tourists and to promote regions under the pressure of competition. The three southern states of Brazil – Santa Catarina, Parana, and Rio Grande do Sul – which are taking advantage of their border with the three MERCOSUR Member Countries to attract investors and transnational corporations, are a case in point (Landau, 1999b).

Rosenau recognizes that we are witnessing an emergent epoch marked by

> shifting boundaries, emergent authorities, weakened states, and proliferating nongovernmental organizations, at local, provincial, national, transnational, international, and global levels of community. International and domestic no longer adequately describe the new era in which there is authority without territoriality, and governance without government (Rosenau, 1997: 27).

Loci and foci of activities have moved. Rosenau (1997: 39) prefers to speak of a congeries of spheres of authority or different units of governance. In this sense, a bifurcation has occurred: a state-centric world coexists with a multi-centric world in which authority is diffused among a vast array of actors and levels (Rosenau 1993: 117; Holsti 1990: 55). Actors are more informed by what Rosenau (1997: 16) calls the microelectronic revolution, that has enlarged the competence of those groups and individuals, and helped them to interact. Accessible and affordable technology has broken the monopoly of governments on the collection and management of large amounts of information and has deprived governments of the deference they enjoyed previously. When the Chiapas rebellion erupted in January 1994, the Internet channeled instantaneous messages from worldwide human rights activists. Activists around the globe prepared the demonstrations against the WTO Ministerial Conference using email or the Internet. Access to information and the ability to put it to use multiplies the number of players who matter (Mathews 1997: 51f). There is a vicious circle playing off: the multi-centric world has challenged the authority of the state. The weakening of the state has paved the way for a new type of production organization, and the bifurcation in two worlds has facilitated globalization of national economies.

Links between domestic and international affairs have become more complex. States must increasingly anticipate actions and decisions adopted abroad and take them into account in adopting their own decisions. As a consequence, domestic measures have greater impact on foreign economies, 'calling forth correspondingly greater offsetting responses which in turn affect the first country' (Cooper, 1968: 158). Issues that were formerly deemed to be national in character or amenable to local resolution gained in external significance (Barry Jones, 1994: 11). Correspondingly, international agreements reduced the number of policy instruments available to national authorities.

Rosenau is concerned about the opposite clusters of globalization and localization (Rosenau, 1996; 251), international and domestic, and internal and external affairs (Rosenau, 1997: 29). In the emergent era, boundaries separating domestic and foreign affairs are porous, and are being transgressed by a variety of diverse types of actors and issues. Issues and actors are no longer constrained by firm boundaries. Networks are more crucial to the conduct of world affairs than hierarchical structures. The cluster of globalization and localization relates to contrary conceptions of territoriality. Globalization renders borders less salient while localization highlights borders. Also, globalization suggests centralization, coherence, and integration, and localization points to decentralization, fragmentation, and disintegration.

Thus, the most accurate label to capture the mosaic of global interactions is 'fragmegration'. It 'indicates the tension between the fragmenting consequences of conflict and the integrative effects of co-operation' playing off simultaneously in the new spheres of authority. This label suggest also 'the absence of clear-cut distinction between domestic and foreign affairs, that local problems can become transnational in scope' (Rosenau, 1997: 38). It is the twin process of integration and fragmentation.

Regionalization instead of globalization

The fragmentation of the world economy could best be epitomized by the increasing regionalization of the world economy. Regional integration arrangements are blossoming in every part of the world. Three macro-regions have emerged around a European bloc, including the East and Central European countries and the Euro-Mediterranean countries; a North American bloc, including Canada, the United States and Mexico (NAFTA), or an extended free trade area (including all countries of the Americas as envisioned by FTAA); and an Asia-Pacific bloc, including Japan and the Newly Industrialized Countries (NICs). These centers of power might well provide a sound base for sharing in globalization. Liberalizing trade within a regional framework would be the best way to open up national economies and integrate the world market. Hirst and Thompson (1996) take a further step. They question the validity and accuracy of globalization, whilst accepting that there have been major structural changes. The most significant change is the formation of economic blocs. Regionalization is the other facet of globalization. On the other hand, regionalization also incarnates fragmentation: it means fragmentation into several regional blocs, competing among themselves to get bigger shares of the world trade; it means uneven regional schemes between the giant EU, and the more vulnerable schemes, mainly in Africa.

Globalization also has an impact on the power relations underlying the structure. According to Cox (1992: 309–10), globalization has generated a global class structure – a McDonaldization of the workforce. At the top is a transnational managerial class which is integrated into the global economy; very similar to the transnational kernel observed by Stopford and Strange (1991). The bottom level is peopled by workers who have been doubly fragmented into those who have a relative security in their jobs, and those who are excluded from the global economy.

In a formulation of this line of interpretation, Brecher and Costello (1994: 78–9) distinguish between a 'globalization from above' and one 'from below'. The former refers to globalization sought and promoted by powerful corporate actors and institutions. It is controlled by transnational corporations thinking globally as they shift from domestic to global competitive strategies. By contrast, globalization from below is a web of transnational networks and connections between grassroots social movements, NGOs, and trade unions in many different states trying to ameliorate and democratize globalization from above. Globalization from below opposes global rules designed to force downward leveling, but supports global rules that, for example, protect labor and environmental rights and standards. According to Brecher and Costello (1994: 21) globalization has malignant effects ranging from failing wages and loss of job security, to global warming and paralysis of democratic government.

This 'peripheralization of the core' is accompanied by an uneven development at the periphery. There is an increasing marginalization of many developing countries, and a bifurcation between those that are better equipped to adapt and have found some niches of production, and those that are irretrievably excluded from the global economy (Hirst and Thompson, 1996; Cox, 1991). The following chapters provide large evidence of this bifurcation. The inter-state power configuration of the globalized world is a coalition centering upon the United States, Germany, Japan, and some OECD countries, and the co-optation of a few industrialized third world countries, such as Brazil, Mexico, Argentina, Singapore, Taiwan, or South Korea. States subordinate to exigencies of the world economy (Cox, 1992: 154). The problem of governance is not so much the end of the nation state as the internationalization of the state (Dunn, 1995; Cox, 1981). This is a consequence of the role of states in adjusting domestic economy to the world economy, deregulating, and striving to gain competitiveness. In a globalized world, the state acts as agent. Far from being a mere buffer against exogenous influences, states effectively become active instruments facilitating the globalization from above determined by the international institutions (Tuathail *et al.*, 1998: 14). They are not autonomous actors but embedded actors. They react to domestic pressures to warrant the existence of firms or to defend domestic employment (Ruigrok and van Tulder, 1998: 222).

Governments, companies and trade policies

In their account of the links between 'core firms', internationalization strategy, and trade policies, Ruigrok and van Tulder (1998: 231) note that governments have played a decisive role in protecting major core firms from international competition. The authors give a detailed account of the trade barriers devised by governments to protect their national core firms: the United States administration negotiated VERs to protect Ford Motors against Japanese competition; from the 1960s onwards, procurement markets from DARPA (US defense) were a major source of funding for IBM and for General Electric; Japan did the same for Toshiba in the 1990s; France supported oil exploration by Elf Aquitaine; Germany gave increasing subsidies to Siemens for developing core technologies; and Baden Würtemberg provided subsidies and training facilities to Daimler Benz (now DaimlerChrysler). One-sixth of DaimlerChrysler's employees work for DAS (German defense) (Ruigrok and van Tulder 1998: 239–70).

An UNCTAD study concluded that 'government intervention aimed at firmly anchoring the country in the world economy by strengthening the export competitiveness of the country, by promoting export and transforming the economy into an open economy by liberalizing trade and investment' (UNCTAD, 1994a: 54–5). Policy makers in developing countries have been striving to attract more global investment by injecting the appropriate ingredients into the economy that include political and macro-economic stability, open trade and investment regimes, better transport and infrastructure, and adequate protection of property rights (World Bank, 1997: 2). D'Andrea Tyson (1992: 91) recalls that in the 1970s the governments of Mexico, Taiwan, Singapore, Malaysia, and Korea established 'export platforms' to encourage FDI, offering a vast array of incentives from tax-free exports to import tax reductions, and tax holidays. States – in Poulantzas' phrasing (1974) – 'take charge of the interests of the dominant imperialist capital in its development within the national'. Rather than a loss of power, the internationalization of the state reflects more power (Panitch, 1996: 91).

Many situate the debate on the internationalization of the state in the specific context of the rise and fall of the hegemonic world order of the Pax Americana, which would not be, by any means, over. For Susan Strange (1989) the United States and the corporations have not lost the structural power made of four interacting facets between finance, security, production, and knowledge. They may have increased their power

> to offer, withhold or threaten security; to offer, withhold or demand credit; to determine the locus, mode and content of wealth-creating activity, and to influence ideas and beliefs and therefore the kind of knowledge socially prized and sought after and to control access to and communication of that knowledge (Strange, 1988: 441).

Gilpin (1987: 379) would not contradict this vision.

Indeed, the United States remains the largest single economy, the one that created the impetus for the liberalization of national economies. Thus, in the absence of any other hegemony – Japan not yet ready for economic leadership, Western Europe still divided, and both still dependent upon the United States for their military security – the role of the United States in the management of the international economy remains crucial.

In 1997, though insisting that the United States still prevailed in the management of financial markets, trade and security, Susan Strange (1997b: 134–40) asserted that the capacity of all governments to manage economy, financial stability, industrial and competition policy, and labor relations had substantially weakened as a result of globalization. States have to master a complex network or web of transnational, bilateral bargains – bargaining among states, accepting and adjusting to diplomacy between firms, and negotiating with firms. This triangular diplomacy suggests that 'international trade and production have been the gearbox or transmission mechanism between the world market economy and the state system' (Strange, 1995: 298). States have abdicated some of their control over national economies. National governments could continue to exercise some of the functions of their authority: taxes, police activities, and other domains wherein they have not experienced a shift and contraction of their jurisdictions (Rosenau, 1997: 40).

Markets rather than states control the financial game. For the optimists, it is a matter of fact and not a bad one; for the pessimists, the world economy is becoming unstable and unpredictable. Some events have taken place that confirm the volatility and unpredictability of the world financial market. Barings Bank, one of the oldest merchant banks, went into insolvency. Another such event is the peso crisis in Mexico, the first crisis which involved many NICs in East Asia and Latin America. International finance is controlled by international regulation, and the shift in control to markets has given more power to the transnational corporations (Strange, 1996: 48).

The debate over who controls and makes the rules – the markets or the states – is an interesting one. Polyani had indeed made his point in stating that:

economic history reveals the emergence of national markets was in no way the result of the gradual and spontaneous emancipation of the economic sphere from governmental control. On the contrary, the market has been the outcome of a conscious and often violent intervention on the part of government which imposed the market organization on society for noneconomic ends (Polyani, 1944: 250).

The space between the faltering state and the nascent civil society can be filled by a 'covert world': organized crime, terrorist groups, arms trade, money laundering banks, drug trafficking. Those also are a result of globalization. They even benefit from it, and design innovative strategies to do even better. They operate transnationally. They substitute for states, use force to impose obedience (Strange 1995: 306), and punish the 'free riders'. James Mittelman and Robert Johnston (1999: 110) show how the rise of transnational organized crime groups is spurred on by technological innovations, communications, and information, all which facilitate operations across frontiers:

like global firms, transnational organized crime groups operate both above and below the state. Above the state, they capitalize on the globalizing tendencies of borderlessness and deregulation. Embracing the processes of globalization, these groups create demand for their services. They become actors in their own right in the global division of labor and power, organized along zone or regional and subregional lines, such as the golden triangle.

They offer their services, and reach down to the marginalized segments of the population that are left out of globalization. These marginalized groups find protection in these criminal groups and participate in the parallel economy.

Summing up the globalization debate

To sum up, optimists and pessimists have opposing visions of globalization. Optimists contend that globalization is a fact of reality; pessimists rather think it is an ideal type (Hirst and Thompson, 1996; Bairoch and Kozul-Wright, 1996). Thus, globalization can only be measured against this ideal type. Optimists portray the process of globalization as unique, unprecedented, and firmly rooted to last in the future. Pessimists contend that global economy is not a new feature of world economy, but a return to the liberal international order that existed before 1914 (Hirst, 1992: 411; McGrew, Lewis *et al.*, 1992). Then as now, capital moved freely. Trade flows were rising under the influence of low tariff barriers and technological changes in transportation and communications.

However, the period of liberalization in the nineteenth century when trade barriers were coming down was short, starting in the 1840s and lasting only until the 1860s and 1870s, when the tide started to reverse. Trade liberalization after the Second World War has lasted longer, and its character is different with closer and more intense ties between countries. The growth momentum encompasses the whole world economy, spreading from the North Atlantic economies to include most of Continental Europe, Japan, and many developing areas. Globalization is also more institutionalized with the WTO governing the world trade, creating obligations between countries, and facilitating the liberalization of trade. Such institutions did not exist in the nineteenth century. Regional arrangements such as the EU, NAFTA, or the MERCOSUR have created 'what Kenneth Boulding called "zone of stable peace" ; what Karl Deutsch called "pluralistic security community"; and what Emmanuel Kant termed "pacific union"' (Hyde-Price, 1999: 114). These zones are important in terms of creating a web of political, economic, and social relationships. The end of liberalization in the nineteenth century took place against a backdrop of great power-struggles in Europe, revival of nationalism, and preparation for war. However, globalization is not evenly spread. It does not impact equally among countries. Some capitals of Latin America – São Paolo, Mexico City or Buenos Aires – owe more to the global economy than some remote areas of Switzerland or the United Kingdom. Trade, investments, and financial flows are spread unequally among countries. Rather, they are concentrated in a triad composed of Europe, Japan, and North America, extending to some of the regional arrangements in Latin America (Hirst and Thompson 1996: 2). If transnational corporations are major players in the world economy, they are not 'the genuine footloose capital without specific national identification, with an internationalized management and willing to locate and relocate anywhere in the globe to obtain either the most secure or the highest returns'. They are concentrated as initiating and receiving flows of trade and investment in the economies of the triad. Thus, globalization has mixed effects. Globalization stimulates forces of integration, as it could just lead to more fragmentation and differentiation within and among countries (McGrew, Lewis *et al.*, 1992: 23).

One of the central sources of contention between optimists and pessimists concerns the role of the state in a global economy. Suffice to say here (see Chapter 3) that an ever-growing list of literature casts no doubt that the nation-state is becoming obsolete, increasingly irrelevant (Ohmae, 1995; Hirst and Thompson, 1996; Ruigrok and van Tulder, 1995). The state's range of duties is receding, leaving to the market the 'commanding heights' (Yergin and Stanislaw, 2000: 212). There is not much left of the territorial basis for the state authority, which is outlawed by trade regulations or financial flows. Nation states are less effective because their governance power is circumscribed by geographical borders, whereas problems they are supposed to solve now have global, or at least transborder dimensions. They are even forced to adjust to global processes or global actors (Lubbers and Koorevar, 1999: 3).

However, to swear by the globalization gospel or proclaiming the end of the state is premature. Although states are constrained by globalization, they are far from powerless. Their sovereignty today might have been subverted but not wholly subverted, as stated by Held (1998: 21). Indeed, the state is squeezed from above – by globalization – and from below by the influence of transnational social movements – the global civil society. Moreover, the international trade regime has further restrained the influence of domestic policy actions. All WTO Member Countries are required to adopt national legislation and regulations to implement the rules prescribed by the three Agreements – GATT 1994, GATS and the Agreement on TRIPS – and other legal instruments. The WTO is responsible for the surveillance of the implementation of these rules by its Members, and it has the teeth to impose decisions adopted by the Appellate Body.

However, for others, this line of thinking is far too simple. Globalization is itself directed by the varying fortunes of national economies (Dicken, 1992: 149). They provide the background conditions and engineer many of the measures that make globalization possible. They have a large array of instruments with which to influence economic activity and attract investment. Dani Rodrik (1997: 105) provides evidence that globalization may increase the demand for social protection while simultaneously constraining the ability of governments to respond effectively to that demand. Global players such as the transnational companies put downward pressure on wages and social welfare. He contends that the solution to counteract this downward spiral would be judiciously to mix intervention and international trade (Rodrik, 1999: 26). A solution which is supported by Geoffrey Garrett (1998).

Transnational corporations are at the core of the debate on globalization. According to some, they are walling off state sovereignty. They are global players, bypassing borders and control (Ohmae, 1995). For others, transnational corporations may not be territorially based, but certainly are the key players. That matters the most (Strange, 1988). Moreover, there is evidence that transnational corporations conduct their business activities and invest mainly in the industrialized states (Hirst and Thompson, 1996; Dicken, 1992). Thus, it would be more accurate to speak of a 'trialization' rather than a 'globalization' (Ruigrok and van Tulder, 1995: 151).

Optimists and pessimists recognize that the main problem of a globalized world is the governance. Global economy is difficult to regulate. Some twenty years ago, most economists or political scientists were convinced that governments had the power to correct the ups and downs of market economies

Table 2.1 Globalization: two tendencies

	Optimists	Pessimists
Evolution	Process, new phase of modernization and internationalization	Process, not inevitable and not unprecedented
Social dominants	Intensification of worldwide social relations	Parochialism
Structure	Global space	National base
State power	Eroding power	Internationalization of state, active agents
Regulation	Global governance	Emergence of regions, collusion between states and international institutions

Globalization and governance

One of the developments that had a great impact on the international system was the growing interdependence and interconnectedness between countries (Rosenau, 1990, Keohane and Nye 1972). Many scholars associate globalization with interdependence (Petrella, 1998; Barry Jones, 1994; Giddens, 1994; Cooper, 1968: 148f). Interdependence alters the nature of world politics by changing the policy options of the states, and makes the pursuit of national economic objectives more difficult. It undermines the process by which national authorities reach their national objectives. Each government has to take into account the actions and responses of others in formulating its own choices, and the achievement of the government's objectives depend upon the behavior and the action of other governments. The states' autonomy in setting up economic, monetary, or fiscal policies have diminished. This is even more true for powerful players.

It could be argued that these limits imposed on a country's monetary and fiscal sovereignty are by no means recent. Drucker (1997: 160) points out that throughout the nineteenth century, nation-states had already lost control over their monetary and fiscal policies being put under the control of the gold standard. However, constraints rose to unprecedented levels.

Globalization has constrained the ability of governments to respond effectively to numerous demands (Rodrik, 1997: 107). Increased trade flows and capital movements – two characteristics of globalization – affect countries' economies and ranges of policy options. Increasing flows of goods, money, and capital make it more and more difficult to isolate states and insulate the domestic from the international sphere. The diminished authority of nation-states to control the flow of capital and commerce across their borders, also diminishes their ability to function as traffic police or central planners directing capital and commerce to specified regions (Kincaid, 1994: 75). Still, states retain power. Rodrik (1997) notes that growth of trade combines with growth of government. Governments have an increasing role as a result of their attempts to minimize the social impact of openness to the international economy. Globalization 'increases the demand for social insurance while simultaneously constraining the ability of governments to respond effectively to that demand'. Bairoch and Kozul-Wright (1996: 22) note also the role of the state as an active agent in technological education and research activities.

However, states are not equal in front of globalization. The gap between the winners and the losers does not superpose on the North–South dividing line. Indeed, a number of developing countries have been growing fast, faster than industrial countries, but nevertheless not fast enough to narrow the absolute per capita income gap. In Africa, the gap is widening. Globalization has resulted in increased polarization among countries and among regions. Only a handful of some Southern African countries has succeeded in joining the 'Club of the Rich'. The global flows are unevenly distributed. Interdependence does not entail equality between countries. Robert Keohane and Joseph Nye (1972) note that interdependence refers to a power relationship. Similarly, Robert Gilpin (1987: 17) remarks that interdependence means mutual albeit not equal interdependence. Many of the distinctive phenomena and developments of globalization engender inequality between countries and fragmentation in the international system. Needless to say that the rapid diffusion of technology and information exert increasing stress upon economies, developed as well as developing, although more technologically advanced economies are better equipped to react to innovation and costs. Susan Strange (1995: 296) summarized the political consequences of globalization as the increased asymmetries of state power. This fragmentation of the system is not easy to regulate. The main problem is to accommodate the interests of each player.

Different strategies have been devised as to how handle the consequences of globalization:

1) Pro-marketers. The pro-marketers advocate the free game of the market economy. The task of the government is to leave the market alone. The government provides some services that are necessary for the market to function properly. President Clinton declared at the 'progressive Governance for the XXI Century', in Florence in November 1999: 'support debt relief, fight child labor, continue to reform international financial institutions, but do nothing to block the daily flow of the trillions of dollars needed to keep the global economy turning' (*International Herald Tribune*, 22 November 1999).

2) National economic governance. It would be a misunderstanding to claim that national states have lost any significance, and that the only solution is to cede more power to transnational forces. They have the power to limit the excesses of globalization. At

the Florence meeting, the French Prime Minister Jospin supported new values, rules, regulations, and institutions to constrain globalization and render it more *socially friendly.* This entails participating more extensively with the institutions managing the world economy. States would help to further the growth and strength of the global economy, by performing what they have already performed, that is in producing new forms of legality.

3) Co-ordination among major powers. The achievement of domestic goals, and many international areas such as money, environment, or health require increased policy co-ordination among major powers. However, the co-ordination processes settled at the international level have hardly achieved any result except when major powers are compelled to find solutions in period of crisis (Ikenberry, 1993: 139; Kapstein, 1994: 65).

4) Global governance. States could contribute to the strengthening of international governance (Sassen, 1996: 33). International institutions could regulate specific dimensions of economic activity. In the trade area, the WTO is overseeing the multilateral trading system. All WTO members are required to adopt national legislations and regulations to implement the rules prescribed by the General Agreement on Tariffs and Trade; the General Agreement on Trade in Services (GATS), and the Agreement on Trade Related Aspects of Intellectual Property Rights (TRIPS). The WTO has an increased power to impose its rules through the dispute settlement mechanism.

5) Regional governance. Regional arrangements provide some flexibility to regulate the economy. Member countries can adapt to requirements of the international economy, and cope with the rapid changes. Regionalization is a response to the internationalization of markets. Governance is improved by the integration process. Regional governance is particularly adapted to the needs of developing countries.

The determinants of globalization

There are many definitions of globalization. There might be disagreement about the dominant causal factor, about what is really globalization and if it is taking place at all, but there is an agreement according to which globalization is the result of a complex interplay between economic, political, cultural, and technological changes. Globalization cannot be labeled by only one determinant, since it would be only a partial explanation. Daniel Bell (1999: xvii) accurately points out that 'the nerves, nodes, and ganglia of the genuinely global economy are tied together'.

Definitions often combine some of these nerves and nodes: technological changes, mobility of capital, interdependence or interconnectedness of the economies (Kapstein, 1994: 65; McGrew, Lewis *et al.*, 1992). Susan Strange for example (1997: 137) lists the accelerated internationalization of production, the increased mobility of capital, and the greater mobility of knowledge and information from communication of messages to the transfer of technology. For Bairoch and Kozul-Wright (1996: 1), open markets, transnational corporations, and new information technologies are the ingredients of globalization. In a list elaborated by Petrella (1996), three concepts are at the core of globalization: finance and capital ownership; markets and strategies; technology, R&D and knowledge. Table 2.2 explains these three elements.

All these processes are mutually reinforcing, and it is their confluence at all levels that makes globalization so pervasive. There is a complex web of interactions among firms, institutions, and governments. The various components of globalization are supported by powerful social trends within society, by players and institutions, and by regulatory structures. This multiplicity of linkages and interconnections generates a structural shift.

Table 2.2 Concepts of globalization

Category	Main elements/processes
1. Globalization of finance and capital ownership	Deregulation of financial markets, international mobility of capital, rise of mergers and acquisitions. The globalization of shareholding is its initial stage.
2. Globalization of markets and strategies, in particular competition	Integration of business activities on a worldwide scale, establishment of integrated operations abroad (including R&D as financing), global searching of components, strategic alliances.
3. Globalization of technology and linked R&D and knowledge	Technology is the primary catalyst: the rise of information technology and telecom enables the rise of global networks within the same firm, and between different firms.

Source: Based upon Petrella, 1996

Globalization and technology

Globalization could not have occurred without technology. Technological change has had a profound influence on globalization. Globalization is technology driven. Yet it cannot be the sole factor explaining globalization. It is a conduit for globalization, it is facilitating globalization, but that does not mean that it is the primary determinant of all other changes (Bell 1999: lxxxviii). Entrepreneurs incorporate useful technologies into innovative products. Technology is harnessed to production and manufacturing systems, to finance, trade, specialized workforces, and political will to promote it. History provides evidence of the role of technology in economic change.

David Landes (1998: 45–55) recalls that division of labor and widening of markets encouraged technological innovation, not the other way round. The Romans innovated when the empire was breaking down. China had an impressive record of inventions: Chinese industries mastered waterpower some five hundred years before England of the Industrial Revolution knew water frames; and China anticipated the Europeans in textiles and iron manufacture. But China failed to realize its potential.

Landes explains this gap by stressing that China lacked curiosity (1998: 96). China did not have to conquer more territories. For a long time, it remained detached from outside competition and technology. The biggest impediment to development is, in Landes' phrasing – social, cultural, and technological unreadiness – want of knowledge and know-how (1998: 269).

Paul Kennedy, in his attempt to understand what made the peoples in the western parts of Eurasia become the commercial and military leaders in world affairs, stressed the 'dynamic involved, driven chiefly by economic and technological advances, although always interacting with other variables such as social structure, geography, and the occasional accident; that to understand the course of world politics' (Kennedy, 1989: 20).

Hobsbawm (1968: 116–17) also noted the benefits of technological innovations on the British Industrial Revolution in the 1840s. Industry cheapened under the input of the technological revolution. But the major technical advances of the second half of the nineteenth century, originating from an increase in the scientific knowledge, the factory system, and the organization of industry did not produce the same effects in Britain as they did in Germany or the United States. The explanation lies elsewhere: in the lack of entrepreneurship, in the conservatism of British society, or in both (Hobsbawm, 1968: 153).

Thus, as suggested by Bairoch and Kozul-Wright (1996: 22), if technological progress is an important source of economic growth, it is not an exogenous one. Two elements seem to be central: the state involvement in the area of technological progress through the creation of demand for new product as well as in the direct funding of technical education and research activities; and the process of capital accumulation. Still, technology is an important instrument of economic activity. Services are a case in point. The growth of services is linked to development in new information technologies. All the sectors that compose services are interrelated: increase in business travel relates to internationalization of business, and financial services. It is no use having a very competitive airline company if it is not connected to a computerized reservation system. France experimented with 'Socrates" weakness – the computerized reservation system for the TGV.

Daniel Bell (1999) gives a detailed account of the trajectory of technology from a mechanical, to an electrical and intellectual technology. The latter revolutionized places and markets. The spread of mini- and microcomputers, the ability to 'download' databases and memories as well as to give access to large mainframes means distance is meaningless. The cost of a unit of computing power fell by 99 per cent between 1960 and 1990. Progress in communication and information technology has made it possible for firms to communicate more information at reduced costs, and to disperse production and service networks. Benetton makes a daily computerized report of its foreign sales in its 4,500 franchised and 450 licensed sales points. The growth of global telecommunications networks has dramatically reduced the costs and difficulties of transmitting funds around the world (Helleiner, 1994c: 6).

After the year 2000, 300 million people, or 5 per cent of the world's population, are expected to be connected to the Internet. Boundaries are transcended. Transactions are made in real time. Electronic commerce over the Internet is the latest development in the emergence of an increasingly borderless economy. It was calculated that approximately 300 million Internet users would be participating in electronic commerce in 2000, an activity that by then would generate a turnover of more than $300 billion (WTO, 1999: 35).

Railways, container ships, and pipelines have boosted trade in bulk products: the application of communication technologies has facilitated the internationalization of capital markets and of production.

Bank transactions are almost instantaneous. In 1973, 239 national banks established the SWIFT (standardized world interbank and financial transactions) system, creating instantaneous transactions worldwide. In 1999, 6,710 banks operated through the SWIFT system in 189 countries.

Reduction of time and costs of time and the rapidity of communication have been accelerated by electronic innovations, promoting interactions and interconnecting people located thousands of miles away. Facsimile, e-mail (electronic mail), ISDN (Integrated Services Digital Network), which combines data, text, and sound, and the World Wide Web (WWW) or Cable News Network (CNN) engender simultaneous reactions all over the world. Conflicts that have erupted since the end of the Cold War – the collapse of the Berlin Wall, the occupation of Tienanmen Square, the Gulf War, Somalia or the war in ex-Yugoslavia – have been broadcast live. However, the development of communication technologies has large socio-economic consequences in marginalizing even more remote countries or regions. The next step will come from integrated communication technologies. The Internet will be offered through television sets or mobile phones. In a recent survey of innovative in industry, *The Economist* (20 February 1999) pointed out that a new industrial revolution – based on semiconductors, fiber optics, genetics and software – is well under way.

Globalization has occurred in national tastes, in international trade and investments, and in labor markets (Salvatore, 1998: 3). Globalization has occurred in production of goods and services with the rapid rise of global corporations. These are companies that have research and production facilities in many countries, use parts and components from the cheapest source around the world, and sell their products, finance their operations and are owned by stockholders throughout the world (Dunning, 1993). This is true in food, automobile, textile, steel, computers, telecommunications, consumer electronics, chemicals, and many other sectors.

Globalization entails elements of both integration and fragmentation. It mesmerizes the public by disseminating and internalizing global norms, common values, and common icons. It stimulates global actors, brokers, yuppies, businesses, the 'happy few'. Information and networks bind the major financial centers: New York, London, Tokyo, Paris, Frankfurt, Zurich. Some are closing the core: São Paolo, Mexico City. What about the others? Globalization marginalizes many countries or peoples unable to catch up with the new technologies. The Internet has spread at a rate never reached before. It has penetrated the public very fast, and has secured public adoption. However, the new technology widens the gap between the haves and have nots.

Indeed, as Fukuyama points out (1992: 275), 'the economic forces are now encouraging the breakdown of national barriers through the creation of a single, integrated world market'. If that is so on the economic side, what about the political side? Politically, from 51 states in 1945, the world is now partitioned into 185 states in 1999. Frank Pfetsch (1998: 173) stresses that this entails a risk since states might pursue their traditional tendencies towards the struggle for self-determination, that is to say safe borders, control of territory over other states, and the temptations of domination. Paul Kennedy (1993: 329) concludes that this tension between two antithetical tendencies – an economic activity on a single unit – and a political structure partitioned in an ever-growing number of units leads to 'a series of jolts and jars and smashes in the social life of humanity'. Integration and fragmentation are indeed two faces of Janus.

3
Assessing the Differentiated Character of States

For many, the most visible consequence of globalization has been the erosion of the state. The conventional Westphalian conception – a single authority governing the territory and representing it outside its borders and with no authority above the state – which has dominated world politics since 1648, is dissolving. It is challenged by the outdated distinction between domestic/international, inside/outside, territorial/non territorial (Held 1999: 50).

For the *'Optimists'*, the state is now obsolete, insignificant, depossessed of its authority, ineffective and, at best, should get out of the way so that the new rules of the game can play out without any constraints for the benefits of all. As asserted by Ohmae:

> so long as the nation states continue to view themselves as the essential prime movers in economic affairs, so long as they resist – in the name of national interest – any erosion of central control as a threat to sovereignty, neither they nor their people will be able to harness the full resources of the global economy. Nation states have become little more than bit actors, they have become remarkably inefficient engines of wealth distribution. States are a nostalgic fiction (Ohmae, 1995: 136).

Scholars list the most important elements challenging the sovereign state: communication technologies, world markets, transnational corporations, and financial globalization (Helleiner, 1999; Kapstein, 1994).

Stephen Krasner (1999: 35) explains that the term sovereignty has been used in four different ways, which are quite distinct. The first one is the most commonly referred to when scholars describe the curtailed latitude for autonomous and purely domestic oriented actions of governments. They associate their arguments with the *interdependence sovereignty*, that is the ability of a government actually to control activities within and across borders (including the movement of goods, capital, ideas, and disease vectors). The other three refer to *domestic sovereignty* – the organization of authority within a given polity; *Westphalian sovereignty* – the exclusion of external authority; and *international legal sovereignty* – the recognition of one state by another.

This chapter makes two claims: that the impact of globalization on states is not so clear cut; and that the political realm has become overpopulated with actors. States remain powerful actors, although they are confronted by some dramatic changes, and have to solve new issues. However, the argument according to which there is an erosion of the state starts from a false assumption that all states have had the same control over their activities. Many weaker states have never had such control. Sub-Saharan countries are a case in point. South Asian and African countries offer two opposite patterns. Policies and institutions have to complement economic strategies to incorporate the global economy.

Challenges to the state?

We should begin by evaluating some of the arguments underlining the decline of state sovereignty. In *The Economics of Interdependence*, Richard Cooper (1968) argued that there is a conflict between nation-states and the international economy. States are finding it difficult to strike a balance between increasing economic interdependence on the one hand, and the pursuit of legitimate national objectives on the other. Because of the intensification of economic interdependence, states have lost control over the central aspects of their economy, and their ability to reach domestic objectives. Their policy instruments are being called into question.

There is no better example than the financial sector. The fast-moving movements of money across the borders, which are taking place in the form of rapid blips on computer screen, are not passive actors (Helleiner, 1994a: 295). The day's play of the casino of global finance, depicted by Susan Strange (1997), has become a powerful player, difficult for governments to master. Build-up of speculative pressures on volatile markets and capital mobility has undermined the ability of governments to control the value of their currency and pursue an autonomous monetary policy (Helleiner, 1999: 139). Hence, the famous words: 'if Wall Street catches a cold, the rest of the world also will be infected'. Rises in dollar interest rates are often followed by similar rises in the European Central Bank's (ECB) interest rate. With greater financial integration, the global impact of interest and exchange rate policies has become much more important. Contagion cannot be ruled out. Uncertainty that rules in the financial markets could change governments' fortunes. The open and liberal global financial order has facilitated tax evasion that can weaken governments. Despite their pretension and their discourse, governments have lost the power to fight unemployment and revive economic growth.

The globalization of business – and the powerful response of enterprises (public as well as private) to it – constitute the second great eroding force on the power of the state. States have lost power because the transnational corporations are more powerful actors than governments. They govern the world economy, and they are equipped with the social and economic infrastructure that facilitate their global control. They have mapped global production networks in a borderless economy in which states are meaningless units of participation in the global economy (Ohmae, 1995: 11; Kapstein, 1994: 8; Petrella, 1996: 74). Economic activities have been denationalized (Mittelman, 1996a: 231). Corporations can base their activity anywhere that money goes furthest. They decide which countries will receive flows of investment and where to locate their new plants.

According to Krasner (1999: 37), these views are myopic. The argument that globalization has meant the erosion of sovereignty suffers from two defects. First, it confounds one meaning of sovereignty – effective state control – with other meanings of sovereignty that are related to issues of authority and legitimacy. Second, it is assuming some golden age in the past, where states could exercise effective control (Dunning 1997: 3).

To assess the situation, it is useful to distinguish between two quite different functions that governments may perform. First, the state is an initiator and a setter-up of the legal and institutional framework within which the resources and capabilities in its jurisdiction are created and deployed. Second it is an owner of assets, and a participator in, or influencer of the way these assets are utilized. These functions have evolved through history from the entrepeunerial to the hierarchical and the alliance capitalism (Dunning, 1997: 32).

Concerning the first function, international financial markets were able to develop only within what Janice Thomson and Stephen Krasner (1989: 196) refer to as 'a broader institutional structure delineated by the power and policies of states'. States have created the conditions which made the globalization possible (Kapstein, 1994: 6). They have leveled the playing field of international competition. To cope with competitive pressures and protect their lagging sectors, states have different answers. First, they can subsidize. Leading US computer, semiconductor and electronic component makers have benefited tremendously from preferential defence contracts (GM, IBM, General Electric, Hewlett-Packard, Digital, and Equipment) (Ruigrok and van Tulder, 1995: 221). States can adopt protectionist measures. They can also grant more freedom to market operators through liberalization and by refraining from the introduction of more effective controls (Helleiner, 1994c: 169).

The argument of the state being unable to control international capital movements does not hold. Individual states such as the US and Britain and also the EU, have forced liberalization and deregulation in financial markets. The US took the lead in deregulating and liberalizing the security markets, prompting similar moves abroad in Britain with the decision to deregulate and liberalize the London Stock Exchange, and Germany's abolition of its withholding tax on foreign holdings of German securities (Helleiner, 1994b: 300–7). If it is true that governments can no longer control international capital movements in the way they did in the era of fixed exchange rates from 1945 to 1970, they have at least retained their national financial regulatory power.

They have also been quite successful in designing co-operative actions. States have prevented financial crises from spiralling out of control by containing them through lender-of-last resort actions. They have extended emergency assistance to institutions, countries, or markets that were experiencing a sudden withdrawal of funds. After the global stock market crash in December 1997, the Bank of International Settlement (BIS), which was founded in 1930 to channel German war reparations to other European states, negotiated the Basle Capital Accord, the 1988 agreement to set international standards for how much capital banks must hold (*The Economist*, 6 June 1998). The Peso crisis was handled by the International Monetary Fund, the BIS, and private banks in December 1994 (*Financial Times*, 30 December 1994). The United States organized a $1 billion loan to Mexico, supplemented by a $1.85 billion from BIS central banks.

When the South Korean financial crisis erupted in December 1997, the United States, Japan, Canada, Australia, and the European countries, in recognition of the potential global implications of the crisis, contributed to the $55 billion rescue package. It is the largest ever rescue package wrapped up in the International Monetary Fund's 50-year history. It exceeds the famous bailouts for Mexico in 1994 and several Latin American countries in the 1980s. The IMF had also arranged bailouts worth $37 billion for Indonesia, and $17 billion for Thailand. (*Financial Times*, 5 December 1997).

Let's turn now to the second function of the state underlined by Dunning (1997: 3; 32): the state as a participator in, or influencer of, the way these assets are utilized. The state continues to accomplish a vast array of functions. It is the main social actor. The state regulates the economies, in designing its social, labor, and industrial policies, and in maintaining institutions that differ from those of its trading partners (Rodrik, 1997). It manages financial resources and public expenditure. Claims for social justice or economic prosperity are addressed to states, so much so that it would be more accurate to speak of the increased role of governments in a globalized world. Dani Rodrik (1997) asserts that by the mid-1990s the increased role of the state was particularly striking. Globalization had increased the demand for social insurance while simultaneously constraining the ability of governments to respond effectively to that demand.

The state is an international actor. In the diplomatic field, it is the main one. In the last decades, meetings have multiplied to an unprecedented extent; agreements and organizations have proliferated. Globalization has made international negotiations more important. Negotiators have to act together and design co-ordinating and regulatory mechanisms at the international level. In international negotiations, the principle of one country–one vote prevails even if it is purely formal: in an international organization like the WTO, Liechtenstein's vote counts as much as that of the United States. States ameliorate their functions and their negotiation capacity by integrating groups or lobbies (Pfetsch, 1998: 175) to expand their policy analysis or expert advice. Dan Esty (1998) points out that in NAFTA's decision-making process, environmentalists were placed on the key USTR public Advisory Committees. They were called before the Congress to testify alongside USTR on progress in meeting environmental goals within NAFTA and in environmental co-operation in parallel with the trade agreement. Congressional committees invited environmental group leaders to comment on the integration of environment concerns into NAFTA.

Thus, according to Panitch (1996: 84–5), there is a problem of tending to ignore the extent to which today's globalization is authored by states and is primarily about reorganization of states rather than bypassing them. A false dichotomy between the national and the international is promoted, which diverts attention from the need to develop new strategies for transforming the state, even as a means of developing an appropriate international strategy. The exigencies of worldwide production, trade, and finance have meant that the nature of state intervention has changed considerably but not that the role of the state has necessarily been diminished.

There is no indication whatsoever that nation states are declining. According to Susan Strange, far from withering 'the state remains' (Strange, 1986: 289). Even though the state is under attack from supranational and transnational entities, these entities have also been busily contributing to the power and authority of the states. There is a symbiosis between state and transnational corporation from which both benefit in that they are allies as well as competitors or opponents (Strange, 1986: 292). In the words of Gilpin:

> a complementarity of interests has tended to exist between the corporations and the US government. American corporate and political leaders have in general believed that the foreign expansion of American corporations serves important national interests of the United States. American policies have encouraged corporate expansion abroad, and have tended to protect them (Gilpin, 1987: 241).

Notwithstanding the wave of deregulation, the 1980s witnessed an extension of the power of all states.

New patterns of governance

Looking back to the Westphalian system, states had a very high degree of autonomy in domestic and external affairs. The contemporary world is also a turbulent one (Rosenau, 1990). States are embedded in an over-populated environment. Social movements are mushrooming everywhere, often leading to loosely organized transnational movements. Non-governmental organizations (NGOs) set the public agenda, from human rights to environmental issues. Intergovernmental organizations, empowered by the end of the Cold War and the extending global agenda, map the global order and channel international co-operation.

Thus, layers of governance are emerging both within and across political boundaries, so much so that it is possible to speak of a multi-layered system of governance. New paths of governance are opening, illustrating that we are moving away from a pure state centric world.

Whether through international agreements, or through international institutions, states have constructed frameworks of rules and practices which enable them to secure co-operation (Keohane, 1984: 25). It is increasingly difficult for states to free ride. They are entangled in a complex network of institutions and organizations that circumscribe their actions. Hedley Bull speaks of the emergence of a 'society of states' (Bull, 1977: 13) to describe the modern international system, which still contains elements of struggle and competition between states, but also elements of co-operation and regulated intercourse.

These new trends have some historical resonance. The medieval era in Europe had some of the characteristics of the contemporary multi-layered system. Then, as now, there was an array of authority structures from evolving local or regional political units to the supranational Christendom. The term 'neo-medievalism' captures the re-emergence of overlapping and multiple forms of authority and identity, which contrast with the distinctive structures of sovereign nation-states which characterized the Westphalian system. The new order is a hybrid situation in which 'states, city-states, region-states, communities and autonomous minorities are intermixing with no clear delimitation of power within these mixed components' (Minc, 1993: 188).

Bringing in international and transnational actors

States are no longer the only actors. Other actors, besides the state, tend to have an important role in international politics. Keohane and Nye (1972), challenging the realist paradigm that once dominated the realm of international relations, have underlined the growing number of regions, NGOs, international and transnational actors, social movements, communities, and coalitions increasingly seeking to influence policies and shaping decisions according to their interests (Risse-Kappen, 1995: 9; Lipsey, 1997: 93). Some groups have transcended the national borders, and have begun the construction of a viable international civil society beyond the direct control of states (Agnew, 1995: 90). The structure of international co-operation channeled through intergovernmental or supranational organizations provides multiple opportunities to help groups and movements pursue their interests and more actively use their leverage to achieve their goals. The existence of power centers, such as the United Nations, offers new political opportunities to social movements.

The international organizations grant consultative status to social movements that are not transnational, allow movements to participate in conferences that are not formally open to them, and offer financial support to organizations that cannot attend UN commissions or working groups. Moreover the UN facilitates transnational linkages between organizations in providing a place where social movements can challenge nation–states and international norms, and in offering them an opportunity to interact and work together (Passy, 1999: 155–61).

Groups and individuals are more informed. The microelectronic revolution has increased the competence of those groups and individuals. Accessible and affordable technology has broken the monopoly of governments on the collection and management of large amounts of information and deprived governments of that monopoly. The information technologies have disrupted hierarchies and have spread power among more people and more groups. Individuals or groups link for joint action without building a formal institutional framework. Groups communicate their demands to each other. As a result, they may find that their demands converge, and these demands may spin off into transnational action. For activist groups or social movements, layers of integration among local, regional, national, and international collective life are lines of power that can be used in the service of their demands. Groups upgrade their action, publicize it, and force the state to take their demands into consideration. However, it would be misleading to consider that these activist groups or social movements act in a vacuum, and that they are disconnected from their national environment. Their actions are constrained by the national setting and institutional framework in which they are located.

The NGOs: newcomers in world affairs

NGOs are a growing universe, but they are not new. Most of the main NGOs started their activity in the late 1950s, but gained more visibility in the 1970s and 1980s. NGOs cover a vast array of interests groups, including agriculture, environment, development, human rights, indigenous peoples, disease, peace, youth, women, and population. Their number and role increased as the scope of international issues grew in the last decades. They range from modest groups to influential ones like Amnesty International, Greenpeace, or CARE with a budget of $400 million. NGOs have increased tremendously from 4624 in 1989; they now number nearly 29000 (*The Economist*, 29 January 2000). Domestic NGOs have grown even faster. There are now two million in United States alone. In Russia, where none existed before the fall of communism, there are at least 65000. The label NGO masks differences between them. Some are local; some are of a truly international character. WWF, Greenpeace, and Friends of the Earth are probably the best known among this category. The World Wide Fund for Nature (WWF) is one of the best financially resourced NGOs. In 1961, the *Daily Mirror*, which advocated environmental issues, carried an article about the WWF. The newspaper received thousands and thousands of answers, and gifts from pence to more important sums of money. As a result, WWF established international headquarters in Gland (Switzerland) in 1962, and is located in 27 countries. It has a turnover of $200 million. WWF was an actor in the Uruguay Round of negotiations, but on the fringe in terms of influence and resources. The way WWF slotted into the negotiations is illustrative of an NGO's potential impact on negotiations. The WWF tracked what was going on inside the GATT, and tried to get information from the different negotiating parties, the GATT Secretariat, and the agencies. When any sensitive issues erupted in the negotiation, WWF created inputs. Most of them were publications, position papers, discussion papers, short position statements, or press releases. WWF formed coalitions with other NGOs, with Greenpeace, and with the European Environmental Bureau. The position statement they formulated turned to be a joint one with 14 other NGOs that was sent around the world. WWF has enough prestige to have a formal alliance with the World Bank relating to timber. The mainstay of that alliance is to take into account whether logging is being carried out in a sustainable manner, and whether concessions have been handed out to responsible companies, rather than to the president's personal ties. The WWF will provide the monitoring and the data (*The Economist*, 26 June 1999).

Greenpeace started in 1969, and achieved visibility during the US nuclear test in Amchitka, Alaska. Greenpeace Canada had organized demonstrations against testing in British Columbia and at one point brainstormed on the opportunities for action. The first boat, the *Phyllis Cormack*, left Vancouver for Amchitka in September 1971. It never made it to Amchitka, but the journey was not vain: it was widely broadcasted and contributed to the dissemination of an 'ecological sensibility' in the words of Paul Wapner (1996: 42). Since 1972, Greenpeace has grown from having a single office in Vancouver to staffing offices in over thirty countries. Greenpeace World organizes massive campaigns, targeted on four issue areas – toxic substances, energy and atmosphere, nuclear issues, and ocean and terrestrial ecology. Each country selects its own targeted campaign. Greenpeace Switzerland organized a campaign to support the popular referendum against Genetically Modified Organisms in 1998. One of Greenpeace's strategies is to plug into the worldwide communications system to advertize its direct action (Wapner, 1996: 51). The group relies on media presence to help with fund-raising.

Friends of the Earth (FOE) began as a consequence of a feud between members of the Sierra Club. In 1969, the group was created with the objective of acting internationally, issuing publications as its central activity. Decentralized, it became everything the Sierra Club was not (Wapner, 1996: 121). The group has grown tremendously since 1969, and has now offices in over fifty countries.

Dan Esty (1998: 7) has listed the variety of roles that NGOs play on the international scene. They may act as:

- service providers, often as government subcontractors
- watchdogs or private enforcement agents
- lobbyists
- stakeholders or countervailing interests
- agents of civil society enriching the public dialogue and representing interests not reflected in national government viewpoints
- policy analysts or expert advisers to governments
- mobilizers of public opinion
- bridges between state and non-state actors connecting local and global politics
- change agents offering new viewpoints
- consultants to industry

NGOs, with their issue-oriented activity, contribute to the network of professionals, 'epistemic communities', who have a specific knowledge of an issue in which uncertainty and lack of information prevail (Haas, 1992; Risse-Kappen, 1995; Elliott, 1999). They build coalitions with like-minded officials and academics, and use these alliances to strengthen their own bargaining leverage vis-à-vis governments. Their scientific and technical expertise helps them gain more access to decision-making. They point out the salient dimension of an issue from which decision-makers deduce their interests. They help to promote new ideas and beliefs that may become widely accepted before they can come up on the agenda. NGOs represent a significant element of opinion-building at the international level. They can express more freely their opinion, and are not tied by any specific mandate other than promoting their values and goals. As argued by Doherty (1994:

201) 'they are not constrained in the same way as governments to satisfy constituencies or preserve sovereignty'. They parallel the action of intergovernmental organizations (IGOs). They bring local experience to national or international decision-making (Gordenker and Weiss, 1995: 359). The reverse is also true. Increased participation of the NGOs in international politics was stimulated by international organizations, which acknowledged that it was essential to enjoy the input of the NGO community and thus encouraged their participation. The NGO community was formalized with the establishment of the United Nations in 1945. Article 71 of the UN Charter provides that:

the Economic and Social Council may make suitable arrangements for consultation with non-governmental organizations which are concerned with matters within its competence. Such arrangements may be made with international organizations and, where appropriate, with national organizations after consultation with the Member of the United Nations concerned.

The United Nations Conference in Rio, in 1992, stated that 'environmental issues are best handled with the participation of all concerned citizens, at the relevant level'. This coincided with the development of a burgeoning civil society around the world (French, 1996: 252). NGOs attempted to get an official voice in IGO deliberations, with unequal success. NGOs attending UNCED or Commission of Human Rights negotiations were disappointed by the number of informal or formal negotiations from which they were barred, and by the results of those negotiations (Doherty, 1994: 199). Accreditation rules have been facilitated. The UNCED conferences, UN conferences on Small Island Developing Nations (1994), Habitat II (1996), the Population summits in Beijing, and in Copenhagen, and UNCTAD X (2000) have witnessed gatherings of NGOs. In the UN Conference on Environment and Development (UNCED) in June 1992, 500 groups were accredited to observe the deliberations of the Commission on Sustainable Development (CSD), which was given the task of overseeing the follow-up action of the Rio Summit (Imber, 1996). Thousands of NGOs attended both the 1993 Conference on Human Rights in Vienna and the September 1994 UN Conference on Population and Development in Cairo (French, 1996: 254). However, accreditation rules are made more difficult in some other conferences. NGOs were denied accreditation and access to specific meetings and annual conferences. Gabrielle Marceau and Peter Pedersen (1999: 10) recall that at the Ministerial Meeting in Marrakesh in April 1994 establishing the WTO, no provisions existed for inviting NGOs. They had to acquire press credentials and register as members of the press.

Environmentalist groups like Greenpeace, Friends of the Earth, or the World Wildfund for Nature were active in the conference on Climate Change, alongside 800 registered industrial lobbyists (*International Herald Tribune*, 4 December 1997). They were facing the 'Global Climate Coalition' composed of 12 groups and companies including Exon, Mobil, Shell Oil, Ford Motor Co, mining and transport companies, steelmakers, and chemical producers (*International Herald Tribune*, 7 December 1997).

Governments react differently. Some of them encourage participation by NGOs, which could foster the government's national position; some vociferously oppose such a participation when the debated topic is more sensitive. When the Commission on Human Rights debated the concept of self determination, governments backed by experts screened any statements made by NGOs.

They benefit international negotiators by disseminating their information: reports, surveys, and newsletters are circulated daily during negotiations. The WWF issued reports during the Uruguay Round, based on in-depth analysis of trade and environment. 'ECO', an NGO-published daily newspaper, was negotiators' best source of information on the progress of official talks during the 1972 Stockholm Conference on the Human Environment, and continued to be distributed thereafter. It became a forum where governments tested ideas for breaking deadlocks in the Climate Change conference.

Agreements on complex and challenging issues require scientific and administrative effort at the national level (Cameron *et al.*, 1996: xiv). Local NGOs were associated with the CITES Secretariat and governments in drafting provisions for a permanent independent task force, empowered to investigate cross-border incidents or illegal trade of endangered species. Similar approaches were used at various conventions spreading from environment to landmines.

NGOs' constant participation in international meetings and their transnational links with locally-based interest groups and grass-roots support provide them with in-depth knowledge of a range of activities, which can benefit governments and instil legitimacy and credibility to their work. The tiny nation of Vanuatu turned its delegation over to an NGO with expertise in international law (based in London and funded by an American foundation), thereby making itself and the other sea-level island states major players in the fight against the control of global warming. Negotiations could be instrumental in the creation of NGOs. The establishment of NAFTA and the Uruguay Round of negotiations saw the emergence of powerful voices in the trade debate, namely the environmentalists (Leebron, 1997: 200). NGOs had different visions in the negotiations on NAFTA, and wanted to see provisions on health and safety, transboundary pollution, environment, and sustainable agriculture included in the agreement. Environmental organizations were not organized when negotiations started. But NAFTA negotiations crystallized concerns addressed by different groups. Coalitions of NGOs were built and endangered the congressional approval of the fast track negotiating authority for the US government. The government gave in and opened the agreement to environment and labor concerns. Environmentalists were placed in key USTR Public Advisory Committees, and Congressional committees invited environmental group leaders to comment on the integration of environmental concerns in NAFTA. Environmentalists have not limited their activity at NAFTA. They were quite active in the dispute between the United States and Mexico, the complainant, in the dolphin–tuna dispute over US action in banning imports of tuna caught by processes that did not meet standards adopted by the US Marine Mammal Protection Act for dolphin safety.

Yet, the picture is quite different in the WTO. There is no formal role for NGOs in the WTO (Marceau and Pedersen 1999; Esty, 1998). Although there is a strong case against NGOs' role in the WTO, because of their special interests, there is indeed a case in favor. Special interests already play out in the WTO negotiations (see Chapter 5), environmental perspectives would help to counteract their influence. Diverse groups would monitor each other, and would diminish the prospect of capture of the WTO by one group. NGOs are likely to generate useful information in the light of the high degree of uncertainty and complexity of environmental decision-making. This requires laboratory resources, skilled personnel, and carefully gathered ecological and epidemiological data. Most WTO members are not equipped to deal with this technical work. NGOs are well-positioned to provide it. The WTO would gain legitimacy because NGOs have public support, and represent widely-shared beliefs and concerns about the environment. A greater NGO role at the WTO would enrich the organization's deliberations and dispute settlement mechanism.

International organisations and international regimes

Since the Second World War, international organizations have come to play an increasing role in the global politics. They gained increasing visibility and freeway at the end of the Cold War. NATO is a case in point. But they still rely upon the states, and their willingness to negotiate.

The number of United Nations' members has increased from 51 at its creation in 1945 to 178 in 1988. The WTO has now 188 members, still excluding Russia and China. However, the vast array of international organizations which were established after WW II by the joint efforts of the United States and the United Kingdom, devoted to promote a liberal economic order, do not ensure equal treatment for countries. Developing countries have been able to express themselves in only a few of them. UNCTAD is a case in point.

International Organizations (IOs) help to structure co-operation among states. They are permanent frameworks for discussions and negotiations. Neo-realist paradigm of international relations has acknowledged the role played by IOs in global politics (Axelrod and Keohane, 1985). It is not a new phenomenon. The nineteenth century witnessed some IOs and some extraordinary conferences including the Conference of Vienna. But since the end of the Second World War, there has been a growth in diplomatic connectedness (Held *et al.*, 1999: 53).

This growth is impressive in the number of international regimes that have emerged since 1945. There has been an intensification of diplomatic activity to regulate, facilitate, and monitor the numerous issues that have erupted onto the international scene and the increases in flows of trade and FDI. According to Stephen Krasner (1983: 2), regimes are:

a set of implicit or explicit principles, norms, rules and decision-making procedures around which actors' expectations converge in a given area of international relations. Principles are beliefs, norms are standards of behaviour defined in terms of rights and obligations. Rules are specific prescriptions or proscriptions for action. Decision-making procedures are prevailing practices for making and implementing collective choice.

For John Ruggie (in Keohane 1984: 59) international regimes are ruled by hegemons. Regimes are 'a set of mutual expectations, rules and regulations, plans, organizational energies and financial commitments, which have been accepted by a group of states. States conform to decisions taken by hegemons'. Regimes exist in many areas, such as security, trade, human rights, or the environment. They encourage the use of negotiation to govern and resolve disputes. They are born of negotiations (Stojstedt *et al.*, 1994: 4). Parties that subscribe to regimes meet to monitor the progress towards assigned goals and to issue warnings to free riders. They indicate their will to co-ordinate action, and engage in trade-off of values. Actors prefer a rule-based system to the uncertainties of power capabilities; they can control the behavior of other actors, both internationally and domestically (Aggarwal, 1994: 44). Regimes give them a sense of predictability – particularly important in the context of the Cold War. Regimes provide a negotiating forum for bargaining, linking issues, and enhancing states' preferences, whilst reducing transaction costs. States bargain among themselves in an effort to realize their interests; diverging interests do not necessarily have a disintegrative effect. They broaden the spectrum of issues, and provide sufficient flexibility for coalition-building and compromises between the member states. Regimes adjust states' behavior. They do not impose order 'above the nation-state', and create valued networks of ties between states (Keohane and Nye, 1993: 3). Thus the existence and operation of international institutions helps to shape the expectations and behaviour of the participants, thereby encouraging the emergence of habits and constituencies that will support a co-operative international regime.

One should not underestimate the role of trust in creating international regimes. Christer Jönsson (1990: 213) underlines the role of beliefs and trust in the persistence of international regimes. Cognitive factors are associated with regime creation and regime maintenance. Transactions become embedded in a network of mutual relationships, which diminish the propensity of states to cheat or to defect. Keohane (1984: 59) shares similar views in stressing that 'principles, norms, rules, and procedures all contain injunctions about behavior: they prescribe certain actions and proscribe others'. They imply obligations, but these obligations are not compulsory. Yet, states obey even though they are not enforceable.

In negotiations, parties are engaged in a continuing relationship. Iklé (1999: 340) argues that diplomats who participate in prolonged conferences develop a certain attachment to the ongoing process of negotiation. Even diplomats who have opposing views, such as those from developing and industrialized countries, begin to feel personal bondings and collegiality with their colleagues. The lengthy process of the Uruguay Round, which lasted seven years, is a case in point. Diplomats fiercely opposed to each others' views developed mutual bondings and they were less likely to employ escalative tactics (Pfetsch and Landau, 2000: 39). Axelrod and Keohane argue that institutions alter the extent to which governments expect their present actions to affect the behavior of others in future actions. They become concerned about precedents, and governments do not treat defection as an isolated case, but as one in a series of interrelated actions, by the attribute of the shadow of the future (Axelrod and Keohane, 1985: 234).

Interdependence is tied to international regimes. It becomes increasingly difficult to consider one state's own interests without taking into consideration other states' interests. States have to improve other states' situations to improve their own situation. Interdependence is instrumental in creating international regimes (Mitrany, 1966; Holland, 1993: 15).

According to Keohane, co-operation or discord will depend on how governments take advantage of international regimes to make new agreements and ensure compliance with old ones (Keohane, 1984: 246). IOs help to support these endeavors, and they might be supported by NGOs, which pursue the same objective of ensuring co-operation. Both serve as important vehicles for individual and social learning. IOs play a role in setting the international agenda, and in framing the issues. Sensitive issues, such as environment or human rights, are propelled towards the top of the international policy agenda. When concentrating on monetary, environmental, or political problems, international organizations gain in importance and visibility.

High officials of the GATT, now the WTO, play a central role in the way the issues are negotiated. They are the main suppliers of information, along with the scientific community, and other intergovernmental institutions, such as the OECD. In 1980 the United States initiated a public campaign aimed at achieving an international consensus for negotiations on services under the GATT auspices. Academic research, high level seminars and a work programme on services in the OECD contributed to shape a body of knowledge, scientifically recognized, which helped the negotiators to adopt a position and anchor their understanding of the problems.

International organizations do not act in isolation, but interact. They constantly consult each other, and participate in each other's meetings. Issues addressed in one organization are often echoed in other organizations. Structural adjustment and conditionality were not solely adopted by the World Bank or the IMF, but were also adopted by the EU regarding its policies towards its peripheries (Landau, 1995b). Most issues are linked to other issues. This means that games being played affect one another (Axelrod and Keohane, 1985). Issues are overlapping. Trade negotiations are linked to monetary relations, foreign investment, energy, debt, and development; they no longer concern only tariffs. Environmental issues overlap with development, finance, or debt issues (Imber, 1996: 142). The multiplication of issues has forced the IOs to extend their agenda. The GATT was charged with intellectual property, which is dealt with by the WIPO. Some countries want labor standards to be addressed by the WTO, however labor standards are already addressed by the International Labor Organization (ILO). Supporters of action in the GATT/WTO argue that these institutions are weak and that the strengthened dispute settlement system of the WTO is needed to make standards effective.

New organizations have been created: the international Agency for Energy, and the UNCED, to deal with new issues. UNCED's creation can be traced back to the first global conference on the environment, the United Nations Conference on the Human Environment, which was held in Stockolm in 1972. The conference produced a set of principles for ecologically sound management of the planet, put environmental issues on the world's agenda, allowed the creation of the UN Environment Program, and the UNCED was established in 1989.

However, even if several regimes have an IO at their core, many are much more fluid and are constructed around several institutions. That is the case of environment or security regimes. The European security regime involves several institutions: the North Atlantic Treaty Organization (NATO), the Western European Union (WEU), the EU, and the Organization for Security and Co-operation in Europe (OSCE). They can co-operate, and lead joint operations. That occurred during the war in former Yugoslavia. After the UN Council of Security issued resolution 913 in April 1994, demanding an immediate cessation of Serb attacks and responding to the massacre in Sarajevo's market-place, NATO, the WEU, and EU Member Countries participated in joint operations of air strikes.

The end of the Cold War had a deep impact on international organizations. New issues emerged, the problems of migration and other humanitarian affairs as a result of the Gulf War and the Yugoslav crisis, to mention only a few. The Blue Helmets is a consequence of the new tasks facing IOs. Budgetary pressures represent what Childers and Urquhart (1994: 144) call 'a financial syndrome'. In 1992, 39 per cent of the total spending of the UN, which represented $4.09 billion, was going to the Blue Helmets and humanitarian actions. During the last decade, there was a shift away from UN missions in Africa to UN missions in Europe. Missions in Europe outnumber those in other parts of the world. The costs entailed by these operations are high: they can last from two to four or more years.

Bringing power politics back in

Power politics is not absent from IOs. Conferences, meetings, and arrangements are highly uneven in terms of participation and outcome. Indeed, major powers, among them the USA and the UK, have been the founding fathers of the international order. They designed most of the international institutions: the GATT, IMF, the World Bank, the Organization for Economic Cooperation and Development (OECD). Although the GATT has always shown more consideration to the position and to the interests of the developing countries than the inter-

Table 3.1   Selected peace-keeping forces

UN Angola Verification Mission (I, II, III)	UNAVEM	1989–97
UN Mission for the Referendum in Western Sahara	MINURSO	1991
UN Operation in Mozambique	ONUMOZ	1992–94
UN Mission in Liberia	UNOMIL	1993–97
UN Assistance Mission for Rwanda	UNMAR	1993–96
UN Observer Mission in Angola	MONUA	1997–99
UN Mission in Sierra Leone	UNAMSIL	1999–
UN Mission in Haiti	UNMIH	1993–96
UN Transition Mission in Haiti	UNSMIH	1997
UN Verification Mission in Guatemala	MINUGUA	1997
UN Protection Force	UNPROFOR	1992–95
UN Civilian Police Support Group (Croatia)	UNPSG	1992–95
UN Confidence Restoration Organization in Croatia	UNCRO	1995–96
UN Mission in Bosnia Herzegovina	UNMIBH	1995–
UN Preventive Deployment Force	UNPREDEP	1995–99
UN Transitional Administration for Eastern Slavonia, Baranja and Western Sirmium (Croatia)	UNTAES	1996–98
UN Military Operation in Prevlaka (Croatia)	UNMOP	1996–
UN Interim Administration in Kosovo	UNMIK	1999–

Source: http//www.un.org

national financial institutions where power is concentrated in few hands, it has been perceived as a 'club of the rich' by developing countries for a long time. Yet, the politics of international trade is shaped by the interplay of a relatively small number of governments, corporate interests, and technical experts. The WTO is a case in point, so is the International Telecommunication Union (ITU).

The politics of the international telecommunications regime has been revealed since the 1970s. Until then it operated with little controversy (Held *et al.*, 1999: 61). After the deregulation of the telecommunications business in the United States, the communication revolution, and the Agreement on Telecommunications in 1998 at the WTO, the regime has become highly politicized. Managers of firms and the major powers, under the lead of the United States, impacted on the conferences (Strange, 1995: 301).

The decay of the state capacities

States that will be more effective to face globalization will be those that solve their problems on the basis of complex organizational and governance pluralism (Rodrik 1999: 17). According to a prominent member of the neoliberal school, Dani Rodrik, countries that can reap the benefits of globalization are those that have performed reforms in the areas of macroeconomics, trade policy, deregulation and privatization, but moreover have built the complementary institutions – in the areas of governance, the judiciary, civil and political liberties, social insurance, and education. Strong institutions are important for handling social conflicts or mediating distributional conflicts in society. Societies with deeper cleavages (along ethnic, income, or regional lines) need institutions of conflict management. As noted by Dani Rodrik (1999: 3) 'participatory political institutions, civil and political liberties, high-quality bureaucracies, the rule of law, and mechanisms of social insurance can bridge the existing cleavages'. The presence of these institutions will help to face external shocks. Strong institutions require several conditions to make them work efficiently: channels through which societal demands could be aggregated and articulated; solid state apparatus and public bureaucracy; and the wiping out of corruption.

Countries that experienced disruptive conflicts among social groups without having strong institutional conflict management structures could not optimize the effects of globalization. Globalization increases the demand for social protection while simultaneously constraining the ability of governments to respond effectively to that demand. As Dani Rodrik argues, 'as globalization deepens, the social consensus erodes' (Rodrik 1997: 7). Hence the need to have strong institutional conflict management structures. Countries cannot benefit from globalization if they do not first improve the quality of the judiciary and of the public bureaucracy – the channels through which the non-elite (indigenous peoples, workers, farmers) can make themselves heard and brought into the decision-making process and the social safety nets. The most successful economies are those that are accountable and have strong institutions. Some countries are better equipped than others. East Asian countries have very strong governments. They carried out reforms before most of the developing countries; in contrast, African countries suffer from collapsing states.

The East Asian economies: from success to crisis

Asian countries have successfully embraced globalization. State intervention has been quite significant in the East Asian countries, although it has been quite different in the first-tier East Asian countries (Hong Kong, Singapore, The Republic of Korea, and Taiwan Province of China) and the second-tier South East Asian countries (Indonesia, Malaysia, the Philippines, and Thailand). The role of the state has ranged from heavily interventionist in South Korea, Indonesia, and Malaysia to more flexible in Hong Kong. Policies pursued in Asian countries have been coined by terms such as market-friendly (World Bank, 1993: 84); flying geese paradigm (Rowthorn 1996: 1), or investment-profit savings nexus (Singh 1996: 7). Governments have played a leading role in developing new industries, promoting exports, forging linkages with investors, and facilitating the process of technological absorption and learning.

Governments have deployed a wide array of policy instruments combining savings and investment policies and macroeconomic management with trade and industrial policies (World Bank, 1993). Strong incentives were provided to encourage investment and to build up the strength and capabilities of corporations. This was achieved through a wide variety of fiscal incentives including special deductions or tax concessions, or instruments to increase corporate profits (Singh, 1996: 9). Governments selected key industries – high technology information, biotechnology, electro-optics, machinery and precision instruments – provided technology, and channeled financial resources for these key industries. The Republic of Korea adopted the 'picking-up the winners' approach, which helped in the setting up of some successful export chemical and automobile companies (e.g. Hyundai) (Panchamukhi, 1996: 4).

NICs opted quite quickly for export-oriented strategies, although they all passed through an import-substitution phase. But these periods ended earlier than in other developing countries. Governments played an active role in promoting exports, by protecting infant industries from foreign competition, while using various measures to promote exports. These measures varied over time and across economies and included preferential financing; promotion subsidies; tax incentives; tariff exemptions on imported intermediate and capital goods; subsidized infrastructure; and foreign investment incentives (Panchamukhi, 1996: 5).

NICs also had a distinctive way of organizing business systems because of major differences in key social institutions, financial institutions, and societal contexts. Economic activities are characterized by dominant hierarchy market configurations. One of the most striking features of hierarchy market relations is the mutual obligations networks and the high level of interdependence between large firms, subcontractors, banks, and other financial institutions (Whitley, 1992: 25). The business groups, the '*Keiretsu*', or societies of business, which could operate in major sectors of industry, were organized around a leading bank, and in multiple linkages between suppliers and subcontractor firms (Holly, 1996: 34). Japanese '*Zaibatsu/Keiretsu*' and Korean '*Chaebol*' developed with considerable state support, and came to dominate many sectors of the economy: 8 Chaebol accounted for 92 per cent of all sales in the petroleum and coal production industries, 13 accounted for 79 per cent of transportation equipment, and 7 large trading companies – all members of the leading 10 Chaebol – accounted for almost all of the Korean distributors and retailers (Whitley, 1992: 43).

Governments relied on meritocratic and well-organized central government bureaucracy (World Bank, 1993: 143). Political and bureaucratic elites underwrote major investment decisions and provided considerable infrastructure and financial supports for new projects, so that firms could play ahead with confidence. The role of the financial system was crucial for guidance of industrial development, and for firms' strategic choices and risk management. Credit-based financial systems enabled state agencies to play a major role in the allocation of resources, and thus directed firms' choices, especially where the banking system was dominated by the state (Whitley, 1992: 233).

Government intervention was so pervasive that bottlenecks emerged. Signs of strain were becoming increasingly visible from 1996 onwards. To pursue the ambitious development programs that targeted investments in heavy and high-tech industries, credit access was facilitated. The tight relationship between governments, banks, and firms encouraged excessive borrowing and a wasteful use of resources. States were directing banks to make cheap loans on the basis of personal relationships. Firms took risks, and invested in the belief that the government would always bail them out. Korean Chaebol borrowed an average of four times their worth with little accountability (*International Herald Tribune*, 4 December 1997). Firms also invested abroad. Prior to the crisis, which erupted in 1997, debt for non-financial corporations was two or three times higher than equity in Indonesia and Thailand. The debt equity ratio in Korea was over 500 per cent for the 30 largest conglomerates (*The Economist*, 7 March 1998).

There was a lack of transparent accounting practices, and lack of oversight by banks and regulatory authorities. Reliable information would long ago have revealed the perverse effects of business practices in East Asia. Measures were urged to improve the corporate governance and avoid loose payments among Chaebol subsidiaries, which commonly bought and sold a wide range of products between them. A study on East Asia by Dani Rodrik (in *The Economist*, 7 March 1998) concluded that the quality of an economy's institutions makes a difference to growth. His findings were based on an index of institutional quality (e.g. the effectiveness of legal systems, the quality of bureaucracy, and the extent of corruption), adjusted for different levels of income per head and educational standards.

The Asian crisis has affected groups of countries in very different ways. The first group consists of open countries, in which companies are free to borrow abroad and where the government plays only a small role in the economy: Taiwan, Singapore, and Hong Kong. Taiwan's prudent management of the banking sector and diversification of investment risks over a variety of areas have come through the financial windstorm relatively unscathed (*The Economist*, 24 January 1998). Though affected, these countries have not suffered to the same extent as a the second group composed of Thailand, Indonesia, South Korea, and Malaysia. Companies are free to borrow abroad, but the government retains a considerable influence on the economy. It is this structure that many reckon was to blame for the Asian crisis. Thailand allowed the baht to fall in July 1997, the effect spreading quickly to Indonesia, the Philippines, Malaysia, and South Korea. Recovery will depend crucially on governments' abilities to impose structural economic change that could in some places have far-reaching political consequences (Korea, Singapore). India and China have been unscathed by the crisis. Companies have only restricted access to international capital markets, although they are not closed to world trade. But government intervention in the economy is widespread (*Financial Times*, 23 December 1997).

Africa: bleak prospects

The prospects for Africa are looking gloomy. Chains of institutional authorities and political legitimacy have been too weak to promote economic development. Many donor countries have pointed to the endogenous reasons that account for the slow development and stagnation of African economies, and their failure to follow the development recipes recommended by the IMF and the World Bank. Indeed, nearly all the former colonial powers, bar France, now regard Africa as marginal. France alone seems to be willing to provide military and financial aid to its former possessions, which account for one-third of Sub-Saharan Africa's area but only one-fifth of its population. The EU is reconsidering its relationship with Africa, reviewing the Lomé Convention (which guaranteed to African, Caribbean, and African countries (ACP), a privileged access to the EU's markets), and providing financial aid, including special provisions for regional co-operation. Conscious of the fact that the Lomé Convention had failed to enhance ACP trade, the EU in the 1990s started to rethink its special relationships with ACP countries. Instead of offering a privileged access to its markets, the EU adopted conditional aid for sound political governance, and attempted to help ACP countries integrate into the world economy. The new policy was one of selective aid, allocated only to those countries taking strong measures to promote market-based, export-led growth.

The convention may be split into its regional components: Caribbean countries could integrate with Latin America, whereas the Pacific Island states could turn to Asian countries for trade. To a certain extent, Caribbean states have started to move closer to Latin American countries in the context of the creation of NAFTA and the MERCOSUR.

Aid has often delayed reforms. It has not made much of a difference in Africa. Trade between Africa and Europe, though protected by preferential arrangements, has plummeted in recent years. As quoted in *The Economist* (12 December 1998) 'aid has become a way of life for many countries'. African countries tend to think that the explanation for their lagging economies lies in the declining aid. Output per head fell 0.5 per cent between 1978 and 1987 – far below the faster-growing developing countries. Many of the Sub-Saharan countries have lower incomes per head than in 1970. Life expectancy has also diminished with an HIV prevalence of 10 per cent of the population (UNDP, 1998).

The disastrous economic situation prevailing in most African countries cannot be attributed to exogenous causes or the configuration of the international economic system. The state is collapsing, and instability and insecurity pervade in the continent, bar only a few safer places. Most of the governments have failed to impose their legitimacy. Strategies of escape are widely adopted by the population. As noted by Daniel Bach (1999: xvii) 'deficient territorial control and alternative forms of allegiance contribute to the reintroduction of margins of autonomy, which are denied to African states in the formal conduct of their external affairs'. In such weak states, opportunities for survival and accumulation rely on the exploitation of boundary disparities and distortions on a rent-seeking basis by inter-personal networks (Bach and Hveem, 1998: 8). The centers of civilian power are located outside the state. Some are regional, others commercial. They are based on ethnic kinship, or on influential bodies such as the church. They have no connections with the state. They run their trade and provide their own services. Regional institutions may have comparative advantages where the nation–state offers insufficient governance (see Chapter 10)

Democratic practices – particularly within the public sector – are not fully implemented. The participation of society, or transparency, are not widespread over the continent. South Africa constitutes an exception, peopled by a wide range of interest groups, including organized labor and business, non-governmental and community-based organizations, state bodies, political parties, and civic associations.

The end of the Cold War has exerted a catalytic effect in opening up new opportunities for expressing identitarian, ethnic or religious demands. That further challenged the incumbent regimes. The 1990s witnessed new waves of civil unrest and armed conflicts.

Nearly a third of the 42 Sub-Saharan countries have been embroiled in cross-border wars or civil conflicts, which were fought mostly between national armies and guerillas. Angola experienced 20 years of war followed by four years of uneasy peace (*The Economist*, 11 April 1998). To make things worse, conflicts are spilling over to neighboring countries: see Table 3.2. In Namibia, the Caprivi Liberation Army (CLA), which was fighting for the independence of the Caprivi Strip, received

Table 3.2 Countries with major armed conflicts

Location	Inception	Principal combattants	Deaths
Angola	1975–	Government of Angola vs UNITA	500 000
Burundi	1993	Govt of Burundi vs Hutu (FDD)	150 000
Chad	1966	Govt of Chad vs CSMPD. MD	100 000
Mozambique	1992	Govt of Mozambique vs FRELIMO	
Namibia	1999	Govt of Namibia vs CLA	100
Nigeria	1999	Yoruba vs Haussa-Fulani	
Kenya	1992	Govt of Kenya vs tribal resistance	1 500
Rwanda	1990	Govt of Rwanda by Hutu	1 m
Sierra Leone	1989	Govt of Sierra Leone vs RUF	20 000
Somalia	1991	USC (Mahdi) vs USC (Aidid)	400 000
South Africa	1996	ANC vs IFP	15 000
Senegal	1999	Govt of Senegal vs MFDC	
Sudan	1983	Govt of Sudan vs SPLA, NDA	1.5 m
Uganda	1994	Govt of Uganda vs LRA	1 000
Western Sahara	1973	Govt of Morocco vs POLISARIO	15 000
Zaire	1993	Govt of Zaire vs ADFLCZ	20 000

Source: Miall, Ramsbotham, Woodhouse 1999; *The Economist* various issues; Heidelberg Conflict-Barometer (http://www.hiik.de)

support from the Angolan rebel movement (UNITA). Senegal helped rebels in Guinea-Bissau. The conflict in Eritrea between the government of President Issayas Afewerki and the Islamic Salvation Movement operated out of Sudan (Heidelberg Conflict Barometer, 1999). Laurent Kabila, Congo's ruler, who overthrew Mobutu Sese Seko, had been supported by Angola, Namibia, and Zimbabwe, followed by Chad and Sudan, while rebels had been backed by Rwanda and Uganda. Many of the fighters were attracted by Congo's resources. Angola, whose troops had occupied an oil town on Congo's coast, formed a joint oil-exploration company with the Congolese government.

Regional schemes such as the Southern African Development Community (SADC), or the Economic Community of West African States (ECOWAS) are playing a security-building role. Some countries are faring better. Mozambique is at peace: after 15 years, the war between Frelimo and Renamo ended in 1992. Relations between Uganda, Kenya, and Tanzania have also improved. Nigeria and Equatorial Guinea settled their border problem. In Uganda, the conflict between the government of Museveni, which supported a rebel group in Southern Sudan, and the rebel organization Lord's Resistance Army (LRA), supported by Sudan, ended after Iran, Malawi, and President Carter mediated between Uganda and Sudan. An accord was signed in

1999 between the governing party of Zanzibar in the Federal State of Tanzania and the opposition party Citizens' United Front (CUF), that ended the conflict for Zanzibar autonomy.

Ghana is a success story. Since 1983, the military regime has been implementing the reform program of the IMF and the World Bank. Ghana has been one of Africa's biggest borrowers with aid amounting to 11 per cent of GDP in 1996. Mauritius has drawn investments, and switched away from sugar production and tourism to textiles and clothing. Coats Viyella and Floreal, two clothing companies, have implanted factories in the country. The GDP of Mauritius grew by an annual average of 5.3 per cent between 1990 and 1994.

Yet, political stability and civilian rule can never be taken for granted. For a long time Cote d'Ivoire had a stable political regime ruled by the charismatic leader of Houphouet Boigny, whose death ushered in an era of instability. Zimbabwe, one of Africa's healthiest economies, has suddenly become inflation-ridden, debt-burdened and plagued by a 50 per cent unemployment rate, with riots erupting after a steep rise in the price of basic foods. The reverse is also true. Political instability and economic stagnation can end and give way to better prospects. Following its independence, Mozambique's civil conflict was backed by white supremacists from Rhodesia and South Africa. It ended in 1992, and the economy has recovered very fast. In 1997, growth attained was nearly 8 per cent.

The situation in Nigeria is emblematic, reflecting many of the evils plaguing Africa. Since the country's independence, political power has resided in the North. Oil revenues are concentrated in the hands of the government with numerous tenders being distributed according to personal ties. The vast public sector needs to be privatized to prevent rampant corruption and the civil service needs to be paid properly.

Indeed, economic reforms require strong institutions. Governments in Africa have to undertake a democratization process and economic reforms concurrently. However, political upheavals, and civil unrest are unlikely to help reforms. Foreign investments are unlikely to flow into countries with a weak local private sector, corruption, uncertain legal framework, strict exchange controls, civil unrest, and political instability. Congo is a case in point.

American Mineral Fields (AMF), a small mining company listed in Canada, signed a $1 billion deal with the Zairean rebel movement led by Laurent Kabila. Soon after the latter took power, Congo's state mining company, Gecamines, backed out of the deal. Tenke Mining, another Canadian mining company formed a joint venture with

Gecamines with a view to exploiting the biggest copper deposit in the world. The bid was reopened at the request of South Africa's Anglo American Corporation. The deal with AMF was finally set. But the minister of the economy, a member of Mr Kabila's inner circle, wanted to reopen the contract. Mining companies were asked to deposit money in the Banque de Commerce et de Développement. Most of them complained that Kabila's government was seeking bribes. In January 1998, the contract with AMF was cancelled and AMF sued Anglo American and related companies for more than $3 billion, on the grounds that Anglo had wrecked its deal with the Congo (*The Economist*, 17 January 1998).

Concluding remarks

South Asian and African countries offer two opposite examples. In the former, states have played an active role in the economic growth of the region, by orchestrating industrial development and promoting investment in the selected sectors. Economic performance was not the result of the opening up to trade and investment, but of the government's ability to engineer investment (Rodrik, 1999: 45). In Africa, the state is weak. In some cases, it has impeded economic growth in failing to provide a positive and predictable environment for trade and investment. Population has been delinked from governments, and has run trade and provided services away from the state. Many transnational companies have been reluctant to invest in states where extortion and bribery are widespread and where overall political outlook is bleak. As noted by Maria Livanos Cattaui, Secretary General of the International Chamber of Commerce (ICC) 'good governance, a transparent and predictable regulatory framework, the rule of law and a stable society all contribute to a hospitable investment climate'. Indeed, policies and institutions complement economic strategies to incorporate the global economy. The building up of a predictable environment for economic growth requires robust institutions and an active involvement of the state. Globalization is likely to provoke tensions and inequalities within the state as well as among the states. These problems must be addressed in institutional terms. As noted by Rubens Ricupero, the UNCTAD Secretary general at UNCTAD X (2000: 20): 'the State should enhance its role in providing macroeconomic stability, and a legal system, which in the case of the poorer developing countries and countries in transition involve extensive reform of the legal environment'.

4
The Stratification of Global Trade

Many observers of the world economy have recognized the qualitative and quantitative changes in the nature of trade, investments, and capital flows (Held *et al.*, 1999, Dicken, 1998). There could be some disagreement as to the beginning of globalization. Some trace it back to 1860 (Hirst, 1992; Sachs, 1996), others to 1913 (Bairoch, 1996), the 1950s (Dicken, 1992), or the 1960s or 1970s (Rowthorn and Kozul-Wright, 1998: UNCTAD, 1997a). However, no one would contest the magnitude of the changes and the increasing interactions between the components of globalization. As put by Boyer, 'today's globalization is qualitatively and quantitatively different from that of previous periods' (Boyer and Drache, 1996: 13). From 1973 to 1994, the volume of world exports grew at an average annual rate of around 4.5 per cent with lower rates over the years 1973–1985, but with a marked acceleration after 1985. During the same time, world GDP increased annually of 3.1 per cent. Trade multiplied by the factor 17, while GDP grew approximately six-fold between 1948 and 1997. FDI grew at an even faster rate than trade.

During the 1970s, annual flows of FDI averaged $27.5 billion, rising to $50 billion in the first half of the 1980s and $318 billion in 1995 (Rowthorn and Kozul-Wright, 1998: 3). Finally, cross-border financial flows grew at a faster pace. The fixed exchange rates were abandoned in the 1970s opening the path to short-term capital flows. Daily trade rose from $15 billion in 1973 to $880 billion in 1992 and to over $1300 billion in 1995. From 1980 to 1993, cross-border sales and purchases of financial assets rose from less that 10 per cent of GDP in the United States, Germany, and Japan to 135 per cent, 170 per cent, and 80 per cent respectively.

These figures are important as indicators of a rapid changing global economy, and especially of its greater openness and interdependence which are the landmarks of globalization. Increased trade, capital flows, and investments translate into global integration and convergence among countries. However, these figures mask significant geographical variations. My contention here is that globalization is unevenly spread over the countries both geographically and by sector. International trade and capital flows are highly concentrated on the countries, which are already the wealthiest and the most dynamic, while low-income countries have been bypassed in the process.

Trade, investments, and financial activities depend upon a country's resource endowments, institutional arrangements, and policy choices (Bairoch and Kozul-Wright, 1996: 4; Rowthorn and Kozul-Wright, 1998: 4; UNCTAD, 1997a: 70). There are still islands of poverty and marginalization in an ocean of hectic activity. If by 1913, four countries only – the United Kingdom, Germany, the United States, and France – accounted for 45 per cent of world trade, the situation today is similar. By 1995, Germany, the United States, France, and Japan still lead the world trade. Their share of world exports have decreased to 36 per cent and Japan has replaced the United Kingdom in the top four (Yarbrough and Yarbrough, 1997: 83).

However, the declining share of the top four suggests that participation has broadened to include some exporting countries, among them some developing countries. These are increasingly divided by the impact of globalization. Latin America is a case in point. In Mexico, both imports and exports accounted in 1996 for more than 20 per cent, or four times faster than all other Latin American countries (WTO, 1997). East Asian countries have been remarkably successful in increasing their trade with industrialized countries. This suggests whether globalization is a smooth and converging process, or a discontinuous and conflicting one.

Globalization and trade

From 1973 to 1994, world exports of goods and services grew more rapidly than world output. World exports in relation to world output rose from 12.1 per cent to 16.7 per cent over the period, increasing the degree to which national economies rely on international trade. A study conducted by UNCTAD (1996a: 4–5) explained the development in the relationship between trade and output growth by four new aspects of world trade which are the result of greater integration of the markets:

1) The rise of intra-trade. One third of the trade today is intra-industry trade. Intra-industry trade encompasses two types of trade (Yarbrough and Yarbrough, 1997: 83). The first is composed of trade in similar but differentiated finished goods (exchange of Japanese Toyotas for German BMWs). The second includes trade in components (import of components from a country and re-export of finished goods).

   The intra-industry trade has added a deeper layer of integration than was previously the case since it extends the number of countries involved in the production process. It is also associated with intra-firm investments and intra-firm alliances. A new international division of labor is taking place in which the industrial process is no longer concentrated in developed countries. A small fraction of developing countries benefits from intra-industry trade – constituting as much as one-third of NICs' total manufactures trade (Held, 1999: 174). A much higher share of trade among developed countries is intra-industry trade than among developing countries and NICs. Yarbrough and Yarbrough (1997: 87) report that intra-industry trade among developing countries, NICs, and developed countries account for 14.5 per cent, 41.9 per cent, and 58.9 per cent respectively.

   Intra-regional trade expanded faster than trade with all other regions especially for APEC, NAFTA, and MERCOSUR (see Chapter 10). Since 1980, trade within Asia has grown even faster than trade within NAFTA or MERCOSUR. By 1990, intra-Pacific Basin trade had risen to almost 69 per cent of the region's total trade, from about 58 per cent only ten years earlier. Intraregional trade remained more modest for Africa, with the sole exception of SADC. Between 1980 and 1997 intra-European trade decreased slightly.

2) The ability of producers to slice up the value chain, breaking the production process into many geographically separated steps. In a globalized world, it is increasingly difficult to trace the exact origin of a product. The production process is increasingly separated between pre-assembly and assembly activities on a global basis (OECD, 1994: 5). The *maquiladora* crossborder assembly operations of US companies accounted for $23 billion – almost half – of Mexican exports to the United States in 1994 (World Bank,

1997: 43). Virtually all manufactured products that are available in markets today are produced in more than one country. More than 80 per cent of the semiconductors shipped in the United States are assembled and tested overseas, mainly in the five South East Asian countries (D'Andrea Tyson, 1992: 93). Three-quarters of Taiwan's electronic production is eventually sold under someone else's brand name (*The Economist*, 7 November 1998).

US computer companies parceled out across national borders to highly specialized producers. Companies in Thailand and China assembled printed circuit boards, software was written in India's Bangalore, Malaysian and Philippine companies assembled components, and Taiwan and Korea specialized in higher value-added services and products such as digital design services and semiconductor memory (Steinberg and Stokes, 1998: 25).

For the production of a particular car manufactured by one of the three US autofirms, no fewer than nine countries are involved in some aspects of production, marketing and selling. Thirty per cent of the car's value goes to Korea for assembly, 17.5 per cent to Japan for components and advanced technology, 7.5 per cent to Germany for design, 2.5 per cent to Taiwan for advertising and marketing activities, and 1.5 per cent to Ireland and Barbados for data processing. This means that only 37 per cent of the production value of this 'American' car is generated in the United States (WTO, 1999: 36).

International 'sourcing' that is the purchase of intermediate inputs from foreign sources has grown faster than domestic 'sourcing'. Yeats (in WTO, 1999: 36) estimated that global production sharing accounted for more than $800 billion, or some 30 per cent of world trade in manufactured products. This highlights the increased interdependence of countries. Production sharing is of crucial importance for developing countries. They import components and parts, and re-export them in assembled form to the original country. But in the car example, this production sharing benefits mostly the East Asian countries.

3) The emergence of large exports of manufactured goods from low-wage to high-wage countries. Export success in East Asia was possible through the process of rapid capital accumulation, learning and productivity growth. However, a significant ingredient was that the industrial dynamism went hand-in-hand with rising real wages (UNCTAD, 1995: 149). This explains also the shift in East Asia trade patterns. Rising wages eroded the cost advantages in

unskilled labor industries such as textiles and clothing or chemicals, which provided the initial push on foreign markets. One of the responses was to relocate in other countries in the region, such as Malaysia, Thailand, and China. The other response was to upgrade towards more capital and technology-intensive industries such as electronics, machinery, and transport equipment (UNCTAD, 1995: 151). Over the past nine years, some 80 000 Taiwanese businesses have moved offshore, about half to China and half to South-East Asia (*The Economist*, 7 November 1998).

4) The emergence of super traders, countries with extremely high ratio of trade to GDP. This is the case for the Asian countries. The share of 10 Asian economies (China, Hong Kong, India, Indonesia, Malaysia, Philippines, Republic of Korea, Singapore, Taiwan, and Thailand) in world trade (exports plus imports) in 1995 (excluding trade among the EU countries) was over 19 per cent, which is greater than the United States (17.7 per cent), or Japan (10.2 per cent) and very close of the share of the EU (19.5 per cent). In 1965, the share of East Asian countries in total manufactured exports from developing countries was about 13 per cent; by 1990, it has risen well over 60 per cent. In 1996, the Asian countries were the United States' second trading partner (about $240 billion) just after the EU (about $274 billion) and before Japan (about $185 billion).

As Table 4.1. shows, the growth in the value of world merchandise trade over the period 1990–96 was greater in Asia than in any other region. Western Europe was lagging far behind, whereas exports from African and Latin American countries were similar. The table also shows that in the 1990s, imports were high in Latin America as trade liberalization in Latin America resulted in an increase of imports. The bulk of this was accounted for by

Table 4.1   Growth in the value of world merchandise trade by region (1990–96)

	Exports (per cent)	Imports (per cent)
North America	6	6
Latin America	12	11
Western Europe	3	2
Africa	12	3
Asia	16	8

Source: WTO, 1997

Brazil (facilitated by a certain degree of currency appreciation) and Columbia (UNCTAD, 1994a: 15). Brazil and Mexico reduced their import tariffs from 35–50 per cent to 14–15 per cent, and non-tariff barriers from 12–40 to 1–2 per cent (World Bank, 1997: 37).

Changing pattern of trade in developing countries

Developing countries have undergone sea-change since the 1980s when they abandoned the *import-substituting industrialization* strategy under the pressure of the debt and the balance-of-payments crises. Closer integration into the world economy through rapid liberalization of trade, finance, and investment was deemed to be the condition for success. As quoted by UNCTAD:

> trade liberalization was expected to lead to greater efficiency and competitiveness, thereby boosting export earnings needed to finance imports of capital and intermediate goods. It was also thought that greater openness to private foreign capital, including FDI, would further accelerate growth by supplementing domestic resources and lifting the rate of accumulation, as well as by enhancing productivity through the transfer of technology and organization skills. Such policies were expected not only to overcome the payments difficulties associated with the debt crisis, but also to set developing countries on a growth path that was faster and more sustainable, and more resilient to external shocks, than that of previous decades (UNCTAD, 1999a: 73).

Liberalization has not resulted in even benefits for developing countries. From 1970 to 1995, the share of developing countries in world industrial output rose; however this was almost exclusively due to industrial growth in East Asia. Since 1980, the share of Latin America and Africa has fallen, while at the same time, industrialized countries' shares in world industrial output fell. Interestingly, Table 4.2 shows that in 1970, Latin America and Asia started with similar shares in world manufacturing output; 25 years later Asia finds itself far ahead of Latin America. However, Asia is not so homogeneous a region as some have previously suggested (World Bank, 1993).

There are differences between a first tier composed of Hong Kong, the Republic of Korea, Singapore, and Taiwan and second-tier Asian countries, including Malaysia, Thailand, Indonesia, and China (Jomo,

Table 4.2 Share of different regions in world manufacturing output since 1979 (percentage)

Country/region	1970	1980	1990	1995
Industrialized countries	88.0	82.8	84.2	80.3
Developing countries	12.0	17.2	15.8	19.7
of which				
Latin America	4.7	6.5	4.6	4.6
South Asia*	1.2	1.3	1.3	1.5
East Asia	4.2	6.8	7.4	11.1
Sub-Saharan Africa	0.6	0.5	0.3	0.3

* South Asia is composed of Bangladesh, India, Nepal, Pakistan, and Sri Lanka
Source: UNCTAD, Trade and Development Report 1997

1996: 1). The difference is clearly discernable in the structure of first-tier and second-tier East Asian NICs.

The first-tier East Asian countries undertook a dramatic change in their exports structure from labor-intensive manufactured goods such as textiles to capital-intensive goods such as machinery and transport equipment or electronic goods (Jomo, 1996). They also developed sharply focused export niches. In the footwear industry for example, South Korea has specialized in athletic footwear, Taiwan in vinyl and plastic shoes (Gereffi, 1996: 59). Second-tier South-East Asian NICs have been less successful in anchoring in high-technology niches than the first-tier East Asian countries.

The composition of exports of developing countries has undergone a rapid transformation since the early 1980s. The share of developing countries exports practically doubled between 1982 and 1992 (Rodrik, 1995: 32). In 1982, exports of commodities constituted the bulk of their exports. As shown in Table 4.3, in 1992, agriculture and mining had diminished, while exports of manufactured goods increased.

African countries remain commodity-exporting countries. They have suffered large terms of trade losses over the period 1980–90, estimated at $350 billion a year for the period 1980–92. Commodity prices in real terms have now been depressed for two decades, resulting from an increasing volume of commodity exports from African countries. For many commodities exported by African countries, there has been a substantial substitution by synthetic materials over the past two decades (Maizels, 1999: 1–3). However, concentration is having an effect in Africa. Some countries such as Tunisia, Mauritius, Morocco, South Africa, and Zimbabwe have succeeded in increasing their market share in textiles and garment. But the main African export portfolio includes

Table 4.3 Share of developing countries in world exports, 1982, 1987, 1992
(per cent)

	Agricultural products	Mining products	Manufacturing	Total merchandise exports (excl. fuels)	Commercial services
1982	29	30	11	16	21
1987	28	25	14	17	18
1992	27	26	19	20	18

Source: GATT 1996

cut flowers, frozen fish, T-shirts, women's trousers, footwear, and transistors. Sub-Saharan Africa (excluding the SACU) is the world's largest net exporter of fresh food and agro-based products (International Trade Center, 2000). Commodities – especially food and fibers – and their processed products face high barriers in importing countries. High protection for the food industry impedes diversification of activity in developing countries, and food exports such as meat or fish products face sanitary and phytosanitary measures in the industrialized countries' markets, notably in the EU. Tanzania complained that the EU had banned imports of fresh, frozen, and processed fish products alleging health concerns, so did Kenya, Uganda, and Mozambique. The EU agreed to withdraw the ban, following consultations that were held with the exporting countries.

The shift to manufactured goods has mostly benefited the Asian countries. In 1990, about three-quarters of their exports were in those goods (UNCTAD, 1996a: 124–5). In contrast, the proportion for Latin America was only 38 per cent, and only 24 per cent if Mexico is excluded.

This gap is even more striking when analysing a list of 20 product groups (at the three-digit SITC level), which had the most rapidly rising shares of OECD imports in 1963–92.[1] The first-tier and second-tier NICs have, in general, been more successful than other developing countries in moving into these products. The Latin-American region could not keep pace, and its share of the OECD markets abruptly diminished over the period 1963–93. In 1963 Latin America accounted for 15 per cent of all OECD imports, or for 60 per cent of all developing country exports of these products. Its share in 1993 of the 20 most dynamic products stood at only 2.5 per cent of total OECD imports of such goods, and only 16 per cent of total developing countries (UNCTAD, 1996a: 125).

The analysis of import penetration by developing countries of the OECD market for selected groups of manufactures illustrates some of the changes performed by developing countries between 1978 and 1992, and also shows the gap between the two categories of East Asian countries. As shown in Table 4.4, import penetration of textiles and clothing more than doubled from the late 1970s to the early 1990s, from around 7 per cent to 16 per cent. Import penetration was more striking in the United States: around 21 per cent of imports came from developing countries, the largest proportion of whose manufactured exports is made up of textiles and clothing. However, as trade barriers remained high in developed countries developing countries began to move into the higher technology end of industries. Textiles and clothing is one of the most heavily protected sectors in industrialized countries (UNCTAD, 1996a: 151). Trade barriers in these countries have impeded imports of developing countries.

From the 1950s onwards, the textile regime stood outside the GATT discipline, and was ruled by the Multi-Fibre Arrangement (MFA). The MFA provided guidelines for bilateral export-restraint agreements, and encompassed quotas and countervailing duties (Dickerson, 1995: 308). The Marrakesh Agreement on textiles provides the procedure for integrating trade in textiles and clothing fully into the GATT system by requiring countries to remove the restrictions in four stages over a period of ten years ending on 1 January 2005. A study conducted by UNCTAD has reckoned that if the Uruguay Round obligations in textiles is implemented as envisaged, imports from developing countries could increase from $88.8 billion in 1993 to $264 billion. It is assumed that production in the North will fall by 60 per cent by the end of the transition period, and that consumption will grow by 3.25 per cent per annum from $258 billion to $355.2 billion during this period (UNCTAD, 1996a: 150).

Compared with textiles and clothing, imports of developing countries in office and computer equipment increased significantly. Imports of computer and office equipment, negligible in the late 1970s, accounted for nearly 14 per cent of all OECD countries in 1992. Graph 4.1 shows the performance of first-tier East Asian NICs in penetrating the OECD markets in office and high-technology goods. The market share of developing countries almost tripled from 1985 to 1992. More than 90 per cent of these imports came from East Asia.

By the early 1990s first-tier NICs moved into the high tech industries: from only 1 per cent of the market in the early 1970s, by the late 1980s they had captured nearly 10 per cent of the market (UNCTAD

Table 4.4 Import penetration by developing countries of the OECD marked for selected groups of manufactured products, 1978–92

| | Imports from developing countries | | | | OECD imports from | |
	United States	EU	Total OECD	First-tier NICs	Second-tier NICs	Other countries
Textiles						
1978	8.1	6.5	6.6	3.9	0.3	3.8
1980	8.8	7.7	7.7	4.5	0.4	3.9
1985	14.3	9.7	11.2	6.7	0.8	6.9
1990	20.1	14.2	15.0	6.8	1.8	11.5
1992	20.9	17.5	16.3	6.3	2.6	12.0
Office and computer equipment						
1978	1.9	1.8	0.9	0.7	0.0	0.2
1980	2.8	2.3	2.0	1.4	0.1	0.5
1985	5.5	6.7	4.6	3.8	0.1	0.7
1990	17.3	14.9	11.1	9.6	0.7	1.2
1992	21.0	14.6	13.4	10.9	1.7	0.8

Source: UNCTAD 1995

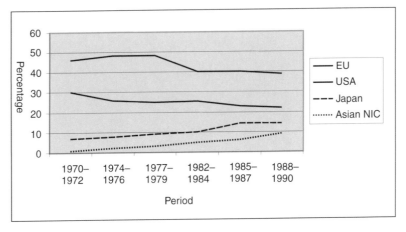

Source: P. Guerrieri and C. Milana, 'Changes and trends in the world trade in high-technology products', in UNCTAD 1995: 151.

Graph 4.1   Share of Asian NICs and other regions or countries in world trade in products of high-technology industries, 1970–1990

1995: 151). First-tier NICs are also catching up with industrialized countries in chemicals, and mechanical products and instruments.

In some technologies, the leap forward of first-tier NICs has resulted in an erosion of the American and European position, especially pronounced in electronics (D'Andrea Tyson 1992: 25; Ostry and Nelson 1995: 11). Leading in high technology products such as electronics and pharmaceuticals (Ostry, 1995: 3) since the 1960s, the United States was losing control of high-tech trade by the mid 1980s. Japan has been catching up the US leadership in high technology, and now registers more than two and a half times the number of patents as the US, eight times as many as Britain. Japan's 147 per capita, resident patents, compares with 28.8 in the US, 35 in Britain and 64 in Switzerland (McMillan, 1996: 121). The Ministry of International Trade and Industry (MITI) focused on overcoming energy constraints, improving quality of life, and developing materials technology, biotechnology and new functional technology. The aim was to spend up to 4 per cent of GNP on research and development in 1995 (McMillan, 1996: 128).

Shifting patterns of trade: services

Economic rivalry among industrialized countries has shifted around services, which cover a wide range of economic activities. The WTO secretariat has divided these divergent activities in 12 sectors: Business (including professional and computer); communication; construction and engineering; distribution; education; environmental; financial (insurance and banking); health; tourism and travel; recreational; cultural and sporting; and transport (WTO, 1996). Growth of services is linked to development in new information technology, which affects all activities, all of which have a strong information content. Services play a central role in facilitating trade in goods as a result of transportation, telecommunications, marketing, and distribution services. Services account for around 60 per cent of GDP in developed countries. In the United States, this figure is 80 per cent of GDP.

International trade in services is growing constantly. The value has increased at an average rate of more than 6 per cent over the period 1992–94. Services account for a quarter of international trade in goods; around $700 billion. In 1993, trade in services represented $154 billion in Japan, approximately 7 per cent of the world trade. In 1996, the share of services in the added value exports accounted for 37 per cent for low income countries, 53 per cent for middle income countries, and more than 70 per cent for developed countries.

Industrialized countries are dominating trade in services. Some developing countries have comparative advantages in services and are firmly developing niches. India is a case in point as regards computers. In some developing countries such as Brazil and the Republic of Korea, services account for 50 per cent and 64 per cent of their GDP respectively. Hong Kong, Singapore, and China are among the 10 first exporters in services. In Brazil, half of the GDP is concentrated in the service sector. In Latin America, Mexico is the first exporter of services followed by Brazil (20.3 and 13.9 per cent of total Latin America exports in services respectively), whereas it is the opposite for imports: Brazil is first followed by Mexico (25.6 and 18.1 per cent of total Latin America imports in services respectively) (WTO, 1999: 38).

Concluding remarks

Some conclusions could be drawn from the analysis of trade flows in the context of globalization. In terms of division of labor, developing countries are no longer exporters of raw products and receivers of manufactured goods from the industrialized countries. They are increasing their share of manufactured goods. Some have done better than others: the East Asian countries are engaged increasingly in high tech exports; thus are competing with industrialized countries. Africa remains marginalized. There are some islands of success in the continent: South Africa is a case in point. In Latin America, trade is unevenly distributed. Mexico, Brazil, and to a lesser extent Chile, are significant players in world trade, including the services.

Indeed, there is an uneven pattern of trade between regions, and a stratification of world trade between winners and losers. Increased trade flows resulting from globalization have mostly benefited the East Asian countries and some Latin American countries. African countries, bar a few, remain marginalized, and bypassed by the increasing trade flows which characterize globalization.

5
The GATT/WTO:
Instrumentalizing Globalization

The WTO, the successor of the GATT, is undoubtedly one of the main instruments of globalization. It contributes to globalization in removing barriers to trade and in pushing liberalization ahead in more and more sectors of the economy, including the key sector of services. Lowered tariffs have reduced national frontiers as barriers to trade, and have facilitated transnational production and distribution. From the Geneva Round in 1947 to the Uruguay Round from 1986 to 1993, tariffs on industrial products diminished from 40 per cent to 3.8 per cent. The WTO provides stability of access to export markets by a uniform set of rules elaborated in the various agreements. These rules apply before the border (inspection procedures); at the border (customs valuation and import licenses); and after the border in adopting harmonized market requirements. Each member country implements the same rules, and the rule-based system provides business enterprises or exporters with a predictable environment in which they can plan and develop their production without fear that foreign markets may be lost or disrupted by government practices such as the raising of tariffs or the imposition of prohibitions and restrictions on imports. The WTO has transformed the global playing field for international players. Is the WTO successful in transforming it for developing countries? Is it contributing to integration or to fragmentation? Before answering these questions, we will explore the GATT/WTO trade regime, the results of the Uruguay Round of Negotiations, and the built-in provisions.

The GATT: adapting to the transformations in the world economy

The International Trade Organization (ITO) was conceived to be the third pillar to the Bretton Woods Agreement, besides the IMF and the BIRD. When the United States failed to ratify the ITO, the GATT, which was a provisional arrangement, became the international trade treaty. The GATT adapted to the transformations in the world economy which took place after its creation as new issues emerged: the EEC in 1958; escalating trade disputes between the United States and the EC from the 1970s onwards; and the segregation of textiles from the GATT discipline. The Contracting Parties tried to find flexible interpretations to the GATT legalism, which prevailed in the first decade of its existence. Hence, Article XXIV and the Enabling Clause Decision of Differential and More Favorable Treatment, Reciprocity and Fuller Participation of Developing Countries, which allowed regional agreements to coexist with the General Agreement, or the Multi-Fiber Agreement to provide guidelines for bilateral export-restraint agreements.

The GATT regime is built on several principles:

- The Most Favored Nation (MFN), according to which each contracting party to the GATT is required to provide all other contracting parties with the same conditions of trade as the most favorable terms it extends; that is each contracting party is required to treat all contracting parties in the same way that it treats its 'most favored nation'.
- The National Treatment principle complements the MFN principle. It requires that an imported product which has crossed the border after payment of customs duties and other charges should not receive treatment that is less favorable than that extended to the like product produced domestically. In other words, the principle requires member countries to treat imported products on the same footing as similar domestically produced products.
- Reciprocity according to which the benefits of any bilateral agreements between contracting parties regarding tariff reductions and market access are extended simultaneously to all other contracting parties. The principle of reciprocity is closely associated with that of MFN.
- Transparency, that is to harmonize the system of import protection, so that barriers to trade can then be reduced through the process of negotiation. The GATT therefore limited the use of quotas, except in

specific conditions widely used by agriculture. The Uruguay Round reinforced the transparency principle in multiplying notification procedures. Countries should notify any new laws, or any new regulations to the concerned WTO committees. Protection is only granted if countries have complied to the notification procedure.

When the GATT was established tariffs were the main form of trade protection, and negotiations in the early years focused primarily upon tariff reductions. The GATT has been remarkably successful in diminishing tariffs through the eight Rounds of negotiations (see Table 5.1). While the GATT stands for liberal trade, it recognizes that countries may wish to protect their industries from foreign competition. It urges them to keep such protection at reasonably low levels and to provide it through tariffs. The principle of protection by tariffs is reinforced by provisions prohibiting member countries from using quantitative restrictions on imports.

Many developed countries have deviated from the GATT rules, whether in agriculture or in textiles and clothing. However, the GATT provides for some exceptions to the rules to restrict imports for countries considered to be in balance-of-payments difficulties. The GATT rules provide developing countries in balance-of-payments difficulties with a greater flexibility to use quantitative restrictions on imports.

Starting from the Kennedy Round and the Tokyo Round, the focus of negotiations has been extended to other non-tariff barriers (NTBs) as governments have devised other barriers to trade to limit foreign entries. These refer to administrative barriers or 'Grey area' measures that took place outside the legal framework of the GATT, and in

Table 5.1 The GATT Negotiating Rounds

Round	Date	Member countries	Value of trade ($ million)	Number of tariff concessions
Geneva	1947	23	10	45 000
Annecy	1949	33	–	5 000
Torquay	1950	34	–	8 700
Geneva	1952	22	2.5	–
Dillon	1960–61	45	4.9	4 400
Kennedy	1962–67	47	40	
Tokyo	1970–83	118		

Source: WTO, various issues

different guises such as 'voluntary export restraints' (VERs), 'orderly marketing agreements' (OMAs), or similar measures on the export or import side. Exporting countries with rising exports were required by importing countries to restrain their exports to agreed limits. Though these arrangements were called 'voluntary', in reality they were not always so. As the restraints were applied only to imports from certain countries, they were also inconsistent with the rule that restrictions on imports should be employed on a non-discriminatory basis.

These arrangements have affected mainly agricultural products, textiles, footwear, steel products, machinery, vehicles, and electronic equipment originating from Japan and Korea among others (UNCTAD, 1994b: 55–7). By the early 1990s, VERs affected 15 per cent of world trade. More than 33 per cent of Japanese exports to both the EU and the United States were subject to VERs, which were imposed in addition to tariffs, MFA restrictions, antidumping and countervailing measures (Ruigrok, van Tulder, 1998: 229; UNCTAD, 1994b: 51). Table 5.2. lists the main instruments used by developed countries to restrict imports. Antidumping measures outnumber any other instruments, and have replaced previous restrictive practices.

Devising new trade restrictions

The liberalization process has moved beyond its primary concern with the removal of tariffs and quantitative trade restrictions on goods at the border to focus more closely on an ever-growing range of policy measures affecting the terms and conditions of market access, such as standards and regulations, subsidy practices, intellectual property protection, or restrictions on personnel movement. The WTO is increasingly dealing with new layers of restrictive practices that have come to

Table 5.2 Measures used to protect imports from 1979 to 1988

Country	Safeguards	Antidumping	Countervailing duties	Other	Total
USA	2	427	371	78	878
EU	6	406	13	33	458
Australia	22	478	1	–	458
Canada	1	447	22	–	470
Total in percent	0.5	76.9	18	4.6	

Source: Patrick Messerlin, 1990, 'Antidumping' in Jeffrey J. Schott (ed.), *Completing the Uruguay Round*, Washington: Institute for International Economics

the forefront. Barriers to trade are generally embedded in domestic regulations. That is the case for some of the areas covered by the WTO trade regime, such as technical barriers to trade (ecolabels), sanitary and phytosanitary measures, and regulations in services.[1]

In services, most of the barriers to trade are composed of domestic regulations, which, unlike tariff barriers to trade in goods, do not take the form of transparent barriers imposed at the border against foreign services. Governments have tried to protect their local service suppliers from foreign competition, by focusing on the local consumption of services, or the local provision of services. For example, regulations may stipulate that only car insurance provided by a local firm satisfies the compulsory insurance requirement for car registration, or that only locally owned and established firms may sell car insurance to consumers (Feketekuty, 1999: 4). Also, domestic regulations frequently limit trade even if they do not explicitly discriminate against foreign providers. These regulations have made difficult the designing of a regime for trade in services.

According to Mattoo (1999: 22), the weakest provisions of the General Agreement on Trade in Services (GATS) are those dealing with domestic regulations, although they have such an obviously powerful influence on international trade in services. The reason is not difficult to see: it is extremely difficult to develop effective multilateral disciplines in this area without seeming to encroach upon national sovereignty and unduly limiting regulatory freedom.

Developing countries argue that environmental standards of the North that often translate into the establishment of technical standards, packaging or labeling requirements, aim to keep out some of their exports. Some ecolabels function as serious non-tariff barriers. The EU ecolabel for tissues, T-shirts, bed linen made of cotton or blends of cotton and polyester, or for timber, harm developing countries' exports. According to Brazil, it is unfair to penalize wood from sustainably managed plantation forests as the EU does. Eucalyptus forests in Brazil renew faster than many other rainforests. Ecolabels may reduce the competitiveness of unlabelled products in a particular market. Imports of paper originating from Brazil declined significantly after the introduction of an ecolabel (Motta Veiga *et al.*, 1997: 65–79).

The ecolabelling schemes are related to the life cycle of the products and therefore include the production process, in particular the raw materials used in the production process (use of power, air, soil, and water). As such, they embody a massive potential for discrimination between imported and domestic products based on the assessment of the various uses of inputs as well as processing and production methods. Many of the disputes brought to the WTO are related to the Product and Process Methods (PPMs): the United States argues that non-product PPMs are allowed under the WTO (Raghavan 1996: 11); and developing countries reject the argument.

The WTO rules under the Agreement on Technical Barriers to Trade (TBT) may fuel disputes (Markandya 1997: 29). Although the GATT rules do not allow one country to take trade action for the purpose of attempting to enforce its own domestic laws in another country – even to protect animal health or exhaustible natural resources (extra-territoriality) – it never adopted the panel results in the Tuna–Dolphin case opposing the United States and Mexico, backed by the EU.[2] The panel result infuriated environmentalists who concluded that the WTO put trade rules ahead of environmental goals, and was against saving the planet. From an ecological point of view, damage resulting from a product or damage resulting from a process to produce it are part of the same problem. The WTO should have ruled on the killing of the dolphins and not on the tuna fish as a product. However the WTO as a legalistic organization judged the dispute on the ground of the WTO obligations, which do not give primacy to environmental considerations.

In the future, the Sanitary and Phytosanitary Agreement (SPS) rules may fuel trade disputes in the WTO. Many have already involved the United States and the EU (use of growth hormone for beef),[3] but could potentially involve other countries. The requirement of scientific evidence is at the core of the dispute. How much and what type of scientific evidence is required remains unclear. Where the relevant scientific evidence is insufficient, the SPS Agreement allows Member countries to adopt provisional measures on the basis of the precautionary principle. The EU's application is quite stringent, and has made a large use of the precautionary principle; hence, the disputes between the United States and the EU so far. Further disputes may arise in the future from the sensitive issue of genetically modified products. One is already brewing between the United States and the EU, in response to public concerns that genetically modified foods endanger public health, limited product approval to a maximum of 10 years, and is adopting a directive tightening labeling and monitoring of such goods. The EU has recently postponed a decision to approve new GM crops.

The Uruguay Round of negotiations

The Uruguay Round of negotiations presented strong links with the Kennedy and Tokyo Rounds, by dealing with some of the same issues, such as government procurements, antidumping regulations, counterfeit goods, and customs valuation. However, the agenda of the Uruguay Round was also very different from the previous negotiations in opening the door for measures in new issues, services, intellectual property rights, and investments. The agreement was novel in bringing these new areas into an international organization, and in facilitating transparency and liberalization in highly sensitive issues (Landau, forthcoming).

The WTO system, which has emerged from the Uruguay Round of negotiations, encompasses the GATT and twelve associate agreements, the GATS, and an Agreement on Trade-Related Aspects of Intellectual Property Rights (TRIPS).

One of the main achievements of the Uruguay Round of negotiations is to replace the patchwork of previous GATT obligations with a *single undertaking* that is binding on all the Member countries. As a result, developing countries are now required to assume substantial obligations from which they had been exempt in previous GATT rounds.

The negotiations of the 32 countries for accession are more complex to achieve.[4] Acceding members have to embark on a vast array of measures and laws compatible with the WTO agreements. To comply with WTO terms of accession, China had to open its telecommunications sector, fund management and brokerage services, auto finance, and areas of distribution that have been largely off-limits to foreign investors so far.[5]

The WTO

The WTO is better equipped to monitor international trade. The dispute settlement mechanism deals with all disputes arising between member countries. The dispute mechanism settlement of the GATT was based on very meager clauses, but became quite sophisticated in the 1980s. The WTO dispute settlement mechanism induces adherence to international norms by member countries, by a technique of surveillance of the trade activity, by correcting deviant behavior. Conflict resolution is ensured by consultation procedures, good offices, conciliation and mediation, arbitration, adjudication by a panel, and an appeal structure (Qureshi 1996: 100). The Dispute Settlement Understanding (DSU) also ensures that conflict resolution will intervene in a reasonable period of time (Art. 21.3).

The Dispute Settlement Body (DSB) administers the rules, and ensures enforcement through authorization of retaliatory measures

Table 5.3　Main legal instruments negotiated in the Uruguay Round

---

A.　Marrakesh Agreement establishing the World Trade Organization
B.　Multilateral Agreements
　　Trade in Goods
　　　General Agreement on Tariffs and Trade 1994f (GATT 1994)
　　　Associate Agreements
　　　　Agreement on the Implementation of Article VII of GATT 1994
　　　　(Customs Valuation)
　　　　Agreement on Preshipment Inspection (PSI)
　　　　Agreement on Technical Barriers to Trade (TBT)
　　　　Agreement on Sanitary and Phytosanitary Measures (SPM)
　　　　Agreement on Import Licenses
　　　　Agreement on Safeguards
　　　　Agreement on Subsidies and Countervailing Measures (SCM)
　　　　Agreement on the Implementation of Article VI of GATT 1994
　　　　(Antidumping) (ADP)
　　　　Agreement on Trade Related Investment Measures (TRIMs)
　　　　Agreement on Textiles and Clothing (ATC)
　　　　Agreement on Agriculture
　　　　Agreement on rules of origin
　　　Agreement on Trade in Services (GATS)
　　　Agreement on Intellectual Property Rights
　　　Understandings and Decisions
　　　　Understandings on Balance-of-Payments Provisions of GATT 1994
　　　　Decision regarding cases where customs administrations have reasons
　　　　to doubt the truth or accuracy of the declared value (Decision on
　　　　Shifting the Burden of Proof)
　　　　Understanding on Rules and Procedures Governing the Settlement of
　　　　Disputes
　　　　Understanding on the Interpretation of Article II: 1(b) of GATT 1994
　　　　(Binding of tariff concessions)
　　　　Decision on Trade and Environment

---

by the aggrieved member. However, it is not empowered to adopt interpretations of the Multilateral Trade Agreement or the Agreements established by the WTO. The DSB is reliant on the consent of the parties, particularly in implementing its decisions (WTO, 1999). Table 5.4. gives an overview of the State-of-play of WTO disputes.

One of the most difficult areas facing dispute settlement mechanism today is the question of implementing the result of panel rulings, whether at the first-level panel report, unappealed, or after an Appellate Body report has been adopted. The Banana case or the Hormone beef cases were cases which most deeply affected the problem of dispute set-

Table 5.4 Overview of the state-of-play of WTO disputes (2000)

	Consultation Requests	Distinct Matters	Active cases	Completed cases	Settled or inactive cases
Number	185	144	26	30	40

Source: www.wto.org/dispute settlement

tlement's implementation.[6] The EU refused to comply with a WTO ruling to open its market to US hormone-treated beef.

The Uruguay Round provides 'built-in provisions' for starting new rounds of negotiations, and continuing review or negotiations of specific sectors or subject areas. Table 5.5 lists some of the most important dates and deadlines. Explaining the agreements is beyond the scope of this chapter; however it is important to stress the most important features of the Marrakesh Agreements and their impact on developing countries.

The WTO: towards an open and liberal multilateral trading system

The WTO is built on two basic rules. In addition it is complemented by rules of general application and other rules, which are intended to avoid the trade-distorting effects of practices pursued by governments.

The basic rules

The first rule is to ensure that protection at the border is only established through tariffs at low levels. Thus, it prohibits countries from using quantitative restrictions, with specified exceptions (balance-of-payments). Even in this case, the Understanding on Balance-of-Payments Provisions (BOPs) of GATT 1994 urges Member countries not to use quantitative restrictions to safeguard their BOP situations, but to prefer in such situations price-based measures as their impact on the price of imported products is transparent and measurable.

The second rule is to reduce and eliminate tariffs and other barriers to trade through multilateral negotiations. The tariffs so reduced by each member country are bound against further increases by being

Table 5.5   Schedule for revisions of the Marrakesh Agreements

1998	• Sanitary and Phytosanitary Measures (SPS): review of the operation and implementation of the Agreement by 1998.
	• Technical Barriers to Trade (TBT): review of the operation and implementation of the Agreement by 1998.
	• Intellectual Property Rights (TRIPS): further negotiations starting in 1998, with a view to broadening and improving the Agreement on the basis of mutual reciprocity.
	• Dispute Settlement Understanding: full review of dispute settlement rules and procedures.
1999	• Government Procurement: possible extension of its coverage among all parties on the basis of mutual reciprocity.
	• Investment Measures (TRIMS): review of the operation of the Agreement and discussion on whether provisions on investment policy and competition policy should be included in the Agreement.
2000	• Agriculture: negotiations for continuing the process of substantial progressive reductions in support and protection.
	• Services: new round of negotiations, achieving a progressively higher level of liberalization.
	• Intellectual Property Rights (TRIPS): review of the implementation of the Agreement after 1 January 2000.
	• Trade Policy Review Body.
2001	• Textiles and Clothing: review of the implementation of the Agreement by 2001.
2002	• Textiles and Clothing: review of the implementation of the Agreement by 2004.

Source: WTO *Annual Report*, various issues

listed in national schedules; thus creating enhanced and more secure access to the markets of members.

However, there are some exceptions to this rule in case of the General System of Preferences and regional arrangements (Article XXIV: 5 and Article XXIV: 8) for which some reductions applied to member countries are not extended to other countries. More than 98 per cent of imports of industrial goods in developed countries and countries in transition are bound; around 73 per cent in developing countries.

The rules of general application

These basic rules are complemented by rules of general application for goods entering the customs territory of an importing country. These include rules:

• determining the dutiable value of imported goods where customs duties are collected. The agreement on customs valuation lists six methods to determine the value of merchandise among which the main one is on an ad valorem basis;

- applying mandatory standards, and sanitary regulations to imported products. These standards or regulations should not be so applied as to create unnecessary barriers to trade. They should be based on scientific information and evidence, and on internationally agreed standards. The Agreement on sanitary and phytosanitary measures (SPS) constitutes a considerable strengthening of constraints imposed by the WTO on national regulations and standards for trade in food products. The principles of national treatment, scientific proof, harmonization, equivalence and mutual recognition, risk assessment, and transparency are clearly stated. The SPS agreement requires transparency by systematic notifications to the WTO Secretariat when technical regulations are not based on existing international standards. Major importing and exporting countries have notified their SPS measures during the first two years of enforcement of the Agreement (a total of 724 measures) (Mahé, and Ortalo-Magné, 1998: 6).

  International standards are recommended as they avoid distortions in competition. However, a country can introduce or maintain measures corresponding to a level of protection, which is higher than international norms if there is a scientific justification (Art. 3) and provided that a risk assessment justifying the measure is carried out (Art. 5). The agreement encourages mutual recognition of conformity. Some disputes have occurred over the scientific evidence, and what scientific evidence is needed for the government to ban imports. The hormone-treated beef dispute between the EU and the United States is a case in point;

- applying technical regulations that should not be so applied by countries as to cause unnecessary obstacles to trade. The Agreement on Technical Barriers to Trade (TBT) complements the SPS Agreement, and they should be taken together although they are governed by separate agreements. The TBT Agreement is more comprehensive, and encompasses measures necessary to protect human, animal and plant life, national security requirements, the environment and consumers. The TBT Agreement covers public compulsory regulations such as Process and Methods of Production (PMP), standards with either a voluntary private status or an infra-national public status, and conformity assessment procedures. The TBT Agreement covers technical rules and standards, including matters of packaging, branding, labelling, and procedures of conformity assessment. The TBT Agreement encourages harmonization, equivalence and transparency in adopting technical regulations;

- Issuing licenses for imports. The Agreement on Import Licensing Procedures lays down principles of transparency and rules to ensure that the flow of trade is not impeded by the inappropriate use of import licensing procedures.

Rules over the trade-distorting effects of practices pursued by governments

The Uruguay Round of negotiations spells out other rules, which would avoid the trade-distorting effects of practices pursued by governments.

The grant of subsidies by governments

The Agreement on Subsidies and Countervailing Measures (SCM) and the Agreement on Agriculture clarify the rules on subsidies elaborated in the Tokyo Round, and restrain the right of governments to grant subsidies that have significant trade-distorting effects on competition in international trade. The Agreements divide subsidies into prohibited and permissible subsidies. Prohibited subsidies include export subsidies; permissible subsidies are classified into two categories: those that are actionable – that causes serious injury to the domestic industry or serious prejudice – and those that are not actionable. Subsidies for R&D, non-specific to certain firms, and for disadvantaged regions, are not actionable. They cannot be subject to countervailing duties or dispute settlement challenges although they can be brought to the Committee on Subsidies and Countervailing Measures if they result in serious adverse effects in another country. All other subsidies are 'actionable', that is they may be subject to multilateral dispute settlement challenges or to countervailing action if they adversely effect another WTO Member.

The Agreement on Subsidies and Countervailing Measures contains provisions dealing with issues relating to investment liberalization and competition, which will provide grounds for settling issues in future negotiations. The Agreement also requires that countries notify their specific subsidies (as defined under the Agreement) on an annual basis, and countervailing duty activities on a semi-annual basis.

Safeguard actions

The Agreement on Safeguards clarifies and reinforces Article XIX of GATT 1947 in particular in determining the criteria of 'serious injury' caused by an increase of imports. It prohibits the imposition of new grey area measures over a period of four years. Safeguard actions must be temporary and non-selective. They should be progressively liberalized by the member applying them, and a trade compensation should be agreed on. The Agreement on Textiles and Clothing contains special provisions for safeguards regime.

Antidumping measures

The Agreement on Antidumping is central to the WTO framework: the removal of grey area measures has resulted in an increase of anti-dumping measures. A number of VERs were replaced by anti-dumping measures (UNCTAD, 1994b: 63). Now more than 50 WTO members have adopted anti-dumping legislation. Developing countries are increasingly using anti-dumping actions, and now initiate about half of the total number of anti-dumping cases. Thus, for example, South Africa initiated 41 proceedings, India 30, Brazil 16, and Mexico 10 (Vermulst, 1999: 1). The Agreement on Anti-dumping agreement spells out the criteria to establish the presence of anti-dumping: export prices set below domestic prices and the intention to monopolize the market by the foreign firm. As with the Agreement on Safeguards, the criteria of injury and investigations are clearly codified by the Agreement.

Rules of origin

The GATT 1947 did not contain any provision on rules of origin. All manufactured products that are available today are produced in more than one country. Rules of origin are crucial for deciding the treatment given to imports, some of them sensitive (textiles and clothing, chemicals) especially when trade restrictions (safeguards, antidumping, or countervailing duties) are in force (Croome, 1998: 32). The basic objective of the Agreement on Rules of Origin is to require countries to adopt uniform set of harmonized rules to determine origin of goods imported on MFN basis. This is a massive task, and the basic work is done by the Technical Committee on Rules of Origin of the World Customs Organization, which passes its decisions on the WTO. The Agreement recommends transparency in adopting rules of origin (notification).

Trade-related investment measures

The Agreement on Trade-Related Investment Measures is fairly limited. It does not rule the admission of foreign investments, nor are the incentives offered by governments included. The agreement requires countries to phase out TRIMs that are considered to be inconsistent with GATT rules on the national treatment principle (Art. III) and the rule which prohibits the application of quantitative restrictions to imported products (Art. XI). It does not go beyond existing GATT rules. However, as noted by Hoekman and Saggi (1999: 5), the discipline entailed by reiterating GATT principles is quite powerful, notably when transition periods for developing countries are due to expire. The measures covered by the Agreement, which tend to be concentrated on specific industries – automotive, chemical and petrochemical, and computers (Low and Subramanian, 1995) – cover performance requirements imposed by countries. These include domestic sales, fiscal incentives, remittance restrictions, tax rebates, licensing and local equity, provisions of land and other services on preferential terms, and local content requirements, which require the investor to utilize a certain amount of local inputs in production. Export performance requirements are another example; they compel the investor to export a certain proportion of its output. The complaint that has been recently made by Japan, EU, and the United States against Indonesia concerning its 'National Car Program' is an illustrative example of discriminatory local content requirement.[7]

The General Agreement on Trade in Services (GATS)

The Agreement applies the basic rules of national treatment, non-discrimination, and transparency on trade in goods, to trade in services. However, the rules have been suitably modified to take into account the differences between goods and services. The national treatment does not apply to trade in services as it does to trade in goods. While international trade in goods involves the physical movement of goods from one country to another, service transactions entail four different modes of supply of services (cross-border trade; the movement of consumers; the establishment of a 'commercial presence'; and the movement of physical persons). National treatment and market-access commitments are listed in the individual schedules of commitments relating to sectors, sub-sectors and modes of supply. Thus, the country indicates that it will apply to trade in the sector market access and national treatment obligations, and that it will not take any new measures to restrict entry into the market or the operation of the service. It is, however, open to a country to indicate the sectoral exemptions from the MFN treatment.

Yet, GATS achieved modest progress on liberalizing trade in services. Some observers have pointed out some of the flaws in designing the Agreement: overlapping between modes; the possibility that a commitment on a particular service in one mode can be undermined by the absence of a commitment in another mode; clarification between market access and national treatment; strengthening of provisions on domestic regulations (Mattoo, 1997).

Four separate negotiations on issues of market access for services have taken place since the Uruguay Round. Sectoral negotiations on liberalization of maritime transport were suspended in 1995–96; negotiations on movement of natural persons (mode 4) failed. In February 1997, members of the World Trade Organization concluded an annex to the main agreement that significantly liberalizes trade in basic telecommunications services; 67 governments made significant liberalization commitments in 56 Schedules of Specific Commitments. The agreement on financial services was concluded in December 1997 after 70 WTO Member governments agreed to open their financial services sectors. This agreement covers more than 95 per cent of trade in banking, insurance, securities and financial information.

Trade-related aspects of intellectual property

The TRIPS Agreement builds on the main international conventions on intellectual property rights (Paris Convention, Bern Convention for the Protection of Literary and Artistic Works, Rome Convention on protection of integrated circuits) by incorporating most of their provisions. The Agreement reaffirms the basic principle of national treatment. In particular, it states that in regard to the 'availability, acquisition, scope, maintenance and enforcement' of intellectual property rights, foreign nationals shall not be accorded treatment that is less favorable than that accorded by a country to its own nationals. Countries are required to extend MFN principles to intellectual property rights. The Agreement spells out uniform minimum standards and periods for which protection should be granted to each of the intellectual property rights: patents; copyright and related rights; trademarks; industrial designs; layout-designs of integrated circuits; undisclosed information, including trade secrets; geographical indications, including appellation of origin. The regime ruling intellectual property rights seeks to secure an appropriate rate of financial return for intellectual property owners on their investment in knowledge. This could be to the disadvantage of developing countries.

Agriculture

In the past, a number of developed countries maintained quantitative restrictions in agriculture which went far beyond those warranted by the exceptions provided in the GATT. The EC applied variable levies instead of fixed tariffs to imports of temperate zone agricultural products such as wheat and other grains, meat and dairy products. The primary purpose of those levies was to ensure a reasonable income to farmers and to maintain a certain parity between the income earned by them and that earned by industrial workers. The variable levies thus resulted in domestic production being fully insulated from foreign competition, as the levies completely offset the competitive price advantages of foreign suppliers.

The Agreement on Agriculture provides a general framework of rules and disciplines to govern trade in agriculture, and substantial and progressive reduction in agricultural support and protection over an agreed period of time (market access, domestic support, export subsidies). The developed countries have agreed to replace quantitative restrictions and other non-tariff measures on agricultural products with tariffs. 'Tariffication' of rates and other tariffs are to be reduced by 37 per cent over a period of six years from 1 January 1995. Commitments for domestic support include reductions to the Aggregate Measure of Support (AMS). Amber support (commodity-specific) is subject to AMS reduction with the exception that it is not included if below a 'de minimus' level of five per cent of the production value of the commodity. Green box support is exempt from reductions, as is blue box support. The Agreement allows importing countries to impose special safeguards on tariffied products. The Agreement on Agriculture visualized that negotiations for further liberalization of trade in this sector should begin before the end of 1999, but negotiations on agriculture should resume in 2000. The Agreement has not resulted in lower domestic support. Several countries, including the United States and the EU have increased their use of green box or blue box area payments. Although blue box subsidies are not fully decoupled from production, they were exempted from reduction commitments.

Textiles and clothing

Previous Rounds of negotiations made very little progress in the removal of quantitative restrictions and other non-tariff measures on imports of textile products and clothing. Trade was governed by the Multi-Fiber Arrangement. The Agreement on Textiles and Clothing phases out the restrictions maintained under the Multi-Fiber Arrangement within a period of 10 years, that is by 1 January 2005. From then on, the trade in textiles will be completely integrated into the GATT 1994 and will be governed by it. Thus, the Textiles and

Clothing Agreement is a transitional arrangement, designed to organize the shift between a regime of quantitative restrictions to one in which trade in the sector should be liberalized. The integration process is to be carried out in four stages. At each stage, products amounting to a certain minimum percentage of the volume of the country's imports in 1990 are to be included in the integration process: 16 per cent on 1 January 1995; 17 per cent on 1 January 1998; 18 per cent on 1 January 2002; up to 49 per cent on 1 January 2005. In the meantime, the Agreement provides improved access for textile and clothing products that continue to be restricted by establishing growth rate applied to quotas inherited from the MFA. The Agreement permits countries to take safeguard actions during the transitional period under very strict rules. Developed countries, and some developing countries themselves, have supplemented the effects of quotas by antidumping actions and restrictive rules of origin (Croome 1998: 25).

State-trading

Although there is an increasing trend towards privatization, state trading continues to play a role. However, state trading is different from government procurement which is the purchase by a government agency of domestically produced or imported products. The main obligation imposed by the Uruguay Round is the general principle of non discrimination, that is making purchases or sales solely in accordance with commercial considerations (price, quality, availability and marketability, transportation), and affording adequate opportunity to enterprises in other countries. The second obligation is transparency, that is notification obligations.

The WTO and developing countries: maintaining special and differential treatment or equalizing power?

The Uruguay Round of negotiations broke off the supremacy of the major powers like the United States, the European Community, Canada, or Japan. Without denying the weight of those powerful actors, the Uruguay Round of negotiations were a turning point in the history of the relations of the developing countries with GATT, which were dormant ones. India, Brazil and more generally middle powers have adopted a new look at the way they have approached GATT issues. In the previous negotiations, developing countries stayed on the margins of the GATT. In the Uruguay Round, they took important and major steps towards negotiating the strengthening of GATT disciplines, and the enforcement of system rules.

Until the Uruguay Round, developing countries were largely exempted from most of the disciplines that applied to developed countries. Developing countries were not required to make any commitments on tariffs. They could use subsidies as an tool for development. The Uruguay Round resulted in a dilution of the Special and Differential Treatment (S&D). Developed countries began to insist that 'free riding' on rules and disciplines had to end since some developing countries were increasingly engaged in world trade and were significant players. (UNCTAD, 1995b: 26). The Final Act addressed mainly S&D by allowing developing countries periods of transition to comply with the agreements and by granting them technical assistance (Table 5.6).

What is going to be the impact of the Uruguay Round on developing countries? Is the WTO going to help to firmly anchor the developing countries in the global economy? What it certainly did was to divide more deeply countries who have abandoned import-substitution strategy once for ever and have got on the bandwagon of world trade, and those who have not succeeded in doing so.

The first group includes many Latin American countries – Mexico, Brazil, Chile, and Argentina – Asian countries, and very few African countries. These have unilaterally liberalized their economy. The second group includes countries who have clearly not abandoned the spirit which once prevailed in the 'third world', namely that of special and differential treatment.

As regards market access, the balance of the agreements is only modestly favorable for developing countries (UNCTAD, 1994b: 4). Tariff reductions on industrial goods do not apply to the primary-based and labor-intensive industries on which developing countries are primarily dependent (UNCTAD, 1996a: 28). In developed countries tariff reductions for industrial goods average 38 per cent, but only 34 per cent for imports from developing countries (UNCTAD, 1994: 4). This is due to the fact that tariff cuts on products of export interest from developing countries (averaging around 20 per cent *ad valorem*) are more modest than those applying to products traded between developed countries (which range from 43 to 62 per cent).

Despite eight rounds of tariff negotiations, there are still substantial tariff peaks in some sectors, such as textile, glass, agricultural products, and manufactured food products. It has been estimated that a 50 per cent reduction in remaining industrial tariffs would yield approxi-

Table 5.6 Special dispositions for developing countries

Subject	Provisions
Institutional	– More time when brought under a trade dispute
	– Technical assistance
Tariffs	– Ceiling bindings at higher levels (25–30 per cent)
	– Fewer concessions offered by developing countries
Agriculture	– Smaller reductions in tariffied NTBs and domestic support – around 2/3 of developed countries
	– Longer transition periods: ten years instead of six; greater number of permitted subsidies
	– The least developed countries are not required to notify their domestic support each year
Textiles	– Commitments to reduced the export subsidies and domestic support are not required for the least developed countries
	– Special treatment for least developed countries, small suppliers and fiber-producing countries
Safeguards	– No safeguards measures applied to low-volume imports from developing countries – representing no more than 3 per cent of total imports and more than 9 per cent of all imports of the goods originating from developing countries
	– Can maintain their own measures for a maximum of ten instead of eight years
	– Can re-apply measures more often
Subsidies	– The Agreement extends the rules to developing countries
	– Phase-out of export subsidies within eight years
	– Exemptions for countries with GDP per capita below to $1,000
	– Phase-out period of seven years for transition economies but providing some leeway to apply programs and measures necessary for transformation from a centrally-planned to a market, free enterprise
	– De minimis provisions for export markets.
Antidumping	– Special regard for developing countries before action is taken
	– De minimis provisions
Trade-Related Investment Measures (TRIMs)	– Longer phase-out period (five years for developing countries; seven years for transition economies and least developed countries)
	– Possibility of seeking extensions in individual cases
Trade-Related Aspects of intellectual property Rights (TRIPs)	– Longer transition period in order to adjust: five years for developing countries and transition economies; eleven years for least developed countries
	– Technical assistance
Balance of Payments	– Simplified consultations for least developed countries

Table 5.6   Special dispositions for developing countries *(continued)*

Subject	Provisions
Services (GATS)	– Principle of increasing participation of developing countries; less market opening measures required; assistance in strengthening services sectors. – For financial services, less stringent provisions
Technical barriers to trade	– Technical assistance for adjusting to international standards and technical standards in exporting markets. – Technical assistance by international institutions (Codex, WHO, CIPV).
Sanitary and Phytosanitary Measures	– Developed countries should take care of special needs of developing countries in implementing sanitary and phytosanitary measures.

Source: Landau, Alice 1999, *The World Trading System*, unpublished manuscript; UNCTAD 1995b: 27

mately $270 billion in global income (welfare) gains per year (François and McDonald in Laird, 1999: 3).

Tariff peaks have not been eliminated in specific sectors such as agriculture or textiles. In Canada customs duties on dairy products are 600 per cent; the United States imposes 132 per cent customs duties on peanut butter, and 14–32 per cent on wool, cotton or synthetic fabric. Japan imposes 550 per cent on rice; the EU 215 per cent on frozen beef, and the United States 179 per cent on milk powder. The EU maintains between 46 and 215 per cent on fruit juices. Developing countries are not exempt from high tariffs. Tariffs in Malaysia have diminished from 15.2 per cent in 1993 to 8.1 per cent in 1997. But tariffs on agricultural products or cars average 145 per cent. These high tariffs have resulted from the 'tariffication' of the NTBs agreed on in the Agreement in agriculture. The tariffication process implies a sharp rise in rates over and above the agreed cuts in existing rates.

The assessment of the impact of the Uruguay Round on developing countries is particularly important in the new issues brought in by developed countries, and very often opposed by developing countries at the outset of the negotiations. The intellectual property protection system introduced by the Uruguay Round is a case in point since the protection of intellectual property does have some effect on decisions of TNCs and firms to invest in a given country, and is often conducive to the transfer of technology and FDI. It is even more important as developing countries are far more users than generators of technological innovation. One of the consequences of the Agreement would likely be an increase in the price ticket on imported items such as pharmaceuticals for which patents have been relaxed in the South. A balance must be struck between the financial return on investment knowledge and the larger benefits that would result from rapid and unrestricted knowledge flows (UNCTAD X, 2000: 27). TRIPs granted a 20-year protection for patent rights in pharmaceuticals.[8]

However, a protection system has some advantages for developing countries. East Asian countries have recognized that the adoption of intellectual property in advanced technological innovations by them impedes infringement by competitors in their own and other countries.

Developing countries do have assets in the field of geographical indications. As an example, there is a debate over the label of Basmati rice originating from India or Pakistan, or tequila from Mexico. Indeed, it would have been a source of income for countries like India or Pakistan to protect their resource endowment for future exploitation. France and Switzerland did it with success for champagne and gruyere. Textiles is also a case in point. Many of the printed designs on fabrics sold on the American and European markets have been imitated from African countries such as Mauritania or Senegal. But these countries do not receive the benefits because they do not have any proprietary rights in this field. A protection system is particularly accurate in the field of biotechnology. A number of developing countries may find their competitive status enhanced by promoting their genetic endowment for future exploitation or developing plant breeders' rights (UNCTAD, 1994b: 199).

Significant loopholes also exist in some other important agreements to the detriment of developing countries. First, the benefits are less than were expected. One of the reason lies in the lack of clarity of the clauses concerning market access or Special and Differential Treatment granted to developing countries. Developed countries claim that developing countries' interests will be taken into account when applying some of the WTO agreements. However, they are implemented all the same. There is nothing compulsory in the WTO about taking into account the developing countries' interests.

In the Agreement on Textiles, the developed countries took the commitment to bring products accounting for 16 per cent of their imports into the WTO discipline. However, the Agreement does not mention the distribution of items to be integrated. Developed countries have taken advantage of this loophole: when the Agreement was implemented in 1998, they chose only such products that were not under restraint (Landau 1999b). The EU and the United States have chosen those products to reach the volume target listed in the Agreement. Also clothing which is of export interest for the developing countries accounted for only a small proportion of the liberalization process. The integration process has had very modest achievement so far, as shown in Table 5.7.

As noted by Laird (1999: 12) in the Major Review of the Implementation of the Agreement on Textiles and Clothing in the First Stage of the Integration Process, held in February 1998, besides the back-loading of the integration process (holding off the more difficult adjustments till last), concerns were raised on the

> exceptionally large number of safeguard measures in use, more restrictive use of rules of origin by the United States, tariff increases, the introduction of specific rates, minimum import pricing regimes, labeling and certification requirements, the maintenance of balance of payments provisions affecting textiles and clothing, export visa requirements, as well as the double jeopardy arising from the application of anti-dumping measures to products covered by the agreement.

The tasks ahead

Despite their opposition to some of the Uruguay Round issues, developing countries have taken important and major steps towards negotiating the strengthening of GATT disciplines. Services is a case in point. The agreement on services provides flexibility for developing countries not only in the timing and choice of sectors to open up, but also by enabling them to attach market access conditions (performance requirements, joint ventures). However, the commitments undertaken in the Round by some developing or even least developed countries as

Table 5.7   Clothing as a percentage by volume of products integrated in stages 1 and 2

Member	Percentage
United States	12.4
European Union	7.2
Canada	7.9
Norway	10.6

Source: WTO Doc. G/L/179, p. 29

shown by Table 5.8 were as extensive as those of some OECD members. Moreover, five developing countries used the ratification process following the extended negotiations on basic telecommunications, in 1997, to submit schedules voluntarily, without external prodding (Barbados, Cyprus, Kenya, Suriname, and Uganda).

It remains true that developing countries have comparative advantages in services. As recalled by Mattoo (1999: 18), health services

Table 5.8 Structure of commitments by WTO Members

Sectors committed	Number of members	WTO members
Below 20	44	Angola, Bahrain, Barbados, Benin, Botswana, Burkina Faso, Cameroon, Central African Republic, Chad, Congo, Congo (Republic), Costa Rica, Cyprus, Fiji, Gabon, Guinea, Guinea-Bissau, Guyana, Haiti, Honduras, Madagascar, Malawi, Maldives, Mali, Malta, Mauritania, Mauritius, Mozambique, Myanmar, Namibia, Niger, Paraguay, Rwanda, St. Kitts & Nevis, St. Lucia, St. Vincent & Grenadines, Solomon Islands, Sri Lanka, Suriname, Swaziland, Tanzania, Togo, Uganda, Zambia
21–40	23	Bangladesh, Bolivia, Brunei Darussalam, Burundi, Côte d'Ivoire, Djibouti, Dominica, El Salvador, Ghana, Grenada, Guatemala, Kenya, Macau, Mongolia, Nigeria, Papua New Guinea, Peru, Qatar, Senegal, Sierra Leone, Tunisia, Uruguay, Zimbabwe
41–60	10	Antigua & Barbuda, Belize, Cuba, India, Morocco, Netherlands Antilles, Nicaragua, Pakistan, Trinidad & Tobago, United Arab Emirates
61–80	12	Antigua & Barbuda, Belize, Cuba, India, Morocco, Netherlands Antilles, Nicaragua, Pakistan, Trinidad & Tobago, United Arab Emirates
81–100	12	Brazil, Ecuador, Egypt, Hong Kong (China), Israel, Jamaica, Kuwait, Liechtenstein, Poland, Romania, Singapore, Venezuela , Argentina, Chile, Czech Republic, Dominican Republic, Indonesia, Lesotho, New Zealand, Panama, Slovak Republic, Slovenia, South Africa, Turkey
101–120	8	Australia, Bulgaria, Canada, Gambia, Latvia, Philippines, Switzerland, Thailand
Above 120	25	Colombia, EC (15), Hungary, Iceland, Japan, Korea (Rep. of), Kyrgyz Republic, Malaysia, Mexico, Norway, USA

Source: WTO document S/C/W/95, 9 February 1999, p. 11

would seem to be an area in which developing countries could become major exporters, either by attracting foreign patients to domestic hospitals and doctors, or by temporarily sending their health personnel abroad. However, a limited number of developing countries such as Cuba, India, and Jordan are currently competing at a significant level (Wolvaardt, 1998: 63). India has a pool of well-trained doctors compared with other developing countries.

This results in inflows of foreign doctors from developing countries into India as well as outflows of Indian technicians to developing countries. Foreign patients are coming to India for treatment, both from developing and developed countries. They have good financial advantages in doing so. The cost of a coronary bypass surgery is much lower in India than, let's say, in the United States. Several transnationals have linked up with Indian companies to set up super-specialty hospitals and polyclinics in India (Gupta *et al.*, 1998: 228–9). SERVIMED, a trading company created by the Cuban government, prepares health/tourism packages. During 1995–96 25 000 patients and 1500 students went to Cuba for treatment and training respectively, and income earned from sales to health services to foreigners was $25 million. Cost savings for patients and health insurers are likely to be significant.

Negotiating in conditions of asymmetry

The 1999 UNCTAD Trade and Development Report (1999a: 40) questioned whether it was in the interest of developing countries to 'enter into negotiations with wealthier trading partners from a position of chronic weakness not only in terms of economic power but also in terms of research, analytical and intellectual support and negotiating skills'. Many of the world's poorest countries do not have the means to have a permanent representative in Geneva where the trade negotiations take place (Pfetsch and Landau, 2000: 26). Nor do they have the administrative capacity required to face ever more complex and intensely technical negotiations. They remain silent in the sessions, because they do not understand the intricacies of the issues under consideration The lack of participation is visible in many of the bodies, which were created in the aftermath of the Uruguay Round. Developing countries have difficulty to follow the Committee on agriculture. They have very few diplomats in Geneva to dedicate time to examine all the notifications that have been made so far by powerful players. Canada, the EU, and occasionally Brazil, Uruguay or Argentina are the ones who ask questions of the Committee. A developing country can build on questions asked by others when they are of interest for that country, but prefers to remain quiet than to betray its ignorance (Lal Das, 1999: 160). However, it is in the interest of developing countries to exploit the opportunities offered by the WTO, in particular its dispute settlement mechanism.

Developing countries do have a power deficit, not least in the dispute settlement mechanism adopted by the WTO. To defend a case is an onerous process, and to participate in a dispute settlement is also quite complicated, because of the intricacies of the legal interpretation and the technicality of the issues. Developed countries have the best lawyers working full time to defend their cases. Developing countries just cannot afford the costs of the best lawyers. Costs are disproportionately heavy for developing countries. There are some exceptions: Brazil mobilized impressive political and financial resources when the government brought a complaint against EU practices affecting the importation of poultry products, in which they have a comparative advantage, and sent experts and political leaders to Geneva to defend Brazil's case. It could do this because some Brazilian banks agreed to pay the bill. Also, if developing countries hire expensive legal assistance, they may find – as did the Caribbean banana producers – that their private legal advisers are excluded from panel hearings because they are not government officials (Croome, 1998: 18)

Power politics continue to play an important role at the WTO. As noted by Burtless *et al.*, overall the WTO has supported the interests of the United States. The WTO either ruled in favor of the United States or arranged that the target of the complaint make favorable concessions (Burtless *et al.*, 1998: 101). The panels and Appellate Body have often adopted interpretations that constrain the rights of developing countries and enhance their obligations. This has been the case in the Venezuela gazoline case, the India woollen shirts case, the Indonesia car case, and the shrimp-turtle case.

There is asymmetry in the dispute settlement mechanism working against the weaker parties. Recommendations and findings of the dispute panels are normally accepted and implemented; however in some really sensitive cases, a country may hesitate to do so, and the only option is to retaliate. Developing countries may find this ultimate weapon difficult to use both for economic and political reasons (Lal Das, 1999: 157). The United States or the EU may ignore WTO decisions at little cost to themselves except an eroding of the credibility of the organization that ruled against them (Rodrik, 1995: 51). The EU ignored the decision adopted by the body on the regime for the importation, sale, and distribution of bananas as it did concerning the measures affecting meat and meat products (Hormones).

However, developing countries should take the opportunities offered by the WTO to defend their interests and denounce the violation of WTO rules by developed countries. Thus, they will be heeded. Table 5.9 shows that developing countries are increasingly introducing complaints against developed countries.

The Uruguay Round has proven that getting something done is possible when developing countries attempt to equalize power and overcome their power deficit, by negotiating on the same grounds as major powers, difficult as this may be. Thus, they have to move away from their previous preferential treatment status and playing off asymmetry of power by taking accurate actions. As Dani Rodrik emphasized, the most realistic option for developing countries is to 'seek to participate in the WTO as fully-fledged members' (Rodrik, 1995: 49). Developing countries have nothing to gain from maintaining their differential status, but everything to gain by playing a more stringent rules-based multilateral system. The developing countries gain more strength from the rules of multilateralism, and have to stand firm on these rules.

Many of the disputes are related to Technical Barriers to Trade. Exports from developing countries are affected by the increased scope and application of measures aimed at environmental protection. These impose stringent conditions for foreign products.

Some of the cases brought by developing countries at the WTO dealt with TBT, such as standards for gasoline or shrimp products. Some developing countries have successfully contested actions by large players.[9] The WTO found that the United States regulations were inconsistent with GATT Article III.4 and did not benefit from an Article XX exception. Disputes between developing countries, or between economies in transition, have also begun to emerge between Brazil and the Philippines (countervailing duty imposed by Brazil on the Philippine's exports of desiccated coconut); Guatemala and Mexico (antidumping actions on cement); and India and Turkey (textiles), as well as between Singapore and Malaysia, and the Czech Republic and Hungary. However, intra-developing country cases remain limited, and least-developed countries are not involved: there have been no cases involving Sub-Saharan countries.

Table 5.9 Overview of the state-of-play of WTO disputes (as at February 2000)*

Complainant	Respondent	Complaint
Venezuela/Brazil	United States	Standards for reformulated and conventional gasoline
Costa Rica	United States	Restrictions on imports of cotton and man-made fiber underwear
India	United States	Measure affecting imports of woven wool shirts and blouses
Brazil	EU	Measures affecting importation of certain poultry products
Malaysia/Pakistan/ Thailand	United States	Import prohibition of certain shrimp and shrimp products
Brazil	Canada	Import prohibition of certain shrimp and shrimp products
Korea	United States	Anti-dumping duty on Dynamic Random Access Memory Semiconductors (DRAMS) of one megabite
Brazil	Canada	Measures affecting the export of civilian aircraft
India	EU	Anti-dumping duties on imports of cotton-type bed-linen
Korea	United States	Anti-dumping measures on stainless steel plate in coils and stainless steel sheet and strip
Brazil	EU	Measures affecting differential and favorable treatment of coffee
India	EU	Anti-dumping investigations regarding unbleached cotton fabrics
India	EU	Measures affecting import duties on rice
Argentina	EU	Tariff rate quota for imports of groundnuts
Panama/Ecuador/ Guatemala/Honduras/ Mexico	EU	Regime for the importation, sale and distribution of bananas
Chile	United States	Countervailing duty investigation of imports of salmon
Colombia	United States	Safeguard measure against imports of broom
India/Malaysia/Pakistan/ Thailand	United States	Import prohibition of certain shrimps and shrimp products

Table 5.9 Overview of the state-of-play of WTO disputes (as at February 2000)* *(continued)*

Complainant	Respondent	Complaint
Korea	United States	Anti-dumping duties on imports of color television receivers from Korea
Philippines	United States	Import prohibition of certain shrimps and shrimp products
Developing countries vs. developing countries		
Philippines	Brazil	Measures affecting desiccated coconut
Brazil	Peru	Countervailing duty investigation against imports of buses
Hungary	Slovak Republic	Measures affecting import duty on wheat
India	South Africa	Anti-dumping duties on the imports of certain pharmaceutical products
Indonesia	Argentina	Safeguard measures on imports of footwear
Mexico	Guatemala	Anti-dumping investigation regarding imports of Portland cement
Sri Lanka	Brazil	Countervailing duties on imports of desiccated coconut and coconut milk powder
Thailand	Colombia	Safeguard measures on imports of plain polyester filaments from Thailand

* The table does not take into account if the case has been completed (most recent list as for January 2000; is going through an active panel, or is still in a stage of pending consultations
Source: http://wto.org

Concluding remarks

The GATT has been portrayed as a 'club of the rich'. In the WTO, there are still imbalances and inequities in the treatment of developed and developing countries. Far from correcting the imbalances of trade, the Uruguay Round has resulted in only modestly favorable treatment for developing countries as regards market access. Agreements in services, intellectual property rights, and textiles are also full of loopholes, and developed countries are taken advantage of. The special and differential treatment for developing countries has also been diluted. Special provisions are restricted to periods of transition or technical co-operation.

The WTO, which should have helped to open markets, and liberalize trade did not end the main difficulties facing exporting developing countries. It might be right to say that in the past, developing countries have often played security against creativity, and preferred the preferential treatment status. They have nothing to gain from maintaining their differential status, but everything to gain by playing a more stringent rules-based multilateral system When they do play the multilateral game, they are finally able formulate their interests and pursue constructive proposals in many areas of negotiations. The developing countries have also been very unsuccessful in developing an effective cohesiveness. Here again, they are trying their best to co-ordinate. The MERCOSUR Member countries met many times before the Seattle Meeting to co-ordinate their position; and ASEAN Member countries co-ordinate on a regular basis. They achieved some results during the Conference.

African countries, which were quite marginalized in the Uruguay Round, took a firm stance at the Seattle Meeting, against the efforts to put labor on the agenda, arguing alongside many developing countries that this was simply a cover for protectionism and that it would undermine their comparative advantage. Latin American countries and English-speaking Caribbean countries joined the Organization of African Unity in threatening to walk out from the negotiations, and in warning that they would reject an agreement forged without their input (Pfetsch and Landau, 2000: 34). Developing countries have been offered some compensation as a result of the Seattle Ministerial Conference.

Many problems still subsist in the field of international trade. Reaping the full benefits of open markets is within reach of Mexico, Chile, Brazil, and the East Asian countries. But the developing countries as a group have not been able to exploit the benefits of open trade (OECD, 1999: 29). Sub-Saharan Africa, which accounted for 3.1 per cent of world exports in the 1950s saw its share fall to 1.2 per cent by 1990. More generally, Africa's share of world exports, for example, was half its 1985 level in 1996. Similarly, Latin America lost 14 per cent of its share during the same period (from 5.6 per cent to 4.9 per cent), whereas Western Europe increased its share of world trade by 11 per cent (from 40.1 to 44.6 per cent). Low, Olarreaga, and Suarez (1999) have argued that marginalization is not the result of 'globalization', but is more likely to be explained by domestic policies in relatively closed countries. But it is true that the increase in international trade has been mainly restricted to a handful of countries. The OECD shares these views, 'benefits from trade and access to foreign markets do not come automatically and require strong domestic policy frameworks' (OECD, 1999: 29).

Many of the issues addressed by the trade agenda are pushed forward by the private sector. The first push for disciplines on services in GATT was made by American International Group (AIG) during the Tokyo Round. In 1978, AIG was joined by American Express Company (AMEX) in the efforts to open services. AIG devoted substantial effort and funds to ensure that trade in services and investment would be placed on the trade agenda of the Uruguay Round (Gibbs and Mashayekhi, 1998: 9). Similarly, the Intellectual Property Committee, including a dozen of big companies or pressure groups, such as the Pharmaceutical Producers Association, the Motion Picture Association of America, the Audio-Visual Industry, the Californian Chemical Industry, and the Californian Wine Industry, exerted strong pressure upon the US administration to place intellectual property on the agenda (Landau, 1996). These initiatives were strongly supported by the US executive branch, notably the United States Trade Representative (USTR). Developing countries need to mobilize their private sector to make a better contribution to their trade agenda. That means that national governments have to gather information on the needs of the private sector, and the market access barriers met by exporters in foreign markets. Some countries still succeeded in mobilizing the private sector; Brazil is an illustrative example.

The WTO has transformed the global playing field for international players, but has failed to transform it for developing countries so far. The new agenda will have to be considerably more development-oriented than was that of the Uruguay Round (UNCTAD X, 2000: 23). Is the situation better in the field of FDI and capital flows?

6
Foreign Direct Investment and the Global Economy: Why, How, and Where?

The definition of globalization lays stress on trade and Foreign Direct Investment (FDI) flows. Over the period 1945–1973, there was an increase of trade, but since the 1980s trade has not been the most important element of globalization. Trade has been eclipsed by the growth of FDI,[1] which is the driving force of globalization. The global FDI stock increased twenty-five fold during the last quarter-century (OECD, 1999). Between 1982 and 1994, FDI doubled as a percentage of world gross domestic product to 9 per cent. In 1996 the global FDI stock was valued $3.2 trillion, rising from $1 trillion in 1987 and $2 trillion in 1993. It increased at an average annual rate of 34 per cent compared with an annual rate of 9 per cent for global merchandise trade (UNCTAD, 1997b: 3). In today's global economy, FDI has superseded trade with global sales by multinational enterprise affiliates worth $5.2 trillion in 1992 compared with world-wide exports of goods and services of $5 trillion in 1992 (UNCTAD, 1995a).

But these figures mask significant geographical variations. My contention here is that FDI is unevenly spread over the countries. FDI is highly concentrated on those countries that are already the wealthiest and the most dynamic, while low-income countries have been bypassed.

Explaining FDI

FDI is attracted for a variety of reasons: access to specific factors of production (resources, technical knowledge, patents and brand names) or cheaper factors of production (investment incentives, subsidies, grants, tax concessions). International competitors could undertake mutual investment in one another company (through shareholdings of joint

109

ventures) in order to gain access to each other's product range. FDI could also aim to secure access to customers in the host country market. FDI should be stimulated by the relaxation of ownership and entry requirements and other liberalizing measures to open markets to greater competition.

Raymond Vernon (1977, 90–1) formulated the expansion and trajectory of the firm that leads a national firm to establish overseas. According to Vernon, the first stage of the product life cycle takes place in the firm's home market. In a later phase, the firm settles overseas by establishing sales and representative offices. Then, the overseas office develops into foreign production subsidiaries, producing the bulk of the goods concerned. If these overseas markets are protected by high tariff barriers, this shift of production takes place earlier.

The increase of FDI is also fuelled by cross-border mergers and acquisitions. The cross-border M&A activity accounted for between a half and two-thirds of world FDI flows in the 1990s (UNCTAD, 1999b: 118). The value of all cross-border M&A sales (and purchases) amounted to $544 billion in 1998, representing an increase of about 60 per cent over that in 1997 ($342 billion), doubled between 1988 and 1995 to $229 billion. These trends have increasingly been associated with a more elaborate system of intra-firm flows of goods and services as well as inter-firm alliances, thereby adding a deep layer of integration to the global economy.

To some extent, FDI is also an answer to domestic or regional policies. FDI could be attracted by the trade diversionary aspect of regional integration. This is commonly known as 'tariff jumping' FDI, and occurs when firms are prevented from exporting into the host country by the existence of tariffs and other barriers to trade. Foreign firms jump the barriers by establishing a local presence within the host countries. Roger Strange (1996: 19) argues that the relationship between regional integration and FDI depends upon the underlying entrepreneurial motivation for the investment and upon the liberalization provision of the integration. Decreasing tariffs in the EC have propelled US investment projects in Europe to take advantage of economies of scale and prospective extended consumer markets.

FDI: pros and cons

Developing countries were also winners at this game. Held *et al.* (1999: 243) recall that in the 1950s, US companies started to invest in mining and agriculture around the globe. They sought to circumvent prohibitive tariffs and other protectionist measures adopted by developing countries. As Latin America industrialized behind high tariffs, US firms started to locate their production in that region. Some decades later, the motivation for locating production abroad has changed, but is nonetheless important for developing countries. Because of increased international competition firms have been constantly searching for new production locations where costs were lower. This has been a strong rationale behind FDI flows from North to South. Intra-firm trade expanded considerably between northern parents and foreign subsidiaries in developing countries (UNCTAD, 1995a: 153). Indeed, FDI has integrative aspects around the globe. Valuable intangible assets – technology, organization skills, and research and marketing knowledge – get transferred as part of FDI (WTO, 1999: 320). Besides its contribution to the capital shortage faced by developing countries, FDI is supported for its 'technological spillover', both within and across industries, the development of managerial and marketing skills, and the training of labor (Fransman, 1985: 577). Firms and sectors where FDI is intensive have higher average labor productivity and pay higher wages. A McKinsey study found that in eight sectors of the economy, ranging from steel and telecoms to food manufacturing and housebuilding in which FDI are important, productivity was rising by at least 9 per cent a year (*The Economist*, 27 March 1999).

FDI is channeled through joint ventures, management contracts, and licensing and other technology agreements. Faure notes that China gets a substantial advantage from foreign capital investment brought by bringing in technology and know-how (Faure, 2000: 157). Almost 300 000 joint ventures had been approved by the Chinese administrative authorities in January 1998 and $468.8 billion have been introduced in China as direct foreign investment during the two last decades. A study of OECD countries found that each $1.00 of outward FDI was associated with $2.00 of additional exports, and a trade surplus of $1.70 (OECD, 1999: 4). Brazil-based TNCs' exports to Latin America accounted for 47 per cent of their total exports in 1997, up from 26 per cent in 1990 (*The Economist*, 27 March 1999).

However, according to Rodrik (1999: 37) 'systematic studies from countries such as Morocco and Venezuela find little in the way of positive spillovers'. As far as technological spillovers are concerned, developing countries were often incapable of utilizing the technology because of unskilled labor. There was a lack of experienced indigenous managers, qualified engineers, and skilled workers.

Transfer of technology could be inappropriate to the real needs of developing countries. Either products introduced locally are high technology products with highly specialized uses that few consumers could use; or they are mass consumption items geared towards the tastes of Western consumer markets that distorted consumption patterns in developing countries by persuading consumers to spend what little income they had on unnecessary products, such as soft drinks, consumer goods. The balance-of-payments and growth effects of FDI are inconclusive. Relative to domestic investment needs of developing countries, the contribution of FDI is relatively modest. FDI is not always good for a country's development and a liberal policy is not always sufficient to ensure positive effects (Milberg, 1999: 111; Agosin and Mayer, 2000: 14). FDI cannot be a substitute for stronger domestic industrial policies or mobilizing domestic resources (Kozul-Wright and Rayment, 1995: 25). If the location presents opportunities to innovation production through indigenous firms, intellectual property, national treatment, skilled labor, and geographical location, opportunities exist for technological spillovers.

There is more evidence that growth leads to FDI. As a matter of fact, firm location decisions depend on various factors: domestic economic policy, privatization achieved in the developing countries, size of the market, political risks, rate of growth, dismantling of barriers in capital movement, skill of labor forces, legal infrastructure of property rights, and patent protection. It also requires satisfactory policy and legal frameworks.

Developing countries and FDI: shifting pattern

Developing countries have undertaken a dramatic change in the way they deal with FDI. The current attitude of developing countries facing foreign investment breaks away from the one which prevailed some decades ago. In the past, developing countries had been quite reluctant regarding FDI, and were unanimous in castigating and condemning it. Many of the demands addressed by developing countries and grouped under the New International Economic Order (NIEO) were linked to investment rules. Developing countries claimed the control of their national resources and the right to 'full permanent sovereignty'; the regulation of transnational corporation in accordance with their own domestic policies; and the right of nationalization or expropriation of foreign holdings (Jordan, 1982: 71–2). The import substitution strategy followed by many developing countries, which combined import restrictions with FDI regulations, was quite prohibitive against FDI. Protected economies in the past required a restrictive investment framework. Most developing countries, including export-oriented developing countries, adopted restrictive laws towards FDI. Measures tended to concentrate on specific industries with automotive, chemical, petrochemical, and computer industries leading the list (UNCTAD, 1996a). These measures ranged from restrictions on inflows of foreign investment at ownership level (Malaysia, Taiwan province of China, Korea, Chile, Mexico), to the reservation of certain activities to nationals (Thailand, Korea, Mexico), to the control of repatriation of investment income and capital (India, Brazil, Chile) (Jomo, 1996). Korea and Taiwan imposed restrictions on entry, ownership and a categorization of industries in limited sectors (defense, transportation, finance, and communications), and non limited sectors such as sophisticated technology, petroleum refinery, or synthetic fibers, or labor intensive export industries generating foreign exchange and jobs.

Even in these sectors accessible to FDI, governments favored joint ventures under local ownership. Governments consistently sought to keep control firmly in local hands. In Korea, foreign ownership above 50 per cent was prohibited except in areas where FDI were deemed to be of strategic importance, which covered 13 per cent of all the manufacturing industries (UNCTAD, 1996a: 5). Singapore directed the flows towards government-designated priority sectors (Chang, 1996). Only Malaysia and Hong Kong had a more liberal policies.

One of the most restrictive law was Decision 24, adopted in 1970 by the Commission of the Carthagena Agreement (Andean Group). All investments were screened by a national office, and foreign companies shared ownership with local partners. The governments selected the economic sectors in which to invest (Mace, 1981: 212–5). Decision 24 sought to limit access to local credit for foreign companies. Some member countries such as Colombia and Chile, and foreign companies – notably US companies – criticized Decision 24. Chile, who applied a liberal investment regime, which did not require any local partnership for foreign companies and applied the national treatment, was excluded from the Andean Pact in 1974. Decision 24 was reversed by Decision 220 of May 1987, effectively leaving the bargaining relating to investment to the individual states (Bolivia, Peru, Ecuador, and Venezuela).

As shown in Table 6.1, from the 1990s onwards developing countries have adopted liberalization policies and have unilaterally liberalized FDI. In 1996, 98 liberalizing changes were made to the regulatory FDI

Table 6.1 National regulatory changes, 1991–98

Item	1991	1992	1993	1994	1995	1996	1997	1998
Number of countries that introduced changes in their business regimes	35	43	57	49	64	65	76	60
Number of regulatory changes of which	82	79	102	110	112	114	151	145
More favorable to FDI	80	79	101	108	106	98	135	136
Less favorable to FDI	2	–	1	2	6	16	16	9

Source: UNCTAD, 1999a

frameworks of 65 developing countries, whereas only 35 developing countries undertook these changes in 1991 (UNCTAD, 1997b: 18). The changes included the opening of industries previously closed to FDI, the streamlining or abolition of approval procedures, the provision of incentives, and the establishment of liberalization schemes. Measures to boost profits above free-market levels were introduced, and fiscal instruments were used to supplement corporate profits to accelerate capital accumulation. Tax exemption and special depreciation allowances were applied. In Brazil, Rio Grande do Sul and Parana have been granting huge tax breaks to multinational car companies to build factories (*The Economist*, 27 March 1999).

In 1989, Mexico relaxed restrictions on foreign ownership up to a level of 100 per cent in some three-quarters of 654 sectors. In Brazil, repatriation of capital could be carried out freely, and in Mexico there were no more exchange control regulations designed to segregate current from capital transactions (UNCTAD, 1994a: 105). Among the Central and East European Countries (CEECs), Hungary went very far down the road of liberalization of foreign investment, and granted tax concessions, exemptions of restrictions on profits, and 100 per cent foreign ownership (Csáki *et al.*, 1996: 18). Some $21 billion FDI has flowed into the country since 1990, the highest level per capita in Central and Eastern Europe. Table 6.2. shows the largest FDI achieved so far.

Table 6.2 Largest Foreign Direct Investment in Hungary ($ in millions) – 1999

MagyarCom (Ameritech, Deutsche Telecom)	$1 727
General Electric	760
RWE Energie	720
Audi	600
KPN Telecom	500
General Motors	440
Bayernwerk	430
Banca Commerciale Italiana	381
MediaOne	304
Coca-Cola	300
Hungarian Telephone and Cable	300
Siemens	300
Alcoa	270
Electricité de France	270
Matel	260

Source: Budapest Business Journal 1999

Measures for attracting FDI have been related to privatization programs in most developing countries. Oil, steel, transport, and public utilities have been, or are being privatized in Latin America or in the CEECs. More than 70 countries had privatization programs in 1990.[2] If, from the developing countries perspective, FDI is desirable, its conduct should be firmly controlled and subject to some restrictions and regulations, in order to maximize benefits for host countries. This ambivalence towards FDI is described by Robert Madelin (1997: 39):

> there is a paradox that very often investment-promotion activities by developing countries are moving in the right direction whereas the rhetoric that you sometimes hear from the very same developing countries governments can still rather be anti-investment.

Many developing countries have opted for increasing foreign ownership of existing firms rather than allowing new entry. One reason for the reluctance of governments to liberalize immediately is the perceived need to protect their domestic firms from immediate competition. From the investor's perspective, national frameworks may raise a number of concerns about the commitments made by the host government, the security of investment, and the resolution of investment disputes. Investors want to be sure that domestic rules concerning foreign investments are there to stay.[3] The conclusion of international agreements are increasingly viewed as a means of maximizing profits for the parties concerned, and a mechanism through which the government makes irrevocable commitments, and offers guarantees against reversals. International agreements also lock in liberalization schemes and reforms.

Multiplying investment rulemaking

Three possible venues exist for negotiating international rules to govern FDI: a bilateral venue, which has already manifested in a proliferation of bilateral treaties; a regional venue such as the NAFTA or the EU; or a multilateral one, such as the WTO (Graham and Sauvé, 1998: 105). Each of them suffer from flaws; but at the same time each has positive aspects on which to build on a more comprehensive agreement. Bilateralism is not a realistic option, as the number has reached the point of treaty congestion. By the end of 1996, 1332 such treaties existed compared with less than 400 at the beginning of the 1990s, of which 824 were concluded by developed countries with other countries (UNCTAD, 1997b: 19).

Yet bilateral investment treaties (BITs) have some advantages: they are closer to the reality of different countries and to their specific situations, and they provide more flexibility. The definition of investment is broad, and BITs give to the host country the right to ignore certain conditions for public purposes. They also provide an investor-to-state dispute settlement provision (UNCTAD 1998). However, BITs deal mostly with standards of treatment and legal protection for foreign investors after their entry and establishment in their host countries. BITs provisions cannot be taken as statements of general international law since they bind only the contracting parties. Also, and more important, the key question is the impact the BITs have on investment flows since the main purpose of these treaties is to provide strong legal guarantees in order to attract foreign investment. BITs are confidence-building signals to foreign investors (Sauvant, 1998: 2), but, they often reflect power asymmetry between partners.

Starting in the 1990s, regional investment agreements have multiplied. A number of instruments and agreements were initiated at the regional level in Asia and Latin America. In 1998, ASEAN Member countries concluded a framework agreement on the ASEAN Investment Area. Its purpose was to create a more transparent and liberal investment environment, and to enhance the attractiveness of the region. Two elements are worth mentioning: a provision of national treatment for ASEAN investors, and an opening of all industries to ASEAN investors by the year 2010 and to all investors by the year 2020, subject to the exceptions provided for in the agreement. Framework agreements were also concluded in SADC and MERCOSUR, as well as between the Andean Community and MERCOSUR and individual countries, including Canada, the United States and Mexico and the two integration schemes.

NAFTA took a substantial step in developing a set of rules for cross-border business. NAFTA provides a innovative approach to an investor-to-state dispute resolution, which can be carried out by the World Bank's International Center for the Settlement of Investment Disputes, or the United Nations Commission on International Trade Law, if consultation and negotiations fail (Graham and Sauvé 1998: 130). NAFTA's coverage of investment provisions is broad and includes a definition of investment encompassing portfolio investments and commercial real estate, provisions on the national treatment, and restrictions on performance requirements. The most comprehensive regime has been established in the EU. Freedom of investment was part of the four freedoms of the Internal Market (capital, goods, persons, and services) agreed on in 1987 and applied in 1992 for all investments originating within the EC Member States and later for the EEA (European Economic Area). It was all the more necessary, as the end 1980s witnessed a wave of mergers and acquisitions. It is supervised by a supranational body. The task of establishing a widely accepted regime for investment must not be underestimated. Hart (1996: 58) has listed the main provisions to be included in an investment regime:

- a statement of purpose and definitions;
- conditions governing admission or establishment of investments;
- provisions on the treatment of investments once established such as fair and equitable treatment, and often including national and MFN treatment;
- conditions governing nationalization and compensation;
- rules governing the transfer of profits and the repatriation of capital; and
- provisions regarding dispute settlement and subrogation.

Numerous attempts have been made to codify investment rules. Multilateral principles for investment were addressed as far back as the 1947 Havana Conference. With the failure of the Havana Charter to enter into force, multilateral investment issues were caught by the United Nations (Gibbs and Mashayekhi, 1998: 3). In the 1970s, most of the discussions on investment reflected the North–South divide that prevailed at that time and many of the developing countries' grievances focused on the unequal power between developed and developing countries. Investment and TNCs figured prominently among these grievances. The peak was reached in 1974, when the UN General Assembly adopted two resolutions on the NIEO that would guarantee more favorable treatment for the developing countries. The UN Economic and Social Council established a Commission on Transnational Corporations in 1975, and a Center on Transnational Corporations. Table 6.3. lists some of the international agreements negotiated between 1948 and 1997.

The investment issue was brought back to the GATT in the early 1980s and was one of the new issues addressed by the Uruguay Round of negotiations. More recently, there was a heated debate on whether the WTO or the OECD was to contain a multilateral investment agreement.

The WTO has indisputable benefits if the ultimate goal is to establish a uniform set of rules, and the WTO has a dispute settlement mechanism to impose discipline for abusive behavior. The OECD is also an

Table 6.3 Main Multilateral Agreements

Year	Institutional framework	Level	Structure	Form	Status
1961	Code of liberalization for capital movements	OECD	Regional	Constraining	NA
1962	Resolution 1803 of the General Assembly of the United Nations: Permanent sovereignty over natural Resources	UN	Multilateral	Non constraining	Adopted
1965	Convention on the settlement of investment disputes between states and nationals from other states	World Bank	multilateral	Constraining	Adopted
1967	Draft Convention on the protection of Foreign Properties	OECD	Regional	Non-binding	Not open for signature
1969	Agreement on Andean Sub-regional integration	Andean Pact	Regional	Constraining	Superseded
1972	Decision No.24 of the Commission Joint Convention on the Freedom of Movement of Persons and the Right of Establishment in the Central African Nations	OECD	Regional	Binding/ non Binding	Adopted
1976	Declaration on International Investment and Multinational Enterprises Code of conduct on Transnational Corporations	United Nations	Multilateral	Non-binding	Not adopted
1985	Draft International Code of Conduct on Transfer of Technology	United Nations	Multilateral	Non-binding	Not adopted
1991	Decision 291 of the Commission of the Cartagena Agreement: Uniform Code on		Regional	Binding	Adopted

Table 6.3 Main Multilateral Agreements *(continued)*

Year	Institutional framework	Level	Structure	Form	Status
1991	Andean Multinational Enterprises Decision 292 of the Commission of the Cartagena Agreement: Uniform Code on on Andean Multinational Enterprises		Regional	Binding	Adopted
1992	Guidelines on the Treatment of Foreign Direct Investment	World Bank	Multilateral	Non-binding	Adopted
1992	North American Free Trade Agreement		Regional	Binding	Adopted
1994	Multilateral Agreements on trade in Goods: Agreement on Trade-Related Investment Measures	WTO	Multilateral	Binding	Adopted
1994	Multilateral Agreements on trade in Services and Ministerial Decisions Relating to the General Agreement on Services	WTO	Multilateral	Binding	Adopted
1994	Agreements on Trade-Related Aspects of Intellectual Property Rights	WTO	Multilateral	Binding	Adopted
1994	Protocol of Colonia for the Reciprocal Promotion and Protection of Investments in the MERCOSUR (intra-zonal)	MERCOSUR	Regional	Binding	Adopted
1994	APEC Non-Binding Investment Principles	APEC	Regional	Non-binding	Adopted

Source: World Investment Report, 1996

option: it provides more fertile ground for an agreement because of its limited membership of advanced economies. For some countries, like Canada or the United States, the OECD is a key negotiating forum to channel national policies in investments even if the OECD codes could be deposited later on the international trade agenda. The OECD members account for the vast majority of the stock of FDI. The EU favors the WTO forum because in the WTO the EU negotiates on behalf of its member states whereas in the OECD each member state negotiates for itself.

The OECD Multilateral Investment Agreement

The Organization for Economic Co-operation and Development has been most active in promoting a framework for investment. Firstly, a Convention Combating Bribery of Foreign Public Officials in International Business Transactions, initiated by the United States concerned over the freedom of non-US companies to pay bribes to foreign governments, came into effect in February 1999. As noted by Metcalfe, 'bribery in international business acts as a non-tariff trade barrier, deters foreign direct investment, penalizes companies which refuse to pay bribes, corrodes corporate accountability, and arbitrarily affects the choice and design of major infrastructure projects' (Metcalfe, 2000: 134).

The OECD countries negotiated a comprehensive Multilateral Agreement on Investment (MAI) among themselves. The objective was to establish a free-standing treaty which subjects foreign investments to a multilaterally agreed regime. Its aim was to remove all or most of the restrictions on investment and to ensure that FDI is treated by national authorities no differently from domestic investment. There is a consensus within the OECD on a single broad definition of investment, which goes 'beyond the traditional notion of FDI to cover virtually all tangible and intangible assets, and which applies to both pre-establishment and post-establishment'. The definition hence embraces intellectual property and portfolio investment.

The MAI was to be completed in 1997, extended to 1998, but was abandoned soon after. Some deputies in the US Congress could not support an agreement without a national security exemption and language covering expropriated investments. In France and Canada the agreement raised the hackles of cultural lobbies who wanted to protect local media and communications industries from the 'onslaught of the Hollywood behemoths' (Rashish 1997: 11). Furthermore, the agreement was strongly opposed by developing countries, trade unions, and environmentalists altogether. The majority of developing countries, under the leadership of India and Malaysia, was opposed to the idea of an investment agreement they could not shape, and continued to oppose the idea that the issue should initially be one for study in the WTO.

The two main critical issues of the MAI addressed by India from the standpoint of developing countries were the definition of investment and national treatment in the pre-establishment phase (Ganesan, 1998: 2). The definition of investment by OECD goes far beyond the traditional notion of FDI to include portfolio investment, debt capital, intellectual property rights, and every form of tangible or intangible assets. The grant of national treatment in the pre-establishment phase envisioned by the OECD would have curbed the members' freedom and flexibility to pursue their own policies. An agreement on investments is to open market access.

India would not get state of the art technology from the joint ventures and it considers that the existing bilateral and regional agreements provide enough stability and incentives for investments. Incentives can be found in the domestic conditions: telecommunications infrastructure; stable and democratic political regimes; and local skilled workers. India is reluctant to embark on negotiations on investments because many of the existing commitments under the Uruguay Round are not implemented yet, and it expects few benefits from an agreement on investments with the WTO. Investments would, however, flow into sectors that India wants to protect. As one diplomat said, (Geneva Interview, October 1999) 'India wants computer chips, and not potato chips'.

The MAI revealed some sharp differences between the United States and Europe concerning privatization of state-owned companies and exceptions for regional economic groupings. The MAI could not be the starting point for negotiating investments at the WTO. OECD has a membership of twenty-nine states which collectively form a 'rich man's club' of world trade, and does not encompass any developing countries. The WTO is a more universal organization.

The proposals for investment negotiations in the WTO depart from the MAI on several issues: definition of investment, dispute settlements, labor and environmental issues, temporary entry and permission to stay for key personnel. Table 6.4 lists the main differences. However, many countries oppose the idea of a WTO investment agreement, and some belong to the major players in the WTO. The United

Table 6.4 Differences between the MAI and the WTO

Subject	Draft text of the MAI	Proposals submitted in the WTO
Definition of investment	Any kind of asset owned or controlled by a foreign investor, such as shares in an enterprise (including both direct and indirect, portfolio investment), bonds and loans contractual rights, intellectual property rights, etc	Limited to foreign direct investment, i.e. a certain percentage of equity participation in an enterprise that enables a foreign investor to exercise managerial control of the enterprise.
Performance requirements	Prohibition of requirements (local content, export performance, trade balancing, transfer of technology) imposed on foreign investors	Performance requirements may be addressed in a WTO agreement but the need to avoid distorting effects of these measures needs to be balanced with a recognition of their possible importance as tools of development policy
Temporary entry and stay of key personnel	Requirement to accord investors and certain categories of key personnel a right of temporary entry and stay, subject to certain exceptions	Covered already in GATS

Table 6.4 Differences between the MAI and the WTO *(continued)*

Subject	Draft text of the MAI	Proposals submitted in the WTO
Dispute settlements	Ad hoc arbitration; in addition, mechanism for resolution of disputes between private investors and host country governments enabling private investors to have recourse to existing arbitration procedures; possibility of monetary compensation;, enforcement of arbitration awards under domestic law of parties to the MAI	Under WTO dispute settlement mechanism
Labor and environmental issues	Commitment to labor and environmental standards in the preamble; obligation not to lower labor standards in order to attract investment	The WTO should take into account the concerns expressed by civil society regarding investors' responsibilities and regarding the impact of investment rules on labor and the environment
Development dimension	Not specifically covered	Development dimension should be included

Source: WTO Secretariat

States agreed to an informal working group to study the issue, with carefully negotiated terms of reference. Canada does not go further than the WTO work program, while recognizing that the WTO was well-placed to analyse the role of international investment in the trading system. The WTO work program could include complementarity of trade and investment, investment measures affecting trade and trade measures affecting investment, and a comparison of existing bilateral, regional, and multilateral agreements.

The Triadization of FDI

There is a distinctly uneven pattern of FDI. Developed countries accounted for 60 per cent of global inflows and 85 per cent of global outflows in 1996. In 1998, they registered a record level of FDI amounting to $460 billion of inflows and $595 billion of outflows. Their share in inflows rose to a peak performance of 72 per cent. These figures do not reflect the reality: FDI is concentrated on three players: the Triad (EU, Japan, and the United States) dominates the picture. As a result, only 14 per cent of world population in 1990 attracted 75 per cent of FDI; and 72 per cent of the world's population was in receipt of only 8.5 per cent of global FDI. Two-thirds of the population was excluded from the benefits of the system, whilst the limited prosperity it generates was increasingly concentrated amongst the already employed, wealthier 14 per cent of the world and a few client states (Hirst and Thompson, 1996).

Outside the Triad, only three countries remain significant FDI recipients, the latter two also being outward investors (UNCTAD 1999: 33). Thus, 10 countries attract two-thirds of investments, 100 only 1 per cent.

FDI inflows to, and FDI outflows from the United States amounted $357 billion in 1998. The flows are particularly intense between the United States and the European Economic Area. US investments across the Atlantic are higher than the share across Pacific. However, the most striking element is that the US shifts from being a net exporter of FDI to its current position as the largest host country to FDI. There is an increased share of foreign affiliates in its domestic manufacturing. The EU dominates both FDI inflows and outflows.

EU FDI flows accounted for 94 per cent of the total FDI flows in 1998. Japan, which is the most important investor after the EU, suffered from recession and accounted for only 6 per cent of total FDI flows to the United States (UNCTAD, 1998). However the United

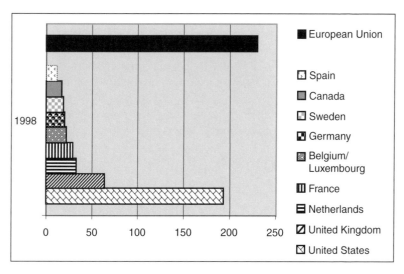

Graph 6.1   Developed countries: FDI inflows (billions of dollars)

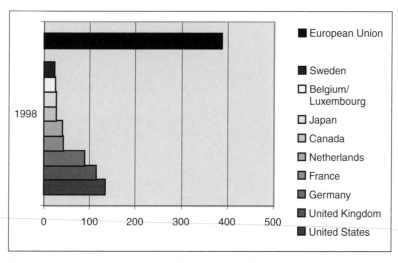

Graph 6.2   Developed countries: FDI outflows (billions of dollars)

States' share of global FDI has fallen from around 50 per cent in 1960, to around 25 per cent today.

The EU was the world's most important outward investor in 1998 with $386 billion outflows. It was also outperforming the United States

Table 6.5 US FDI inflows and outflows (1995) (per cent)

Region/Country	Inflows	Outflows
Total	60.8	93.3
Of which (per cent)		
Developed countries	102.0	72.4
Canada	7.4	8.3
European Union	71.6	49.6
France		6.4
UK		12.4
Germany		2.7
Japan	−1.9	3.9

Source: WTO, 1996

as the most important recipient with $230 billion in 1998 (82 per cent more than in 1997). The United Kingdom maintained its position as the largest EU investor followed by Germany, France, and the Netherlands, whereas the three main recipients were respectively the United Kingdom, Netherlands, France, and Germany. The rising share of intra-EU flows in total EU FDI inflows has been attributed to the poor record in attracting outflows from outside the EU. As shown in Graph 6.3, intra-EU inflows outperformed extra-EU outflows as a percentage of total outflows.

EU FDI outflows focus mainly on the United States. Investments to Central and Eastern European Countries (Hungary, Poland, Czech Republic) doubled to $12 billion in 1995, against $6.6 billion in the previous years. Germany, France, and the UK are the largest investors alongside the US and Japan.

The decline of Japan's FDI outflows continued in 1998 to $24 billion, only slightly over half their peak level of annual average outflows of $41 billion during 1989–91 (UNCTAD, 1999b). In the 1980s, much of the growth of FDI worldwide was attributed to the massive expansion of Japanese multinationals. Japan's direct investment stock in foreign countries grew by nearly 25 per cent annually in the 1980s, and Japan's share of worldwide FDI stocks jumped from 4 per cent to 12 per cent over the same period. However as the result of economic recession, Japanese presence has receded, and developed countries suffered most from this contraction.

The geographical pattern of Japanese FDI outflows has changed since the late 1980s and early 1990s. As table 6.6. shows, FDI outflows have shifted towards South, East, and South-East Asia. Principal

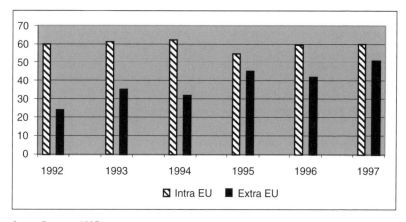

Source: Eurostat 1997
Graph 6.3   Intra-EU and extra-Eu FDI flows, 1992–97

Table 6.6   Geographical distribution of Japanese FDI (1989–91 and 1994–96)
(billions of dollars and percentage)

Region/Country	1989–91	1994–96
All countries (billions dollars)	41.6	21
	83.0	58
Developed countries (per cent)		
United States	51.0	37
European Union	23.0	13
Developing countries (per cent)	17.0	42
South, East, and South-East Asia	11.0	34
China	1.1	12
Central and Eastern European		
Countries (per cent)	0.1	

Source: UNCTAD 1999, FDI/TNC database

recipients are China, Malaysia, Thailand, and in Latin America, Argentina, and Mexico. They received nearly 45 per cent of all direct investments to developing countries in 1991 (Hufbauer, Lakdawalla, and Malani 1994: 40).

Inflows remain at the same level of $3.2 billion as in l997. The level of inflows is no longer the lowest among developed countries. The discrepancy between FDI outflows and inflows has shrunk. Manufacturing is prominent, accounting for the bulk of total FDI inflows to the United States, the EU, and Japan. By contrast, services industries figured more prominently in the US FDI outflows (notably non-bank and insurance) and intra-EU FDI, exceeding manufacturing M&A activities, have been the most important way of entering the US, the EU, and the Japanese markets. They increased by 84 per cent between 1988 and 1995, most of them located in Western Europe and the USA and include strategic industries: telecommunications, energy, pharmaceuticals, and financial services. Half of both EU FDI outflows and inflows during 1994–1996 were related to cross-border M&A (UNCTAD, 1997b: 47).

Between 1986 and 1995, cross-border mergers and acquisitions among EU-based firms increased from 720 to 2296 in industry and from 783 to 2602 in services (WTO, 1998: 18). If M&A have been the most important way of entering the Japanese market as they involve less hustle and transaction costs in a complex environment, there are far more cross-border M&A by Japanese firms (D'Andrea Tyson, 1992: 93).

Intra-triad investment relationships are quite dense, but inter-linkages are also evident. The share of the EU FDI outflows to non-EU countries surpassed the growth of intra-EU flows in 1997 (Hirst and Thompson 1996: 65). Chapter 10 will confirm this pattern of interaction between main regions.

Developing countries and FDI: concentration and shifting pattern

There has been a marked revival of investment in developing countries. However, the upward trend marks wide disparities in performance across countries and regions. As shown by Graph 6.4, high investment rates in East Asia contrast with the low rates of Sub-Saharan Africa (SAFR). Average investment rates in Latin America (LA), Middle Eastern and North African countries (MENA), and South Asia rank between these extremes.

The most troubling aspects of the regional distribution of inflows is the decline of Sub-Saharan Africa. Hence, one could draw an overly pessimistic picture of the perspectives of developing countries in the era of globalization. At present, dynamism is regionally concentrated, namely in Asia. The relatively high concentration of FDI, which focuses on a few advanced developing-country hosts is said to limit the

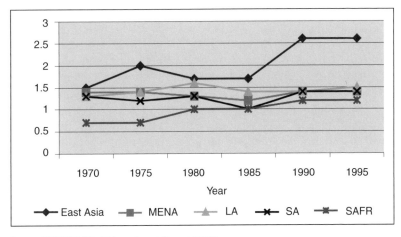

Source: UNCTAD World Investment Report 1999b
Graph 6.4   Investment rates in different regions, 1998

development prospects for the majority of least developing countries
(Grundlach and Nunnenkam 1998: 153).

This is largely because FDI inflows in a number of countries concentrate on the service sector, which is now the largest recipient in these
cases. FDI entails elements of further fragmentation among developing
countries, divided among winners and losers. There is a fault line
between performing developing countries attracting the bulk of FDI,
and the rest of developing countries, which are lagging behind the
front-runners.

Yet the share of world FDI received by developing countries rose
from around 16 per cent in the second half of the 1980s to 28 per
cent in the 1990s. These flows were increasingly concentrated in a
small number of locations (UNCTAD, 1999a: 115) As shown in
Graph 6.5, ten leading emerging countries accounted for three-quarters of the total FDI inflows of developing countries in 1998. China,
Brazil, and Mexico alone accounted for more than half of the total
inflow.

There have been some important changes in the geographical distribution of inflows over the past three decades. Patterns of investment
reflected a decline for Latin America. In 1950, the region accounted for
one-third of direct investment; by 1970, it received less than 16 per
cent, and by 1990, less that 10 per cent. Since the early 1970s, the
East Asian countries have seen a significant increase in their share,
reflecting their increasing attractiveness.

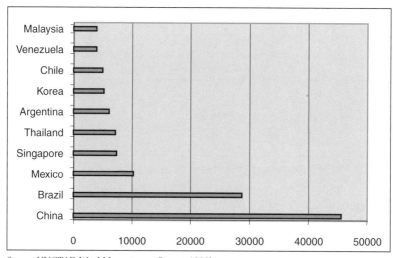

Source: UNCTAD World Investment Report 1999b
Graph 6.5 FDI inflows by economy, 1998 (millions of dollars)

More recently, China has attracted massive investment flows: FDI flows to China have nearly doubled since 1993. In the 1990s China outperformed the few other recipient developing countries and accounted for two-thirds of the total FDI flows of East Asia and one-third of the inflow of all developing countries (UNCTAD 1999a: 116). FDI flows are mainly concentrated on the coastal provinces, especially in the southern Chinese coastal provinces of Guangdong, Shangai, Tianjin, Liaoning, and Beijing (Hirst and Thompson, 1996: 68). This is the result of the government's efforts to promote FDI in the provinces that offer locational advantages (UNCTAD 1997b: 78).

As Table 6.7. shows, East Asia's FDI share of the developing countries' total has more than doubled since 1975, while it has more than halved for Latin America and Africa. Viewed from the perspective of the financial crisis that hit the region in 1997–98, the performance of East Asian countries is all the more remarkable. In 1998, FDI flows to these countries stood up well, and remained well above the average of annual flows recorded during 1991–95. FDI inflows have increased in Thailand and in Republic of Korea, whereas they have declined in Malaysia, Singapore, and Taiwan. In these three cases, the contraction is the result of the recession of Japanese FDI. Argentina, China, Malaysia, Mexico, and Thailand received nearly 45 per cent of all Japanese direct investments to developing countries in 1991 (Hufbauer, Lakdawalla and Malani, 1994: 40). The Republic of Korea received a

Table 6.7   Changing distribution of FDI within the developing countries

	1975		1998	
	% of world trade	% of developing countries' total	% of world trade	% of developing countries' total
Developing countries	24.9	100.0	26.0	100.0
Latin America	12.0	48.3	11.0	13.0
Asia	5.3	21.1	13.0	47.0
Africa	6.7	28.8	1.0	5.0

Source: Dicken 1992; World Investment Report 1998

four-fold increase over its average annual performance during the first half of 1990s.

The second shift is the recent Asian FDI leap outward. Inter-regional investment is the principal source of FDI for the region despite the importance of FDI from developed countries. For the major Asian developing economies, the FDI stock attributed to other Asian economies reached 40 per cent of the total stock. It is far ahead that from developed countries.

The growth of FDI from Asia is an important new phenomenon. Investors from the republic of Korea have invested in the motor and auto-components industry, while Malaysian TNCs are concentrating on services (hotels, property, telecommunications, and petroleum). As Table 6.8 shows, Japan is the largest provider of FDI to East Asia, although there is very little in the opposite direction. Outside the region, North America, Australia, and Latin America remain the most import FDI destinations of Asian FDI. The European Union accounted for only 4 per cent of Asia's outward FDI in the early 1990s. Asian firms are only just beginning to penetrate the European Market (UNCTAD, 1997b: 84; *The Economist*, 7 November 1998).

Since the 1970s, FDI into Latin America has remained strong, although its share of developing countries' total FDI decreased from 48.3 per cent to 13 per cent. MERCOSUR received more than half of all inflows to Latin America and the Caribbean.

Brazil was the largest single host country, receiving FDI inflows of more than $28 billion, equivalent to 40 per cent of all inflows in the region. Mexico maintained its position as the second largest host country. The strong position of Brazil, easily topping Mexico ($10 billion), reflects the wave of privatization undertaken by the country

Table 6.8 Percentage distribution of foreign investment stock in China and ASEAN-4 in 1992

	China*	Indonesia	Malaysia	Thailand	ASEAN-4
Origin					
Singapore	–	4.1	6.7	6.3	
Hong Kong	62.0**	7.4	3.0	6.6	25.3
Taiwan	8.2	7.7	22.8	9.2	
Korea	0.9	5.7	2.9	1.5	
Japan	8.4	15.7	22.7	38.1	26.1
US	8.5	6.5	7.0	11.9	9.5
Others	12.0***	52.9	35.0	26.4	38.6
Total	100.0	100.0	100.0	100.0	100.0

* 1993
** includes Macau
*** Includes Singapore
Source: MITI (1994), Nomura Research Institute

since the early 1990s. The EU has begun to challenge the dominance of United States FDI inflows into Brazil. FDI inflows into Argentina showed the second largest increase of all countries in Latin America in 1998 to about $5.6 billion, although far behind Brazil ($28.7 billion).

African countries lag behind other developing countries in terms of attracting FDI inflows. On average, a Graph 6.6 shows, Africa's share of developing country inflows has more than halved since the 1970s from 28.8 per cent to 5 per cent. Africa has not participated in the surge of FDI flows to developing countries. Furthermore, FDI flows are highly concentrated. Egypt and Nigeria together accounted for about one-third of FDI inflows as shown by Graph 6.6. The oil-producing country Nigeria accounted for 61 per cent of the average annual inflows to Sub-Saharan Africa during 1993–95. South Africa is a promising market for FDI. United States have made by far the largest investment commitments in South Africa since the April 1994 election.

A survey conducted by UNCTAD in 1999 had very ambivalent findings. On the one hand, the creation of a business-friendly environment does not automatically make a country more attractive for FDI. South Africa and Nigeria are exceptions. These two countries are perceived as attractive locations because of factors other than business-friendly environment. On the other hand, factors that are likely to have a positive impact are the profitability of investments, the regulatory and legal framework, and the political and economic outlook

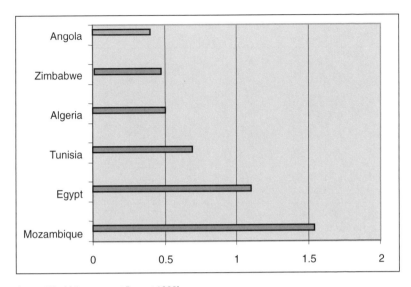

Source: World Investment Report 1999b
Graph 6.6   FDI inflows to ten African countries, 1998 (millions of dollars)

(UNCTAD, 1999b: 49–50). Barriers that militate against FDI are high government ownership, bureaucratic inertia, and complex rules (Kincaid, 1994: 56).

However, out of the six top countries that were the most frequently quoted in the survey – Botswana, Ghana, Mozambique, Namibia, Tunisia, and Uganda – only two are listed in the top ten recipient countries in Africa, and these are not ranked among the most important recipients. FDI in Nigeria, by far the most important FDI recipient in Africa, is a game of 'managing uncertainty' (*The Economist*, 15 January 2000). Companies are prepared to pay bribes, and are spending large amounts of money to accommodate communities.[4]

Central and Eastern Europe: catching up

Central and Eastern Europe is catching up with the rest of the world, as evidenced in the growth rates of FDI inflows in 1993–97. The region has registered an increase since the 1990s, topping $16 billion in 1998. However, the figure masks significant variations. The Czech Republic and Poland are recipients of almost half of FDI. Most investments come from the EU, and are directed towards Slovenia, Romania, Poland, Bulgaria, Albania, and Lithuania.

European agreements played a key role. The United States and Germany have become the two single most important investor countries, each accounting for 7–20 per cent of total foreign investment in many economies of the region, while Japanese FDI accounted for 0.3 per cent of total Japanese investments (Economic Commission for Europe, 1994: 3).

Sectoral distribution of FDI shows that services FDI has been growing over the past years in both developed and developing countries. However, only a cluster of developing countries benefited from inward services FDI. As in trade, FDI tends to increase the gap between the developing countries front-runners and the lagging developing countries. Indeed, FDI has integrative potentiality, raising productivity, bringing technological transfer, and stimulating exports. However, FDI further fragments the developing world into the winners attracted into the orbit of the most powerful states, and the losers, left behind and marginalized.

Concluding remarks

The uneven pattern of FDI is not only reflected in the geographical distribution of FDI (as shown in Graph 6.8), which concentrates on the Triad among developed countries and the most advanced countries among developing countries. More important is the sectoral distribution of FDI: its most striking feature is the decline by half of the primary sector between 1988 and 1997, globally both in developed and in developing countries. The services sector experienced an increase, in both developed countries and developing countries, although the increase is more important in the former than in the latter. The share of manufacturing in total FDI has remained stable in developing countries, while it has decreased in developed countries. Developed countries are the largest recipients of financial services (banks, insurance, securities, and other financial companies).

More importantly, as pointed out by Agosin and Mayer (2000: 15), to benefit from FDI requires capacities that many developing countries do not possess. Some countries have been successful in adopting policies to ensure that FDI contributes new technologies and introduces new products that nest in those countries' policies. Some Asian countries have successfully screened FDI; however, most developing countries do not have the administrative capabilities to implement effective screening.

Finally, transnational corporations, which account for one quarter of world's outward FDI stock, are concentrated in the triad, bypassing the less advanced among the developing countries. This will be the subject of the next chapter.

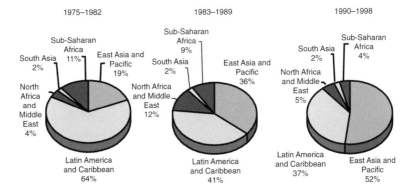

Source: UNCTAD, 1999b

Graph 6.7   Share of different regions in total net inflow of FDI in developing countries, 1975–98

7
The Transnational Corporations: Channeling Disparities

The transnational corporations (TNCs) are portrayed as the main instruments of globalization, although they are by no means a new phenomenon. TNCs emerged quite early, in the seventeenth century. The Vereenigde Ost-indische Compagnie, alias the East India Company, was born in 1602, and was trading cottons from Coromandel to Indonesia and China, silks from China, Tonkin, India, and Persia to Manila and on to New Spain (Mexico), tea and gold from China, coffee from Mocha, and asserted itself as the world's only supplier of nutmeg, cloves, and mace (Landes, 1998: 141–5). The Hudson Bay Company was founded in 1677, and traded furs from Canada to Europe. In the late nineteenth century multinationals such as Singer Sewing Machines, International Harvester, American Bell, Standard Oil of New Jersey, Ciba, Hoescht, BASF, Siemens, and Royal-Dutch Shell started trading. Yet they were still exceptions.

Over the last decades, there has been a quantum leap in the importance of multinationals. The reasons for this lie in the reduction in the cost of international transportation, the development of communication technologies, the innovations in management, and the liberalization of trade that have transformed the ability of firms to organize production transnationally. Technologies have pushed multinationals abroad, and they are able to trade more easily at reduced costs. Air transport has increased over the last decade, and there have been substantial cost reductions. Air cargo rates on long distance routes have reduced by about 15–20 per cent over the 1975–93 period (in Bordo *et al.*, 1999: 17). The introduction of computers has allowed the multinationals to control and handle their global operations with lightning speed.

All these components make multinationals even bigger, and enlarge their playing field. The reduction of impediments to trade achieved by the GATT/WTO negotiations, has facilitated their global activity. Although there are still large pockets of protectionism in textiles, agriculture, and restrictive practices (see Chapter 5), tariffs have fallen. Internationalization of capital and FDI have been very important mechanisms in the process of the internationalization of production, which has simultaneously caused internationalization of capital and FDI. From the 1960s onward, the number of multinationals has multiplied. They now comprise over 500 000 foreign affiliates established by some 60 000 parent companies (UNCTAD, 1999b: 4). In 1974, ECOSOC adopted the term transnational corporations for the activities of multinationals to reflect the essential feature of operation across national borders. TNCs are central to the whole process of globalization. They mould the trade and investment flows. Investments move through intra-firm trade. In 1995, the figure invested by 39 000 parent firms in their 270 000 foreign affiliates reached $2.7 trillion. TNCs account for two-thirds of world trade, with up to a third of world trade being intra-firm trade between branches of the same company. In the USA, 40 per cent of total imports and 31 per cent of total exports could be identified as intra-firm; in the UK it is 30 per cent.

This chapter does not intend to investigate the nature of multinational corporations (TNCs). Some authors argue that TNCs are footloose companies (Ohmae, 1995), capturing most of their activity abroad with their subsidiaries. Others (Vernon, 1977; Hirst and Thompson, 1996) argue that TNCs have the support of their headquarters and have their home base as the center for their economic activities. Our concern is with the uneven distribution of multinationals. TNCs and M&As tend to widen the gap both between developing countries and developed countries and between developing countries. Despite indisputable elements of integration in the global economy, TNCs and M&As entail elements of fragmentation.

Transnationals and national governments: maximizing their interests

The relationship between transnational companies and national governments has always been an uneasy, if not a schizophrenic one. According to Dunning (1993: 9), this is because it is assumed that TNCs normally aim to maximize their profit, while governments are more concerned with maximizing the value added created by multinationals. TNCs are portrayed as profit-driven entities with a global perspective, whose long term interests do not automatically coincide with those of the host countries. If they do coincide, both the TNCs and the governments collaborate in their mutual interest. But this may not be always the case. Even if it is, the host country may wish to maximize the local content of the TNCs' production, or to induce them to produce high-value products and maximize national spillovers by encouraging local firms to enter the industry.

Such objectives may conflict with the natural tendency of TNCs to safeguard their technological advantages and maximize their flexibility to relocate production in line with their shifting global priorities. TNCs are fast moving companies, taking advantage of any opportunities, and looking for safe and profit-driven places.

The recent developments in the globalization of the process of production, and the ability of producers to slice up the value chain into many geographically separated steps, have changed the ability of governments to choose which industries or part of industries to host. It is possible for TNCs to single out specific activities on the production chain according to the host countries' assets. TNCs have the ability to match these assets to their specific needs, and to incorporate the country into their network of affiliates to maximize the corporate profits (UNCTAD, 1996a: 113). The parceling out of the production process has a major effect on the dynamics of a specific sector. Steinberg (1998: 25) notes that in the IT sector, the breaking up of the production chain rescued the US corporations from Japanese competition by providing them with high-speed, high-quality alternative sources of supply with much-reduced demand on capital.

Changing attitudes

There has been a dramatic shift in the developing countries' perception of multinationals. This does not mean that antagonism and fear aroused by multinationals in developing countries have not affected their activity, but the change that occurred in the 1990s, both at the global and national levels, with the emergence of globalization and widespread of liberalization, facilitated their activity. Before the mid 1980s, multinationals were the center of an emotional and ideological debate in developing countries.

Raymond Vernon tried to capture the reasons of the hostility towards MNCs' activity. One of the reasons was ideological (Vernon, 1977: 243). The leaders of countries in which multinationals had activity, reacted against them by way of a set of ideologies and values that rejected the multinationals. That was the case with Dependencia, the main school of thought adopted by many Latin American countries in the 1970s. Multinationals' activity typified the core–periphery model by which the controlling functions of planning, investment decisions, and research and development were concentrated in the core countries, while production was only located in the periphery. Basic decisions about the pace and trajectory of development were being dictated by multinationals (Moran, 1974: 6). Multinationals controlled the exploitation of Third World resources without adequate recompense to the host state.

Multinationals were seen as foreign intruders that sought profits without any consideration for the social and economic needs of the host countries, repatriating earnings, and therefore siphoning off the money which could have been locally reinvested (Cox, 1982: 48; Landau, 1990: 145). The internationalization of production resulted in creating enclaves of production in the peripheral countries, and in enriching local business people and political elites who had close relationships with executives of MNCs and foreign governments, financially and socially coopted by the MNCs. Multinationals' activity resulted in creating a technological dependency and consumer dependency, ensuring that the host country would remain dependent upon inputs from abroad. Either products were high technology products with highly specialized uses that few consumers could use, or they were mass consumption items geared towards the wants of Western consumer markets that distorted consumption patterns in developing countries by persuading consumers to spend what little income they had on unnecessary products, such as soft drinks, and consumer goods (Cox, 1982). The Nestlé scandal about milk powder replacing breast feeding in the developing world, epitomized the distorted consumption pattern in developing countries.

Many of the concerns of the Third World focused on technology. Developing countries were often incapable of utilizing the technology because of unskilled labor, as it was geared to capital-intensive forms of production requiring fewer high-skilled personnel. There was a lack of experienced indigenous managers, qualified engineers, and skilled workers, which was partly due to reliance on multinationals. Raymond Vernon notes that 'the multinational company has come to be seen as the embodiment of almost anything disconcerting about modern industrial society. They were huge, stateless, and ruthless' (Vernon, 1977: 19).

In his account of the Kennecott and Anaconda companies, which extracted Chilean copper, Moran (1974: 55) recalls that from 1955 to

1965, both companies realized $465 million in profits from Chile. When Kennecott concluded a joint-venture with the Chilean government in 1961 (51 per cent for the Chilean government; 49 per cent for Kennecott), Kennecott demanded that the sale amount be made subject to the laws of the State of New York. Any threat of nationalization would result unavoidably in a face-to-face confrontation between the US and the Chilean government (Moran, 1974: 132–5). That happened under President Salvador Allende some ten years later. Kennecott's strategy worked well; pressures on the Allende government came from all directions.

Research conducted in 1975 showed that only 9 per cent of developing countries' negotiators in the multilateral trade negotiations thought that the implications of multinationals were positive; ten years later, 28.4 per cent thought positively about the multinationals; 22 per cent thought that the experience of their country was negative, ten years later this figure was 30.4 per cent (Landau, 1990: 137). Most of the states in which multinationals played a leadership role, lacked bargaining power and decision-making strength to negotiate the terms of investments. Multinationals faced weak government structures and inadequate laws. From the mid 1960s onwards, voices were raised on the national and international levels to monitor the multinationals' activity.

Towards an international regime for monitoring TNCs?

Trade unions started to demand more regulation and more consideration for workers' rights. They brought their influence to the UN agencies, such as the International Labor Organization (ILO) to provide guidelines for multinationals. In 1977, the ILO adopted a 'tripartite declaration of Principles concerning Multinational Enterprises and Social Policy' (van der Pijl, 1993: 43).

The role of MTNs (ITT and US copper corporations) in the destabilization of the United Popular Government of Allende in Chile acted as a catalyst for strengthening the regulation of multinationals in the context of the UN, which was at the forefront of attempts to codify and regulate the TNCs' activity. Multinationals' activity and technology transfer to LDCs became the core components of the New International Economic Order (van der Pijl, 1993: 45). These issues stood out as encapsulating the unequal situation of LDCs. The most comprehensive attempt to codify was made by the UN Economic and Social Council's Draft Code of Conduct on TNCs, which was adopted in 1983, although it came to nothing.

Also, developing countries sought the adoption of an International Code for Technology Transfer (TOT Code), under the auspices of the UNCTAD. This code would be legally binding, would cover all forms of technology transfer transactions, and would give primacy to the recipient state's law and dispute settlement procedures. Developing countries wanted the recipient law to be recognized in case any dispute erupted. Developed countries favored the preservation of the parties' freedom to choose the proper law provided it had a genuine connection with the transaction.

TNCs as conduits for trade and investment

Some 20 years later, the pattern has shifted. One factor behind the shift of attitudes towards the perceived costs and benefits of TNCs was the experience gained by developing countries in dealing with them. States have used their bargaining power to negotiate with TNCs and to adopt policies likely to give the benefits hoped for (Muchlinski, 1994: 11). Increasing knowledge led to a more informed discussion on TNCs' problems. Once regarded as distorting or hampering the developments of poor nations, TNCs are now regarded as conduits for trade and investment, which help developing countries integrate into the global economy. Developing countries that had developed indigenous technological capabilities, such as Brazil in the 1970s, which felt that deepening local capabilities yielded greater benefits than receiving it from TNCs, have stayed at the bottom of the technological ladder. However the building of a local technology is crucial to attract investment. The level of local capabilities determines the benefits of spillovers from foreign presence (UNCTAD, 1999b: 320).

Some developing countries, especially in East Asia have had rather restrictive policies toward TNCs. They supported TNC activity in high-value industries, petroleum refinery, textiles, or labor intensive export industries, generating foreign exchange and jobs. Even in those sectors, the governments favored joint ventures, under local ownership. In Korea, foreign ownership above 50 per cent was prohibited except in areas where FDIs were deemed to be of strategical importance, which covered 13 per cent of all the manufacturing industries.

Retaining control over the assets

TNCs can be found at each stage of the transfer of technology, because of their ability to produce, acquire, master the understanding of, and organize the use of technological assets across national boundaries (Dunning, 1992: 290). The advantages that TNCs bring to the host country depend on the degree of control that they retain over their assets. Too much control prevents the development of indigenous production and export (UNCTAD, 1996a: 113). Patterns are quite diverse, and depend on countries and sectors.

In the 1970s, multinationals retained much control over their networks. US-based companies marked their preference for wholly owned subsidiaries in developing countries (52.6 per cent), whereas European-based companies opted for majority-owned companies (35.6 per cent). Japanese-based multinationals had been setting up joint ventures (77.7 per cent). Various factors pushed the companies to privilege wholly-owned subsidiaries. One was the sector concerned.

TNCs dynamize local companies by subcontracting policy or equipment manufacture contracts, thus forcing local firms to develop their own technological capabilities. They are very effective in improving the local supply base. In Brazil, TNCs have created an incipient cluster of high-technology businesses around Campinas in the State of São Paulo. Automotive TNCs such as Renault, Chrysler, Audi/Volkswagen, Volvo, BMW-Chrysler, and the Detroit Diesel Corporation, motivated by technological conditions, transportation, and fiscal incentives, have invested $16 billion in Curitiba – the capital of Parana, one of the southern states of Brazil. They have had a spillover effect on local suppliers of replacement parts, and have upgraded domestic capabilities of indigenous firms. They have sourced across the state for the supply of electrical appliances, machines, and car parts. After São Paulo, Parana has become the second automotive pole of Brazil. Local firms have selected their industrial niches, sold their products to the foreign company, and used the knowledge obtained to move up the technological ladder (Landau, 1999b). 'Estadual' authorities have provided the state with better domestic skill and infrastructure.

Also, foreign companies play a role in promoting exports from local firms, and linking better local economy to the global market. In 1997, fewer than 600 firms were responsible for 80 per cent of Brazil's industrial exports, and almost half of that total came from local branches of multinationals; in Santa Catarina, 46 companies were responsible for more than 78 per cent of the state's exports, of which 5 realized 40 per cent of the total exports. In Rio Grande do Sul, 20 companies realized half of the total exports (Landau, 1999b).

One of the reasons for the difficulties faced by companies in foreign markets lies in the isolation of Brazil over a period of 20 years, due to its import-substitution strategy and high tariffs. The country started to open to international trade in the 1980s, when it adopted a liberalization program. Brazil is now well ranked among the small number of countries that dominate export activity.

The uneven pattern of TNCs

There are systematic differences in the spread of activity between TNCs based in different countries. In the 1980s, 600 industrial companies accounted for between 20 and 25 per cent of the value added in the world's market economies. TNCs privileged sophisticated manufacturing with high value added, like chemicals, automobiles, and electronics, and kept away from investment in low value-added labor intensive industries like textiles and clothing and food processing. Thus, there is a striking difference between TNCs from developed and developing countries. The latter operate mainly in low-technology products, with high labor intensity.

TNCs originate, and operate in developed countries. Few TNCs come from developing countries: 17 TNCs had sales of $1 billion or more in 1999. When they do operate in developing countries, the TNCs tend to be smaller, and originate from a small number of countries, essentially from the leading NICs: Hong Kong, Brazil, Argentina, India, Mexico and Venezuela, Singapore, and South Korea; and they tend to operate in their own neighborhoods.

A substantial part of TNCs originate from the European Union, United States and Japan. The United States is top with 32 TNCs, followed by Japan with 19, essentially in electronics, and Europe (mostly in Germany, the UK and France) in chemicals and pharmaceuticals. The origin of the top 100 TNCs remains stable. Approximately 89 per cent of parent companies had their headquarters in the Triad, about 10 per cent in developing countries, and only 1 per cent in economies in transition. The top 20, based on the Fortune Global 500 list, are set out in Table 7.1.[1]

TNCs originate pre-eminently from Japan (8) and United States (7), followed by the EU (5). In terms of foreign assets, sales, and employment, the number of companies from the European Union dominate, and even increased from 41 to 45 between 1996 and 1997; companies from United States and Japan ranked second and third. According to the Fortune 500 list, 34 per cent originated from the United States; 30 per cent from the EU; and 20 per cent from Japan. As Table 7.2 shows, TNCs originating in small industrial countries figure prominently in

Table 7.1   List of the top 20 TNCs (*Fortune* 1999)

Rank	Corporation	Country	Industry
1	General Motors	United States	Automotive
2	DaimlerChrysler	Germany	Automotive
3	Ford Motors	United States	Automotive
4	Wal-Mart Stores	United States	Distribution
5	Mitsui	Japan	Diversified
6	Itochu	Japan	Trading
7	Mitsubishi	Japan	Diversified
8	Exxon	United States	Petroleum
9	General Electric	United States	Electronics
10	Toyota Motor	Japan	Automotive
11	Royal Dutch Shell	Brit./Netherlands	Petroleum
12	Marubeni	Japan	Distribution
13	Sumitomo	Japan	Diversified
14	Intl. Business machines	United States	Machines
15	Axa	France	Insurance
16	Citigroup	United States	Banking
17	Volkswagen	Germany	Automotive
18	Nippon tel. & tel.	Japan	Communications
19	Nissho Iwai	Japan	Distribution
20	B. P. Amoco	United Kingdom	Petroleum

the list of the leading 10 corporations ranked by degree of transnationality, which does not include any corporations from the United States and Japan.

In terms of sectoral distribution, the assets of United States corporations have shown substantial changes. In 1996, the services sector, particularly banking, financial and other business services, was almost two-thirds as important as manufacturing, whereas in 1985 manufacturing was almost twice as important as services (Department of Commerce, 1996). Japanese TNCs have exploited their comparative advantages in cars and electronics.

Among the top 100 TNCs listed by UNCTAD, seven TNCs operated in electronics, and four in cars (Toyota, Nissan, Mitsubishi, and Honda). The strategy of internationalizing production and of building factories in Europe and the United States has been very successful for Japanese automakers. In the early 1990, one out of every four cars in the world was Japanese (Steinberg and Stokes, 1999: 71).

Conversely, the nature of share ownership makes it difficult for foreign firms to acquire Japanese companies and foreign firms have often found it difficult to penetrate the closed networks of producers and distributors in the Japanese economy (Held *et al.*, 1999: 252).

Table 7.2   The world's top TNCs in terms of degree of transnationality

Ranking by transnationality index	Foreign assets	Corporation	Country	Industry	Transnationality index (per cent)
1	23	Seagram Company	Canada	Beverages	97.8
2	14	Asea Brown Boveri	Switzerland	Electrical equipment	95.7
3	52	Thampson Corporation	Canada	Printing/Publishing	95.1
4	9	Nestlé SA	Switzerland	Food	93.2
5	18	Unilever NV	Netherlands	Food	92.4
6	82	Solvay SA	Belgium	Chemicals	92.3
7	75	Electrolux AB	Sweden	Electrical appliances	89.4
8	27	Philips Electronics	Netherlands	Electronics	86.4
9	15	Bayer AG	Germany	Chemicals	82.7
10	20	Roche Holding	Switzerland	Pharmaceuticals	82.2

Source: UNCTAD World Investment Report 1999

In the car sector, foreign automakers have had difficulty in setting up their own distribution structure in Japan. As Steinberg and Stokes note, 'few dedicated dealers of any large Japanese automaker will begin to sell a foreign car without the explicit agreement of, or even the request from the Japanese core producer'. Foreign shares of the Japanese replacement parts market are still negligible. US replacement parts manufacturers hold less than 1 per cent of the Japanese market, and the EU portion must be smaller than 1 per cent (Steinberg and Stokes, 1999: 84, 91).

In their account of TNC activity over the periods 1885 and 1992–93, Hirst and Thompson cast doubt on the internationalization of production. They note that transnational activity is marked by the predominance of home region/country activity (Hirst and Thompson, 1996: 80–94). Distribution of sales and distribution of assets are not global, but dominated by home region/country. Home region/country sales comprised two-thirds or over of total company sales. Sales within a region depend heavily on the home country corporation. The Europe/Middle East/Africa category is dominated by the core European countries; Asia/Pacific is dominated by Japan and the United States/Canada is dominated by the United States and Canada. TNCs based in the European Union operate within the region.

Regionalization of markets is evident. US company sales business is concentrated in the US and neighboring countries (US, Canada, Latin America, particularly Brazil and Mexico: US Department of Commerce, 1996). Western Europe's cross-border investments by European firms in 1985–90 totaled $141 billion, compared with $123 billion in North America. Regionalization is even more significant concerning the assets of services TNCs. Japanese corporations concentrate on Asia/Pacific, whereas US corporations concentrate on the United States and Canada.

TNCs and developing countries

TNCs originate from a small group of developing countries, essentially the leading NICs: the Republic of Korea, Venezuela, Hong Kong, China, Mexico, and Brazil. These countries also have a high economic potential. According to the Fortune 500 list, only 22 companies originated from developing countries: 9 from South Korea (Hyundai, Korea Electric Power, LG Electronics, LG International, Pohang Iron & Steel, Samsung, Samsung Electronics, Samsung Life Insurance, and SK); 4 from China (Jardine Matheson, Industry and Commercial Bank,

Sinochem, and Sinopec); 4 from Brazil (Banco do Brazil, Banco Bradesco, Itausa, and Petrobras); 1 from Mexico (Pemex); 1 from Taiwan (Cathay Life); 1 from Malaysia (Petronas); 1 from India (Indian Oil), and 1 from Venezuela (PDVSA). The UNCTAD top 50 TNCs from developing countries lists Petroleos de Venezuela, the Daewoo Corporation (Republic of Korea), and Jardine Matheson Holdings in the top positions.

In the five-year period 1993–97, the group of 50 TNCs from developing countries has become overall more transnationalized. However, in terms of foreign assets, their size remains relatively small. Their median foreign asset holdings were some $1.3 billion, far below the median of the top 100 group ($13.3 billion). TNCs from Asia accounted for an estimated $26 billion in foreign assets with firms from Hong Kong and China. The top 50 TNCs from developing countries include only three African TNCs: Sappi Limited (rank 7, paper), South African Breweries (rank 41, food and beverages), and Barlow Limited (rank 43, diversified) all originating from South Africa. The industry composition of the top 50 remained stable over the period 1993–97. Diversified TNCs, and those from food and beverages, construction, and petroleum industries dominate the group. Therefore, the operations concern mainly unsophisticated, low-technology products with high labor intensity.

The catching up of Central and Eastern Europe is far from complete. Many TNCs remain too small to qualify for the top 25 list for developing countries' TNCs (UNCTAD, 1999b: 89–92). However, Asian TNCs are increasingly interested in investing in that region, and TNCs from East Asian countries have started operating in developed countries.[2]

The regionalization observed by Hirst and Thompson, also applies to developing countries. Most developing countries' TNCs have a more limited geographical sphere of operations, and tend to operate within their neighborhood. Their operations are located in the same region as the source country. This pattern is reflected in the investment of the top 50 TNCs based in developing countries. Daewoo is the largest foreign investor in Vietnam, and the Philippines. Brazilian and Mexican firms are investing in Chile and Argentina.

Mergers and acquisitions: a strategy in its own right

One of the most significant developments in the global economy in the past several years has been the massive wave of M&As. They stem from the sea-changes that have occurred in the global economy, notably: liberalization of trade, investment and capital markets; rationalization of government procurements; deregulation and increased competition; privatization of state-owned enterprises; and intensification of technical changes. Liberalization of trade and investment has widened opportunities for M&As. New rules of competition and technological changes require firms to innovate continuously, to extend their range of products, and to establish their presence on the international market.

M&As are not a new phenomenon. They took place as early as the 1960s, reaching a peak at the end of the 1960s, diminishing few years later and making a comeback in the 1990s (see Table 7.3). What is new is their current scale and their uneven pattern. The earlier M&As were mostly domestic; today's M&As are increasingly cross-border and aim to form a networks of alliances. This last move is due to antitrust laws. Alliances have been increasingly concluded with foreign companies (Ostry, 1995: 25).

Links between investment and technology took the form of joint agreements or international strategic alliances among firms. Many firms also established joint ventures or strategic partnerships, whether in design, research, components, distribution under the form of licensing deals, research consortia, or supply agreements. Strategic alliances are not the same as mergers. Strategic alliances are co-operative ventures that do not involve equity arrangements. In strategic partnerships, only some of the participants' business activities are involved. Partners maintain as much independence as possible, whereas in mergers, identities of companies are subdued (Dicken, 1992: 213).

Table 7.3   Evolution of M&As since 1970

	Total	Value (billions)
1970	5,152	43.6
1975	2,297	11.8
1980	1,889	44.3
1985	3,001	179.8
1990	2,074	108.2
1995	3,510	356.0
1996	5,848	495.0
1997	7,800	657.1
1998	7,809	1 192.9
1999*	9,218	1 418.1

*Through 1/1/00
Source: mergerstat.com

Over the 1980s, strategic partnerships increased noticeably in three areas: biotechnology, information technology, and new materials. Between 1991 and 1992 their number rose from 58 to 90. M&As have different rationales:

- Size has become central to the global strategies of firms, particularly in industries faced with fierce competition. Size very often entails expansion abroad to create financial, operational, and managerial synergies that reduce the vulnerability of firms to economic shocks as it opens possibilities to penetrate a foreign market. Size is also a crucial factor in creating economies of scale. Firms not only look for size but also focus on core activities and rationalize operations across their global production network.

- Size puts firms in a better position to keep pace with a rapidly changing technological environment – a crucial requirement in an increasingly knowledge-intensive economy. In some sectors, such as communications or computers, costs of R&D are soaring, and risks are high. New developments in the field of high technology entail a number of risks: the risk that a competitor will be faster and will get its result patented, which will make it more difficult for other companies to exploit the results of the parallel research; the risk of patent litigation; the risk of the non-feasibility of a new technology (van Tulder and Junne, 1988: 217). Under fierce competition, firms seek to cut costs. Firms have to innovate continuously, to extend product variety and to provide complete solutions to one line of business. M&A enable firms to take advantages of resources and markets world-wide. In some industries, too, it is risky for one firm to develop on its own: IBM is an illustrative example.[3]

- Mergers have too often become a strategy in their own right. If the goal is to absorb shocks, it is also to prevent becoming the target. So much so that one could think that M&A has become the main activity of many firms. The 'power of the example' may also play out. In a competitive world, firms ought to have visions of expansion and competitiveness. The companies that fail to have these visions end up in a strategic impasse that they overcome by bidding against other companies. What seemed to be peripheral to firms, ends up being central to their activity and could develop into a cascade of M&As or a 'merger mania' (*The Economist*, 9 January 1999). Once the equilibrium is disturbed by the move of one firm, rival firms react through countermoves to protect oligopolistic positions vis-à-vis other major competitors.[4]

● Companies hesitate between technoglobalism or technonationalism (Ostry, 1995). Competition has been fierce between firms. However, they also symbolize patriotism and heritage, and as such they attract nationalist acclamation.[5] The American threat in aerospace has been the main motive for European restructuring. The American aerospace industry is composed of four suppliers, although it spends twice as much as Europe on defence. American firms raise strategic concern about European dependence on American technology. Also within Europe, France is afraid of being sidelined by Anglo-German mergers.

It is not a new phenomenon. At the beginning of the 1980s, Japan, Europe, and the United States all faced different challenges regarding their high-tech industries. For Japan, the challenge was to devise a new set of policies so that it no longer lagged behind the United States. The basic goal of Japanese technology and industrial policies since the 1960s had been to enable Japanese firms to catch up with the Americans (Ostry, 1995: 49–50). In automobiles and memory chips, for example, Japanese firms in the 1980s were producing with higher productivity and at higher levels of quality than their American competitors and the rest of the world.

The same situation prevailed for the European countries: they tried to catch up with the Americans. With the exception of aircraft, some areas of telecommunications, and sophisticated chemical products, European firms had not only not gained much ground on the Americans but had been overtaken by Japanese. It became clear in the late 1970s that national policies had failed, and the major European nations began to turn to the idea of intra-European cooperation. The Internal Market was propelled by a consortia of a group of big European companies, concerned about the American and Japanese pre-eminent high-technology industry (Landau, 1995: 272). The Round Table of European industrialists, and a Round Table of the twelve European electronics companies that had given birth to the European Strategic Program for Research and Development in Information Technology (ESPRIT), formulated ideas for action at the European level, which were soon to be carried out by Jacques Delors (van Tulder and Junne, 1988: 213–16).

● European companies have been keen to take advantage of the high demand for euro-denominated bonds. Companies fear that they may not be big enough to compete across the euro-zone. The euro has created a liquid market in European corporate bonds, which grew by 235 per cent in 1999. Many companies are treating indus-trial stakes like other investments (*The Economist* 18 September 1999, 12 February 2000). The danger is that they increase the share price to make M&As possible.

● What seemed to be a single merger ends up forming a network of alliances. Each partner has its own web of arrangements. AT&T, Wal-Mart, and Toshiba are at the hub of overlapping alliance net-works which include a lot of fierce competitors. It becomes difficult to establish the boundaries between firms (Dicken, 1992: 213).[6]

Geographical distribution: transatlantic against Continental Europe

The largest purchaser country in 1998 was the United Kingdom, replac-ing the United States in that position. Table 7.4. shows that there was a dramatic increase in the European Union's M&As between 1991 and 1998. Narula (1999: 717) explains that M&As started to increase in the wave of the single European market. But the 1990s witnessed a change with a propensity for EU firms to conclude M&A with Japanese and US firms, where the technology or market leaders are located. There has been a significant increase for Germany and the United Kingdom.

Table 7.4   Cross-border M&A purchases, by region/economy, 1991–98 (millions of dollars)

| | 1991 | | 1998 | |
Region/Economy	Majority	Total	Majority	Total
World	49 062	85 279	410 704	544 311
Developed economies	47 231	79 900	401 738	526 713
European Union	31 577	50 537	245 965	328 039
of which				
France	11 174	15 904	26 143	40 452
Germany	4 680	7 501	34 092	60 935
Italy	2 119	4 799	12 728	15 235
Netherlands	3 754	6 672	32 356	38 698
United Kingdom	5 901	8 087	110 093	127 716
North America	8 446	15 690	130 450	165 487
Canada	1 349	2 498	38 617	40 707
United States	7 096	13 192	91 832	124 760
Other				
Japan	3 675	8 959	3 835	7 239

Source: UNCTAD 1999

The momentum continued well into 1999 and led to mega deals, such as the acquisition of GEC Marconi Electronics by British Aerospace. M&A have taken place in the industries in which a country's comparative advantages are threatened (such as oil, telecommunications, and utilities). M&A with other firms are the only feasible way to consolidate the firm's position and competitiveness (UNCTAD 1999b: 98). As a result, M&As were in most cases concluded with highly competitive firms in the same industries. Moreover, there is a line of division between the United Kingdom and continental Europe. Only one-tenth of cross-border deals by the United Kingdom took place with European firms in 1998 (*Financial Times*, 18 January 1999).

European firms tend to purchase other European firms rather than concluding deals with United Kingdom firms. Compared with European firms, which are looking to consolidate their European position, United Kingdom firms look to consolidate their transatlantic position. This reincarnates old lines of cleavages within the EU between Atlantic-oriented countries and European-oriented ones (Landau, 1995: 90). However, an intra-European restructuring in various sectors faced by technological challenges could be jeopardized if the United Kingdom approaches United States firms.

Currency is indeed an incentive for promoting M&A. The strong pound has been a major factor in the massive wave of United Kingdom purchases. So as been the case of the dollar for United States and Canadian deals. An unprecedented number of mega-deals in 1998 accounted for the majority of the dollar volume which was reflected in the average purchase price. In 1998, the average transaction price was $211 million compared with $32 million in 1997. Transactions in Canada in 1998 totaled with dollar volume at $148 billion compared to 1264 transactions in 1997 with volume at $102 billion (Canadian Annual Directory, 1998; Mergers & Acquisitions in Canada, 1998: 4).

Mergers and acquisitions are not a significant port of entry for foreign investment into Japan. As Table 7.5. shows, M&As have remained stable in Japan: Japan is the only country among major countries with such stability in M&A activity. However, cross-border M&As by Japanese outward-investor firms declined in 1998. In 1989, Japanese purchases of Japanese firms amounted to 240, whereas Japanese purchases of foreign firms amounted to 404, and foreign purchases of Japanese firms to 17. A comparison of mergers and acquisitions in the USA and Japan shows that in 1991, the number for the USA was 2110, whereas for Japan it was 614 (Ostry 1995: 106–7). Estimates of the spillover effects of trade show that the Japanese

154

Table 7.5 Mega-deals in 1998

Buyer	Target	Sectors	Date
Bellsouth (USA)	Sprint (USA)	Telecommunications	1998
Bellsouth (USA)	Electric Lightwave		
US West (USA)	Global Crossing (Canada)	Telecommunications	1998
Seagram (Canada)	PolyGram (NL)	Consumer products	1998
Northern Telecom (Can)	Ray Networks (USA)	Telecommunications	1998
Teleglobe (USA)	Excel communications (USA)	Telecommunications	1998
Merrill Lynch (USA)	Midland Walwyn Inc. (USA)	Financial sector	1998
BP (UK)	AMOCO (USA)	Petroleum	1999
Wal-Mart (USA)	Wertkauf (Germany)	Retail	1999
ATT (USA)	Media One (USA)	Telecommunications	1999
Manhattan (USA)	Merril Lynch (USA)	Banking	1999
	JP Morgan		
National City Bank	KeyCorp (USA)	Banking	1999
Felekom (Germany)	One-2-One (British)	Telecommunications	1999
Alcan (Canada)	Pechiney (France)/	Commodity industries	1999
	Algroup (Switzerland)		
Alcoa (USA)	Reynolds Metals (USA)	Commodity industries	1999
Air Products (USA)	BOC (UK)	Basic chemicals	1999
Air Liquide (France)			
Union Carbide (USA)/	Dow Chemicals (USA)	Basic chemicals	1999
Union Camp (USA)	Unisource (USA)	Paper and pulp	1999
Georgia-Pacific (USA)			
Totalfina (France)	Elf (France)	Oil industry	1999
Assicurazioni Generali (Italy)	INA (Italy)	Insurance	1999
Hoechst (Germany)	Rhone-Poulenc SA (france)	Pharmaceuticals	1999

Source: Fortune various issues, *The Economist* various issues

impact on United States is larger than the reverse effect, although in general the US spillover to other countries is still the highest.

Industry composition

Recent cross-border M&As have concentrated in industries that have high R&D expenditures (pharmaceuticals); have over-capacity and low demand (automobiles and defence); are undergoing technological changes (chemicals); are under pressure of deregulation and liberalization (financial services); or have been privatized (energy, banking). Massive M&As in telecommunications resulted from deregulation, in addition to a growing demand for Internet products.

Trends in M&A are fast moving. In 1998, the largest cross-border M&A by value was in the oil industry, accounting for 14 per cent of the total, followed by the automobile industry and the banking and telecommunications industry (UNCTAD, 1999c: 99).

In 1999, the largest M&A was in the telecommunications industry, followed by pharmaceuticals industry and banking sector. Table 7.6. shows the top 10 M&As in 1998.[7] The largest M&As were in computer software, wholesale and distribution, miscellaneous services, banking and finance, health services, leisure and entertainment, brokerage, investment and management consulting, insurance, and communica-

Table 7.6   Top 10 deals for 1999

Seller	Buyer	Value in $ millions
1. Sprint Corp.	MCI WorldCom Inc.	$115 972.63
2. Warner-Lambert	Pfizer Inc.	$82 399.63
3. AirTouch Communications	Vodafone Group PLC	$62 767.97
4. MediaOne Group Inc.	AT&T Corp.	$55 795.38
5. US West Inc.	Qwest Communications International Inc.	$34 747,99
6. CBS Corp.	Viacom Inc.	$34 454.01
7. Atlantic Richfield	BP Amoco PLC	$26 611.34
8. Pharmacia & Upjohn Inc.	Monsanto	$25 760.32
9. Ascend Communications Inc.	Lucent Technologies	$24 132.39
10. AMFM Inc.	Clear Channel Communications	$17 307.95

Source: Mergerstat.com

tions. Table 7.7. lists some of the largest deals. Prices do not follow the announcements. Banking and finance, insurance, and broadcasting rank lower, but have higher prices. The story does not finish with the conclusion of the deal. Many M&As end in disappointment. The failure of M&As can be attributed to clashes in culture, corporate culture, or management styles. Each of the parties has its own vision of what the M&A comprises, and the method of working jointly. The cognitive gap is particularly dangerous for the M&A because it may lead to misunderstanding. Conflicts may arise in the marketing, the financial, and the human resources functions. As Faure (2000: 173) observed, 'it is extremely difficult to negotiate (and work together) in a constructive way without common references. The most serious misunderstandings reveal at the worst moment, at the moment action should begin'. Very often, ego plays a great role, and corporate managers react to what is perceived as hostile takeover.

Antitrust regulations may come into action in order to limit and control the market power gained by a number of corporations in their M&A activity. Competition authorities have to review the M&A, and to ensure that it does not jeopardize market competition. It might not be an easy task. First, in the newly formed larger corporations, fierce

Table 7.7   Industry analysis, 1996

Industry classification	Net announcements	Price offered (millions)
Computer software, supplies & services	637	20 287.1
Wholesale & distribution	529	11 508.0
Miscellaneous services	518	22 929.8
Banking & finance	371	36 962.2
Leisure & entertainment	330	16 201.2
Health services	325	15 532.5
Retail	242	11 359.5
Drugs, medical supplies & equipment	201	11 166.8
Broadcasting	196	25 245.8
Insurance	193	31 763.8
Printing & publishing	132	6 796.0
Electrical equipment	127	14 441.6
Industrial, farm equipment & machinery	120	4 639.6
Construction contractors & engineering	118	1 036.3

Source: Mergerstat Review

opponents of antitrust legislation will have been created (van Tulder and Junne, 1988: 254). Second, only 80 countries have competition laws. Developing countries with the exception of Latin American countries and South Africa started to adopt competition laws in the 1990s. There is increasing co-operation. The United States antitrust and counterpart agencies in a large number of countries, including the EU, have developed networks of bilateral co-operation, treaties, and agreements that form the basis of day-to-day enforcement relationships that benefit both parties, and provide assistance in a variety of matters including cartels (USTR interview, October 1999).

M&As and developing countries

Most developing countries prefer greenfield FDI over M&As because the latter involve a change in ownership, and there is no addition to the capital stock or production capacity, at least in the short run (UNCTAD, 1999c: 102). However, there has been a boom in M&As in developing countries. Cross-border M&A sales increased more than fivefold between 1990 and 1997 to over $95 billion in sales. However this figure masks wide disparities across regions. More than 90 per cent of the M&As were in South-East Asia and Latin America, as Table 7.8. shows. M&As in Asia have increased more than four times between 1990 and 1997, while growth has been impressive over a one-year period. In some cases, notably in Latin America, they occurred in the

Table 7.8   Cross-border M&A sales, by region/economy of seller, 1990–97 ($ million)

Region/Economy	1990	1994	1997
Developing countries	18 177	60 983	95 620
Africa	254	2 014	2 117
Latin America and the Caribbean	8 426	14 831	43 809
Southern Europe	108	69	1 144
Asia	9 836	44 011	49 377
West Asia	208	1 395	4 870
Central Asia	–	685	5 865
South, East, and South East Asia	9 718	41 932	37 643
Pacific	3	22	173
Central and Eastern Europe	8 355	4 904	9 883
World	159 959	196 367	341 653

Source: International monetary and financial issues for the 1990s, 1999

wave of privatization that has taken place in the region. That was the case in Brazil: mergers and acquisitions in Brazil climbed from 58 deals in 1992 to 372 in 1997. Asian M&As are particularly aggressive, and most concern telecoms.[8]

Building strategic R&D in developing countries

Some new trends could widen the gap among developing countries. Some developing countries have succeeded in building some technological capacity, and mounting significant research effort. India and Malaysia have undertaken R&D activities in establishing a mutually beneficial network between universities and industries.

These networks are similar to the ties existing between Stanford University and Silicon Valley's computer related industry. The highly active university has played a leading role in technological advancement by providing educational services and helping its students to establish themselves and launch a wave of 'start-up' companies. Laboratories and Programs, such as the Electronics Research Laboratory (ERL) and the Industrial Affiliates Program (IAP) constitute a formal way in which knowledge is transferred from Stanford to industry. Stanford University makes a permanent effort to improve its training function by selecting capable students, by adapting its curriculum to the ever-changing environment of electrical engineering, by attracting high level researchers, and by actively pursuing research (Harayama, 1998).

In Taiwan, the Hsinchu Science Park has imitated Silicon Valley with semiconductor factories and software start-ups. It benefits from the Industrial Technology Research Institute, from which many Hsinchu firms have been spun off. It is the third-largest high-tech industry, accounting for a third of Taiwan's manufacturing exports and a huge share of the world's computer production (98 per cent of scanners, 62 per cent of motherboards, 59 per cent of monitors, and 39 per cent of notebook PCs) (*The Economist*, 7 November 1998). The Asian crisis has benefited Taiwan: some Japanese companies have turned to Taiwanese companies to make chips for them on a contract basis (*The Economist*, 4 July 1998).

In India, TNCs provided the initial push as shown in Table 7.9. Texas instruments, Daimler-Benz (now DaimlerChrysler), SGS Thompson, British Aerospace and Elli Lilly established partnerships with research institutes in Bangalore or New Delhi in India to develop generic technologies and products for regional and global markets. They benefited

Table 7.9 Illustrative cases of R&D centers and R&D ventures in India

Institution/location/year	TNC involved	Focus and objective
Texas Instruments India, Bangalore, 1986	Texas instruments USA	CAD software for IC design and other applications.
Asia-pacific Design Centre, India, 1992	SGS-Thompson Microelectronics, France	VHDL design, layout and debugging of custom ICs.
D-B Research Centre, Bangalore, 1996	Daimler-Benz, Germany	Interface design of avionics landing systems and other projects related to vehicles and avionics business.
Ranbaxy Labs, New Delhi, mid-1990s	Eli Lilly, United States	Joint R&D for process development for drugs.
Hindustan Aeronautics Ltd, Bangalore, early 1990s	British Aerospace, United Kingdom	CAD packages, software applications in management, manufacturing, design and real time info. systems.

Source: UNCTAD, 1999b

from the supply of cheap high quality labor, scientific talent with strong background in theoretical sciences and engineering, and the access to leading research institutes. As a result, India developed remote services and back-office jobs. Some 25 000 Indians are employed in remote services, and the number could rise to between one and three million people within the next 10 years (*The Economist*, 16 January 1999). Software business is particularly successful. Indian software exports grew from $225 million in 1992–93 to $2.7 billion a year in 1999 (http://www.nasscom.org). British Airways or Swissair handle an array of back-office jobs for their parent company, including dealing with automatic reservations, or ticket pricing. BA's operation has grown to 750 in two years, and hires 800 more workers in new office in Pune.

Concluding remarks

Similarly to trade and FDI, transnational corporations' operations tend to widen the uneven pattern playing out among developing countries. Transnational corporations, which account for one quarter of world's outward FDI stock, bypass the less advanced among developing countries. Transnational corporations have relied on the flexibility offered by a multiplicity of small and medium-sized contracting companies. As a result, regional nexus are emerging in Brazil or India in such activities as automotives, electronics, and computers. New centers of dynamic production are burgeoning in many Asian and Latin American NICs. In these economies, production activities are fast climbing the value-added ladder from labor-intensive to capital-intensive toward techno-logy-intensive industries.

8
The Globalization of Capital

Charles Tilly (1992) stresses the essential relationships between capital, coercion, and the creation of states. In the medieval age, accumulation and concentration of capital (merchants, entrepreneurs, financiers) generated urban growth and produced cities and the means to make wars. In turn, wars wove the European network of national states.

During the sixteenth century, the ability to borrow money, coupled with mass mobilization and civilian armies, began to make warmaking easier. It allowed the formation of military armies and the use of coercion, which centered on armed force. Capital and coercion produced organizations that controlled power, subordinated neighbors and more distant rivals, and extended territories, capital, and population. Some areas were capital intensive; some coercion intensive. Others such as England used both capital and coercion. From the start, monetary flows entwined city-states, and city-empires across Europe. From the sixteenth century onwards Europe imported large quantities of gold and silver. Much of it was used to finance trade and to obtain spices from the Indies or from China (Landes, 1998: 150). As a result, financial flows soon closely tied Europe and Asia.

From the early ages, financial activity was centered where commerce was concentrated. Europe shifted economic and financial gravity northward, from Spain to the city-states of Italy – Venice, Florence, and Genoa. In the sixteenth century, Italy was preeminent in the commercial and banking services. There was then a further shift from Italy to Holland. Antwerp and Amsterdam became the main financial and commercial places in Europe. In the eighteenth century, Holland ceded its top position to England, which kept its preeminent position over the nineteenth and part of the twentieth century. Britain's power in trade helped London, and the City of London in particular, to occupy a leading position in international finance, before it switched to the United States

Developments in the international financial structure have had a decisive influence on how wealth-creating activities were divided among nations. The argument of this chapter is that globalization of capital is unevenly distributed. Although developing countries have created links with the international financial system, that does not mean that they share the same efficiency. It is concentrated across all countries, and even more concentrated across the developing countries (Felix, 1994: 365).

From the gold standard to Bretton Woods

Global finance is composed of different components: flows of credit (loans and bonds), investment (see Chapter 6), and money (foreign exchange). The gold standard provided the basis a system of fixed exchange rates. It was established in 1878, and came to include European and Latin American countries and Japan, but ended abruptly in 1931, in the wave of the 1929 crisis. The system embodied a mechanism of automatic adjustment so that countries could correct their balance of payments imbalances and be brought back to equilibrium through the flow of gold. Although the system was said to have promoted the liberal, laissez-faire ideal, the gold standard operated quite differently from the ideal. It was not automatically used (Held *et al.*, 1999: 195–6; Gilpin, 1987: 123–5). Some countries evaded the discipline of the gold standard, and were not playing by the rules of the game. There were some recurrent balance of payments surpluses and deficits. Countries with a trade surplus invested in developing countries.

For the gold standard system to work properly, one country had to police the international order. In the nineteenth century and part of the twentieth, England assumed this role and managed the gold standard. Its hegemonic position, its preeminence in trade, money, and capital markets gave England enough power to enforce the rules of the game, and to police the world's monetary affairs. Sterling assumed a leading role in international transactions; there was an increasing integration of local and international currencies. As long as England was a hegemony, countries were committed to the system, and the world economy and financial system were relatively stable. The gold standard strongly complemented trade flows. The period 1870–1913 witnessed a rapid expansion in world trade (Bairoch and Kozul-Wright, 1996: 5). The success of the gold standard was due to a combination of specific conditions, which dictated an emphasis on monetary stability: financial, commercial and military leadership of Great Britain, free trade, and rapid industrialization. The spread of capitalism, free trade, and capital flows generated a growth momentum of the world economy. However, the stability of the system masked some causes for concern. There were deep differences between interest rates: domestic priorities prevailed for most of the developed countries, and those determined domestic interest rates (Held *et al.*, 1999: 197). Also, there was increasing protection all across Europe and the United States. Tariff barriers and discriminatory measures were erected at the turn of the century. After 1873, the situation was one of rivalry between developed countries. Germany, France, and the United states resented the benefits Great Britain drew from the gold standard system. They had to import food and raw materials, but all, bar Germany, were exporters of food-stuffs. They did not rely, as Great Britain did, on exports to supply their industries (Hobsbawn, 1968: 115). For a while, they did not have the capacity to challenge the English leadership, but they disliked the international order built by Great Britain (Gilpin, 1987: 127). This period reached its peak after the First World War, and approximated the situation observed by Ruggie (1998: 65) in which 'neither a hegemon nor a congruence of social purpose exists among the leading economic powers'.

The hegemonic position of Great Britain was eroding. Despite its position in world trade, Great Britain did not have an export surplus in goods at any time during the nineteenth century (Hobsbawn, 1968: 119). Britain's invisible profits from shipping services filled the gap between imports and exports. Latin American countries, and Argentina in particular, were the largest markets for British textile exports. At the turn of the century, India replaced the Latin American countries. Of equal importance, capital exports to the underdeveloped countries doubled by the 1880s. British capital amounted to 60 per cent of the total foreign investment in the country. Capital was not coming only from Great Britain; Western Europe was the major source of capital supply. By 1874, the combined total of Britain, Germany, and France amounted some $6 billion. By 1914, this figure had risen to $33 billion (Bairoch and Kozul-Wright, 1996: 11).

As a result, underdeveloped countries became frustrated with the British hegemony. Great Britain was no longer able to resist the growing discontent originating both from developed and underdevel-oped countries. The First World War swept away the international political order. The gold standard resisted until the Great Depression of the 1930s. Many countries gave greater importance to their domestic welfare than to a stable international order. Attempts were made to restore the gold standard and a stable monetary order, but all of them failed. Great Britain no longer had the power to assume the responsibilities of a hegemon (Cooper, 1968). The economic chaos led to the fragmentation of the international monetary system. Not surprisingly, the first states to control capital flows were the emerging powers: Germany and Japan. They were the first to depart from liberal practices in trade and finance (Helleiner, 1994c: 29).

At the Ottawa Conference in 1932, the British renounced to the gold standard. Great Britain tried to establish a 'sterling zone', with competition soon after from the American initiative to create a 'dollar bloc', and a 'gold bloc' led by France. However, the emergent dominant economic power, the United States, was not willing to assume leadership. After the treaty of Versailles, and the new international political order outlined by Woodrow Wilson, the United States retreated from the international scene despite some positive signals. In 1934, the US Reciprocal Trade Act gave the President to power to negotiate the reciprocal lowering of tariffs. This principle would be at the core of the new international order designed by the United States and Great Britain before the end of the Second World War.

The Bretton Woods agreement: a facsimile of the gold standard?

The postwar international order planned before the war ended by the United States – the sunrise power – and Great Britain – the sunset power – was based on three main key features: a stable monetary system built around the dollar for international exchanges; open markets; and access to the oil market. A stable economic order would avoid returning to the destructive protectionism and economic nationalism of the 1930s. Along the Keynesian theory, market forces were not automatically self-regulating and, therefore, a certain form of government intervention was required from time to time. Consequently, at the international level it was also conceded that government management was necessary. This was the shared perception that the collapse of the 1930s was due to the lack of international consultative mechanisms that had left economic affairs at the mercy of unregulated market forces.

The aim of the Bretton Woods agreement was to re-establish by international agreement a reasonable facsimile of the gold standard system which would secure the combination of currency convertibility, capital mobility, and free trade. Three major institutions were planned to achieve this objective: the IMF, the International Bank for Reconstruction and Development, and the International Trade Organization (Tussie, 1987: 11–12). The first two were created at the Bretton Woods Conference in 1944. The signatories undertook to maintain the inter-convertibility of their currencies, and to refrain from competitive devaluations and from bilateral currency arrangements, which would discriminate among trading partners in current transactions. The commercial policy was not directly involved and this issue went more slowly. The reason lay in the different conceptions of the US and the British: the Americans were ardent defenders of free trade, although some rifts split the Department of State and Department of Agriculture; whereas the British were more inclined to keep the preferential agreements they had with the Commonwealth.

Negotiations on an International Trade Organization (ITO) began in 1946 and successive conferences took place from 1946 to 1948. Paradoxically, the United States disliked some of the instruments which were at the core of the true multilateral organization it wanted to establish: tariff reductions, controls of safeguards, exemptions, and restrictions. Tariff reductions had been negotiated by 22 countries at the Havana Conference in 1947, before the ITO negotiations were completed, and the US Administration proposed to negotiate these trade agreements and to embody them in one multilateral treaty. Thus the GATT was drawn up as the general framework of rights and obligations for the 22 countries – of which nine were LDCs – participating in the tariff negotiations sponsored by the United States. The GATT was envisioned as the first of a number of agreements that were to be negotiated under the auspices of the ITO. When it became clear that ITO would not be ratified by the US Senate, the GATT became by default the underpinning of an international institution. Thus the GATT was not technically an organization of which countries become members, but a treaty with contracting parties.

The GATT was the product of a subtle compromise. It made compulsory the most-favored-nation rule, but allowed for all, especially for Great Britain, existing preferential arrangements. In many respects, the agreement offered 'a blanket escape from any of its obligations' (Ruggie, 1998: 76).

From the start, the Bretton Woods system had inherent flaws. It was a compromise between domestic autonomy and international stability (Gilpin, 1987: 132; Ruggie, 1998: 78–9). It avoided the interwar regime according to which international stability was sacrificed to domestic policy autonomy. The Bretton Woods system wanted it both to be multilateral and to allow domestic interventionism. The state would intervene to ensure full employment. If the state got involved in balance-of-payments difficulties, the IMF would finance the deficits. Indeed, many European countries had to face capital flight and balance-of-payments difficulties in the first postwar years. Efforts to control capital would require exchange controls to prevent capital outflows from exacerbating their balance-of-payments deficits. The United States answered the call of the Europeans to locate funds that had entered the United States, but divisions were deep within the US administrations and in Europe between orthodox thinking and supporters of free market.

Under the seriousness of the situation in Europe, and the 1947 crisis, the United States reappraised its foreign policy in Western Europe, expressing this change in the Marshall Plan. The Bretton Woods system remained dormant until the 1950s. The creation of the European Payments Union (EPU) in 1950 restored a limited regional convertibility between central banks, whereas the Marshall Plan paved the way for the European unification process and the creation of the European Economic Community in 1958 (Landau, 1995: 88–90). Dollar convertibility was established in 1958 after the British tried to restore the pound's convertibility, with the aim of restoring dollar convertibility (Helleiner, 1994c. 69–70).

Establishment of the Bretton Woods system and the Marshall Plan propelled the United States as the principal engine of world economy. As Gilpin put it (1987: 133): 'American monetary policy became world monetary policy and the outflow of dollars provided the liquidity that greased the wheels of commerce. When America grew, the world grew, when it slowed the world slowed'.

Towards financial globalization

After the move to convertibility, the market operators regained confidence in the international financial order. The Eurocurrency market which emerged in the 1960s contributed to expand international finance. The origin of a pool of eurodollars is shrouded in mystery. Some observers think it began in the 1950s with Russians and Chinese transferring dollar reserves to foreign banks; others think it began with the US running a balance-of-payments deficit, depositing dollars in banks in Europe. World monetary reserves increased twelvefold between 1970 and 1980. European banks receiving dollars decided to lend their holdings instead of converting them into their own currencies.

This market grew rapidly, and included other currencies than the dollar, creating a huge Eurocurrency market (Held *et al.*, 1999: 201). It grew from $3 billion in 1960 to $75 billion in 1970, and over $1 trillion by 1984 after oil producing countries deposited dollars in the Euromarkets (Strange, 1988: 105). Investors gained significant advantages over domestic banks. Great Britain provided the physical location for the market. The Euromarket operated in London free of regulation, but not outside the control of the national government. American banks and corporations participated massively in the Euromarket (Helleiner, 1994c: 82). Corporations deposited their foreign currency earnings rather than sending them back home, and placed them under capital controls.

The Eurocurrency market had perverse effects. It led to speculation against the US dollar as confidence in United States' credibility eroded, and proved disruptive to the Bretton Woods stable exchange rate system by the end of the decade. The Bretton Woods system and the US dollar were linked. The Bretton Woods system continued as long as it rested on a firm political foundation. During the 1960s, the United States' balance-of-payments deficit increased. The Western countries and Japan agreed to loan money to the United States to maintain its world position and to maintain its troop commitments abroad. As noted by Gilpin (1987: 136):

> many Europeans and Japanese began to believe that the United States was abusing the political and economic privileges conferred on it by the primacy of the dollar. But they shared a growing concern over inflation, erratic currency speculation, and increasing monetary instability due to the as overexpansion of the world's money supply.

For the United States, the role of the dollar freed it from concern about its balance-of-payments or the management of its domestic economy. But the United States was not able to devalue the dollar to improve its competitive position as it would immediately be followed by parallel devaluations of the pound, the mark, and other currencies (Gilpin, 1987: 137). Confidence in the dollar was rapidly eroding. By the late 1960s, it became clear that the amount of dollars in circulation outnumbered the amount of gold stored in the Federal Reserve Bank. The paradoxical situation according to which the world economy needed the United States to pump dollars into the monetary system to maintain liquidity, although doing so undermined the value of dollar and its role as a global monetary standard became known as the Trifflin Dilemma (Schaeffler, 1997: 45). Throughout the 1960s, the United States initiated a series of stop-gap measures to curtail capital outflows: the interest equalization tax (IET) and the voluntary controls programs in 1965 (Helleiner, 1994c: 86; Ruggie, 1998: 80).

By mid-1971, the dollar had become seriously out of line with other currencies. On 15 August 1971 President Nixon announced that the dollar was no longer to be freely convertible into gold. The result was the devaluation of the dollar in December 1971 (the Smithsonian Agreement). By 1973, the Bretton Woods agreement came to an end with the decision to let exchange rates float. The quadrupling of oil prices agreed on by the Organization of Petroleum Exporting Countries (OPEC) was another shock for the Western countries, and had a deep impact on developing countries.

The debt crisis

The flexible-exchange system was based on a false assumption, that the economy would be insulated from international shocks. Some fundamental changes occurring on the international financial scene had deep effects. One of the first was the increase of the oil prices, which created a huge reserve of dollars. The combination of excess global liquidity, low interest rates, and the absence of profitable investment opportunities in industrial countries in the aftermath of the oil crisis encouraged lending to developing countries (UNCTAD, 1998: 55). Petrodollars were deposited in the Euromarket, and turned over to be recycled into floating rate loans to the oil importing countries. As Graph 8.1 indicates, loans to non-OECD countries increased impressively after the 1973 oil shock.

This increase also meant that developing countries would have to service their debts. The second change was that national economies were linked together so that macroeconomic policies, and particularly American fiscal and monetary policies, had a deep impact on exchange

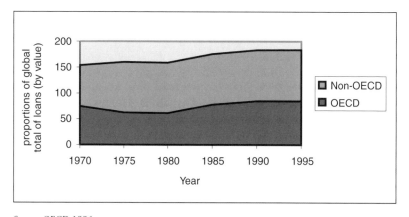

Source: OECD 1996
Graph 8.1 Distribution of international bank loans by borrower, 1970–95

rates and on other economies. The decision by the United States in 1980 to check inflation and the fall of the value of the dollar had tremendous reverberations throughout the world economy. This policy aimed to check money supply, the creation of credit, and an increase of borrowing money from the banks (Strange, 1988: 107). The dollar appreciated, but the world entered in a phase of recession triggered by a second oil price increase and stimulated by an unprecedented wave of protectionism. The falling price of commodities deeply affected developing countries as they also had to face an increase of Euroloans, swollen by the second oil shock of 1979.

As Susan Strange (1988: 110) observed, the banks did not stop to loan money, and tended to lend at shorter and shorter terms. They lent too much, inclined as they were to keep some large developing countries, and substantial importers of Western goods (such as Brazil and Mexico in Latin America, or Poland in Eastern Europe) inside the financial structure. The role of the US banking system and domestic policy played an important role in the debt crisis. In theory, the US rule prevented banks from lending more than 15 per cent of their capital to any borrower. In practice, these rules were not enforced. Some of the banks had already lent 100 per cent or more of their capital to countries such as Mexico or Brazil.

Yet, developing countries would soon be short of dollars to service their debts (Strange 1988: 110). The 1970s and 1980s witnessed a huge debt problem with a debt sometimes accounting for around 60 per cent of a country's GNP. The debtor countries could be divided into three categories:

- The first category included countries like India that had not borrowed heavily in relation to their size. They did not have the opportunity to enjoy rapid growth in the 1970s, but they were quite insulated from the situation that hit some developing countries. India's debt per head in the early 1980s was about $30 compared with Brazil's $480.
- The second category was composed of countries like Kenya, that had never been able to borrow much from the banks. Their need for funding increased as interest charges rose, commodity prices fell, and competition for export market shares from debtor countries increased. Donor countries attempted to ease the weight of the debt crisis by giving them special status or new credit facilities, but it was only just enough to keep them financially afloat.
- The third category was composed of the most heavily indebted countries. Some, like Malaysia, were safe as they had not borrowed beyond their capacity. Some, like Mexico, Brazil and Poland, were also safe because they could benefit from geopolitical or specific interests to attract massive governmental aid. South Korea received special treatment from Japan under the moral guise of reparations.

The Baker Plan (1986) and the Brady Plan (1989) came after the painful adjustment phase of 1983–84, leaving the borrowers with resentment towards the banking system. The Brady Plan proposed financial support from the IMF and the World Bank, supplemented by Japan, to relieve the debtor countries, provided they initiated economic reforms. It sounded good, but 18 months later it only favored four countries: Mexico, Venezuela, Costa Rica, and the Philippines.

Another change in the international world economy was also that volatile exchange rates encouraged speculative activity, which worsened all the problems. The financial speculation concerned the main hard currencies: Dollar, Mark, Yen, and ECU. Since lending in volatile money was a new game for many banks, it proved difficult for them to carry out. They were under constant pressure to increase their foreign exchange limits so that they could meet the demands of their clients. However, they were incapable of giving their managers real-time dates on their positions. Inevitably, they made errors in credit judgement. In June 1974, Bankhaus I. D. Herstatt of Cologne suffered large losses, which it covered up with fraudulent records. It was closed by German authorities. In October 1974, the Franklin National Bank of New York –

the twentieth-largest bank in the United States – was declared insolvent. The Continental Illinois Bank followed some ten years later as the bank piled up huge losses in its various markets (Kapstein, 1994: 39–41). In October 1982, the Bank Ambrosiano was closed by the Bank of Italy after a myriad of illegal activities. Ambrosiano owed various creditors $450 million.

The international financial system today

The 1980s and 1990s were marked by an explosion of new financial instruments, and by rapid innovation. As nicely put by Susan Strange (1988: 108), 'a new language had to be invented to describe new devices – money market, mutual funds, swaps, options, NOW accounts, zero-coupon bonds, off balance-sheet financing, Over-the Counter (OTC), and so on'. Some financial instruments are very esoteric and quite difficult to understand.

Changes have been fast, profound, and contagious. Financial operators want to manage risks that inevitably stemmed from a playing field in which the number of players and amount of money have multiplied. The elimination of capital controls by OECD countries in the 1980s and 1990s meant that the market moved away from official restrictions on this activity. By 1988, the European Community planned the complete abolition of capital controls within two years. Financial centers such as London or New York competed to attract financial markets. The United States wanted to capture off-shore Euromarket business. Deregulation and liberalization succeeded in enhancing the attractiveness of US financial markets. In October 1986, the London Stock Exchange opened up to foreign securities (Helleiner, 1994: 151). London was still the second major center of international financial activity. Japan became the third. In the late 1970s, Japan saw financial liberalization as a key to gaining economic and financial power, and ventured into a spiral of competition, innovation, and deregulation. Liberalization gained a new momentum in the European Community. Germany's first move was to abolish the tax on foreign holdings in 1984.

The Council Directive of June 1988 represented a substantial move towards complete liberalization of capital movements. Prior to the 1988 Directive, governments were allowed to restrict different categories of transactions and to introduce capital controls in response to disturbances in the functioning of capital markets. The 1988 Directive abolished restrictions on capital movements between residents of EU countries, and invited member countries to attain the same degree of liberalization with third countries as with each other. Measures directed at the regulation of banks' liquidity were to be limited to what was required for domestic monetary policies. Removal of capital controls helped member countries to move from the European Monetary System (EMS), adopted in 1978, to the European Monetary Union. At the multilateral level, deregulation and liberalization were likely to be reinforced by the WTO agreement on financial services. Some 102 countries agreed in December 1997 to open their domestic banking, insurance, and securities industries to foreign competition. Negotiations should continue in the year 2000.

In the beginning of the 1990s, speculation increased on movements in floating exchange rates. High rates in Italy and the United Kingdom relative to those of Germany and the United States, and massive flows of funds against a currency, produced notable devaluation crises: Britain and Italy devalued in September 1993, and opted out of the Exchange Rate Mechanism (ERM) and the Irish punt was devalued by 20 per cent. Other currencies also devalued: the Danish krone, the Spanish peseta and the Portuguese escudo, the Mexican peso in 1994, several East Asian currencies in 1997, the Russian ruble in 1998, and the Brazilian real in 1999. The French franc was the target of speculative attack. The EU finance ministers decided during the summer of 1993 to increase the bands for currency fluctuations in the ERM to plus or minus 15 per cent around the central rate.

The debate over risk and contagion has been one of the most heated in the past decades (Eichengreen *et al.*, 1996). The Tequila Effect was very much debated after the crash of the Mexican peso in 1994, the Asian crises in 1997, and the Brazilian devaluation in 1999. Contagion threatened to spread over Asia or Latin America. Some have devised ways of managing risk. Derivatives, which were created in the 1970s, are contracts to sell or buy at a future date at an agreed price. They allowed banks and transnational enterprises a chance to prevent losses from changes in exchange rates, in oil or other commodity prices, and against unforeseen changes in interest rates (Strange, 1998: 30). The contracts allowed a bank to sell to someone else the risk that one of its borrowers might default. Growth of the derivatives market has been astronomical. Trade in international derivatives started in the mid-1980s and, as Table 8.1 shows, the total value of contracts has risen over seven-fold to around $10 trillion (Held *et al.*, 1999: 208). Almost all of the market was accounted for by contracts in currencies or interest rates.

Table 8.1 Derivatives trading, 1986–96

Date	Exchange-traded instruments ($ billion)	Over-the-counter instruments ($ billion)	Turnover of instruments on exchange ($ billion)	Millions of contracts
1986	618.3			315.0
1987	729.9			389.6
1988	1,306.0			336.2
1989	1,788.6			421.2
1990	2,290.4	3,450.3	92.8	478.3
1991	3,519.3	4,449.4	135.2	510.5
1992	4,634.4	5,345.7	181.9	635.6
1993	7,771.1	8,474.6	227.8	788.0
1994	8,862.5	11,303.2	340.4	1 142.2
1995	9,185.3	17,990.0	333.8	1 210.1
1996	9,884.6	24,292.0	321.7	

Source: Held *et al.*, 1999: 208

Part of the explanation for derivatives lies in the regulations. Regulations can have perverse effects. The regulations introduced by the United States to limit the amount of interest payable on short-term bank loans in the United States resulted in the explosion on the Euromarket. Many operators wanted to get around regulations. Non-regulated environments offered new opportunities and profit.

Foreign exchange markets have become delinked from foreign trade and have become a commodity on their own. Foreign exchange business has grown from ten times world trade flows in 1979 to over fifty times today. Business has been facilitated by communications. Deals run over twenty-four hours: London takes over from Tokyo, New York opens as London closes and then hands over to Tokyo.

Securities houses have replaced some banks in providing financial services. Borrowers – non-financial businesses in industry and trade – are increasingly acting for themselves, bypassing banks by going straight to the market (Strange, 1998: 37). They have some means to do so. The money market mutual funds (MMMFs) are allowed to lend to trading or manufacturing firms at competitive prices, and do so by creating credit by buying their securitized commercial paper.

Banks themselves have evolved. They have become huge global corporations, the US banks being the most successful. Between 1960 and 1976, the number of foreign branches of US-based banks grew by 1816 per cent, followed by British, French, German, Arab, and Japanese banks. By 1990, London was host to more than 500 foreign banks, which held more than 87 per cent of international assets booked in that city (Kapstein, 1994: 4). Most top 20 banks are Japanese, followed by two French banks – Credit agricole et Credit lyonnais – and then by Deutsche Bank, Barclays Bank, and Amro Bank (Netherlands). There has been an erosion of American financial institutions. For securities, Salomon is ranked third in the top 20 securities firms, after two Japanese, and followed by two Japanese.

Developing countries: unequal pattern of international finance

Similarly to the situation prevailing in trade and FDI, only a few number of developing countries are increasingly incorporated in the international financial markets. Felix (1994: 365) notes that private capital flows are even more concentrated than in the 1970s lending boom. Some of the main recipients of the capital flows are the same countries that led the way in overborrowing in the 1970s. Lending is concentrated in South and South East Asia and in Latin America. Three Latin American countries (Argentina, Brazil, and Mexico) accounted for 42 per cent of net issues of international bonds by such countries, and six countries of South and South-East Asia (China, India, Republic of Korea, Malaysia, Philippines, and Thailand) for 45 per cent. The latter countries, together with Indonesia but with the exclusion of Philippines, were responsible for 60 per cent of borrowing in the form of international syndicated bank credits, and three countries from Latin America and South-East Asia (Argentina, Brazil, and Republic of Korea) for more than 100 per cent of net issues of Euro-notes. Other countries, particularly African countries, remain marginalized and excluded from private financial markets, relying exclusively on official aid flows (UNCTAD, 1996a: 29).

Indeed, a number of Latin American countries maintained capital account restrictions, which increased after the collapse of the Bretton Woods agreement, and in the wake of the debt problem. In African countries restrictions were applied during the 1970s and the 1980s, while in Asia, liberalization of capital accounts started in the late 1970s. In the transition economies, capital account liberalization has proceeded quite speedily since 1990, especially in the Czech Republic, Hungary, Estonia, Latvia, Poland, and Georgia (Eichengreen and Mussa, 1998: 37). Reforms of the financial sector have included freeing interest on loans and deposits, developing indirect monetary instruments, and abolishing credits ceilings.

There has been a shift in the composition of capital flows to developing countries, as Table 8.2 shows. During the 1970s and 1980s, net private and net official flows were roughly of the same magnitude. From 1971 onwards, private capital accounted for about one-third of the total net inflow in 1971, and almost half in 1981. This trend continued until the break of the debt crisis in the early 1980s, when the share of private inflows in total inflows collapsed as a result of reduced bank lending. In 1991, the flow of long term finance was 25 per cent below that of 1981, when the combined real GDP of the developing countries was also about one-third smaller (Felix, 1994: 366; UNCTAD, 1999b: 103). FDI accelerated rapidly in the 1990s, and predominated in 1998 (34 per cent) but has been quite limited to Asian countries: almost one half of FDI is going to Asia (China, Malaysia, Thailand, Indonesia, and South Korea); the rest is distributed among four Latin American countries (Mexico, Argentina, Venezuela, and Brazil), and to a very few African countries (5 per cent of the total FDI in 1998, see Chapter 4). Official development assistance (ODA) has declined almost

Table 8.2   Gross long-term flows to developing countries: 1971–91 (percentage)

	1971	1981	1991
Official grants*	9.0	7.3	15.4
Official loans	30.9	26.0	31.8
Suppliers and export credits	10.8	11.0	12.9
Commercial bank loans	35.8	46.2	17.9
Bonds	1.2	1.2	4.9
FDI	12.3	8.3	17.1

* Official grants correspond to ODA, while official loans correspond to loans provided by international organizations the World bank, IMF, regional development banks, and other multilateral and intergovernmental agencies)
Source: The World Bank, *Global Economic Prospects and the Developing countries*, Washington, DC: The World Bank, 1993

continuously since the beginning of the 1990s, and is unlikely to rise (Felix, 1994: 366).

International bonds are geographically concentrated, as Table 8.3. shows. Africa is highly marginalized from the bond market, with the exception of South Africa, which accounted for the majority of international bonds. Transition economies have been the most active. 1996 witnessed the largest amount ever raised by the region: $101.9 billion. Latin America has been the most active in the international bond market, doubling from $23.1 billion in 1995 to 47.2 billion in 1996. The three largest borrowers – Mexico, Argentina, and Brazil – raised $18 billion, $14 billion, and $11 billion, respectively, accounting for over 90 per cent of issuance from the region. Asia's international bonds rose from $25.3 billion in 1995 to $43.1 billion in 1996. Korea was the most active issuer, raising $16 billion, accounting for 38 per cent of issues from the region, while Hong Kong, China, Indonesia, and Thailand each raised $4 billion.

Table 8.3   Emerging market bond issues (in $ million)

	1990	1991	1992	1993	1994	1995	1996	1997
Emerging markets	7.7	13.9	24.3	62.6	56.5	57.6	101.9	27.7
Africa	0	0.3	0.7	0.1	2.1	1.9	1.6	0
Asia	2.6	4.0	5.9	21.9	29.8	25.3	43.1	12.7
Middle East	0	0.4	0	2.0	2.9	0.7	2.5	0.2
Latin America	2.8	7.0	12.9	28.7	17.9	23.0	47.1	11.8

Source: IMF 1999, p. 77

As Table 8.4. shows, developing countries have also increased their presence in international equity markets, although these transactions are heavily concentrated on transition economies, namely Latin America and Asia. Since the peso crisis in 1994–95, flows to Latin America have decreased sharply, and a similar decrease occurred in Asia following the financial crisis during the 1990s.

As Table 8.5. shows, the share of bank lending in total for the categories of international financing captured in the table was larger for the

Table 8.4   Emerging equity market issues (in $ million)

	1990	1991	1992	1993	1994	1995	1996	1997
Emerging markets	1.1	5.5	7.2	11.9	18.0	11.1	16.4	3.2
Africa	0	0.1	0.1	0.2	0.5	0.5	0.7	0
Asia	0.9	0.9	2.9	5.1	12.1	8.8	9.7	2.8
Latin America	0.9	3.8	3.8	6.0	4.6	0.9	3.6	0.8

Source: IMF 1999, p. 77

Table 8.5   External Financing for selected developing countries by major categories, 1991–94

Country	Total ($ billion)	of which (per cent)		
		Bank loans	Internationally issued portfolio investments	FDI
Latin America				
Argentina	31.4	8	47	45
Brazil	21.4	8	64	28
Chile	7.9	25	25	49
Colombia	4.7	9	26	65
Mexico	63.0	15	51	34
Venezuela	9.0	27	36	38
South and South East Asia				
China	110.2	18	13	70
India	9.1	30	56	14
Indonesia	37.7	65	14	21
Malaysia	32.2	35	7	57
Philippines	7.2	13	53	35
Republic of Korea	34.0	39	52	9
Singapore	25.6	24	7	70
Thailand	39.0	62	16	22

Source: UNCTAD, 1996

Asian than for the Latin American countries. Bank lending became an increasingly important source of financing in the mid-1990s, particularly for Indonesia, Republic of Korea, Thailand, and Malaysia. With the exception of Philippines, international bank lending for the Asian countries ranged from 18 per cent (China) to 65 per cent (Indonesia), while in Latin America, only Venezuela, and Chile had shares above 25 per cent. The other four countries including Brazil and Mexico had shares in the range from 8 per cent to 15 per cent. In Latin America, all countries relied on FDI, but the range for the shares of Asian countries was wider than for those of Latin America. For the latter, the range varid between 28 per cent and 65 per cent, while for the former the range varid from 9 per cent to 70 per cent. Some of the South and South East Asian countries – Hong Kong, China, Malaysia, and Singapore – still relied heavily on FDI in the 1990s, while others, including the Philippines and the Republic of Korea, had access to external financing mainly through internally issued portfolio investments.

Greater dispersion characterizes the shares of Asian countries in internationally issued portfolio investments, the range being from 7 per cent to 56 per cent. For Latin American countries, shares of internationally issued portfolio investments are above 50 per cent only for Brazil and Mexico.

In Asia, bank lending benefited the non financial borrowers in the private sector. As Table 8.6. shows, Hong Kong has been by far the main recipient of bank lending, followed by Singapore and Korea. In

Table 8.6   Lending by BIS reporting banks to selected Asian economies by sector, end June 1997

	All sectors ($ million)	Bank	Non-bank private sector (percentages)	Public sector
Hong Kong, China	222 289	64.8	33.9	0.5
Indonesia	58 726	21.1	67.7	11.5
Malaysia	28 820	36.4	57.1	6.4
Philippines	14 115	38.9	48.0	13.1
Republic of Korea	103 432	65.1	30.6	4.2
Singapore	211 192	82.8	16.6	0.5
Taiwan, Province of China	25 163	61.6	36.8	1.6
Thailand	69 382	37.6	59.5	2.8

Source: BIS, *The Maturity, Sectoral and Nationality Distribution of International Bank Lending, First Half 1997*, January 1998

Hong Kong, the Republic of Korea, and Singapore most bank lending was directed at the financial sector and, to a lesser extent, at the non-bank sector. Bank lending to the non financial sector was particularly important in Indonesia, Thailand, and Malaysia (respectively 67.7, 59.5, and 57.1 per cent). To give a fuller picture of countries' receipt of different categories of external financing, it is also worth mentioning other categories, including investment in financial instruments issued in domestic financial markets. Such investment by emerging market mutual funds has recently been rising rapidly. Mexico is a case in point. A large proportion of short-term debt instruments recently issued by Mexico has been held by external investors (UNCTAD, 1996a: 33). Holdings of domestically issued financial instruments by both financial and non-financial firms for the purposes of both investment and risk management have increased.

Table 8.7 provides details of private capital flows to Africa and transition economies. FDI flows and net portfolio investments remain low in Africa. They rely on official aid to promote their economic growth. Not surprisingly, banking activity is weak in Africa. Local banks, which can provide benefits to the domestic economies in extending credit to small businesses, farmers, and urban traders have been vulnerable to financial distress and bank failure as a result of non-performing loans. Poor loan quality is attributable to the information problems that afflict financial markets in African countries. Foreign banks or state-owned banks, which have dominated financial markets since indepen-

Table 8.7   Net private capital flows to developing countries, 1991–95
($ billion)

	1991	1992	1993	1994	1995
Africa	3.4	2.9	7.0	12.4	11.8
Net FDI	1.6	2.6	1.2	2.2	2.1
Net portfolio investment	−0.5	−1.0	−0.9	1.1	0.1
Other	2.2	1.3	6.7	9.2	9.6
Transition countries	−2.9	3.5	7.2	11.2	29.7
Net FDI	2.4	4.2	6.0	5.6	11.4
Net portfolio Investment	0.8	−0.8	2.7	3.0	6.0
Other	−6.1	0.2	−1.6	2.7	12.4

Source: IMF in Held *et al.*, 1999

dence, have been conservative in their lending policies, concentrating on the multinational corporations and other large corporate customers (Brownbridge, 1998: 2–4).

Private capital flows have proceeded quite speedily since 1990 in the transition economies. In four years, their share of private capital flows, starting from negative net flows, has more than doubled in comparison with Africa's share. They have succeeded in attracting a growing share of FDI and internationally issued portfolio investment, depending also on official aid. Their capital flows are even above Latin America's share of $22.4 billion. The FDI share of the transition economies is very similar to Latin America's share of $11 billion (UNCTAD, 1996a: 34).

Capital inflows can complicate macroeconomic management and can at worst threaten economic stability. The financial crisis in Thailand was provoked by an excess of short-term loans borrowed in foreign currencies, used by companies to invest in speculative projects, especially land and property. When the currency collapsed, companies were faced with massive debts, especially if they were denominated in a foreign currency (*The Economist*, 12 February 2000). Policy makers must be aware that the capital flows are in volatile forms and are easily subject to reversal. This has been experienced in some countries in Latin America, Asia, and in Central and Eastern European countries.

Policy makers have attempted to overcome the problems in shifting their macroeconomic policy, including by restricting inflows (higher reserve requirements for banks) and by making changes in incentives, or measures bearing more directly on the capital account of the balance of payments. Chile has imposed minimum conditions for external bond and equity issues, and has increased the cost of swap facilities at the central bank; Mexico has placed limits on banks' liabilities in foreign currencies; Indonesia has limited short-term obligations to non-residents and implemented a queuing system to slow external borrowing by private firms. Measures have also included incentives for financial outflows through the relaxation of restrictions on foreign investment by individuals or institutions (pension funds) (UNCTAD, 1994a: 105). These measures have resulted from a reassessment of policy in the financial sector. But it does not indicate any long term trend among developing countries towards greater financial openness. This could be reinforced by multilateral agreements, such as the one reached at the Uruguay Round on financial services, or those resulting from regional arrangements (see Chapter 10).

Agreement on financial services: effects on developing countries

Financial services are critical to developing countries that can benefit from opening their domestic financial services sector. Among the benefits, one of the most important is the expansion of the range of financial services available to domestic firms. Market access to foreign providers may sharpen competition in the domestic economy of host developing countries and may reduce transaction costs. A country that liberalizes its financial services sector is likely to augment its stock of capital (through increased FDI) and, crucially, the stock of human capital and technology that is embodied in or associated with such FDI.

In South Africa, the entry of foreign financial providers, such as foreign insurance or securities trading companies, have expanded the range of products, cut prices, and improved services. As a result, firms have been able to manage risk and to lower the cost of capital. Industry regulation has been improved through strong support for initiatives from the regulatory authority and access to international capital has been facilitated. Local companies have been forced to respond to increased price competition. Foreign entrants offer better analysis of international markets while bringing new techniques and competitive pressure to local research. Market expansion in all financial services has significantly expanded employment in South Africa. In addition, foreign entrants across all segments of the market have played an important part in developing South Africa as a regional financial center.

In many developing countries, foreign-trade financing is scarce, futures markets do not exist, insurance premiums are expensive and risk coverage is narrower than in developed countries. The entry of foreign financial providers could help correct the situation. However there are grounds for caution as the entry of foreign financial providers may also impede the development of domestic industry. In many developing countries, financial services are infant industries (Agosin *et al.*, 1995: 24). Governments are often reluctant to liberalize to protect the incumbent suppliers from immediate competition.

However, infant industry policies have failed in the past, and have led to perpetual infancy. The objective was to adjust the entry of foreign financial services to the needs of domestic financial services, and to create adequate mechanisms for regulation. Such regulation is clearly necessary to fully benefit from liberalization. The appendix on financial services in the GATS recognized the right of Governments to adopt prudent measures, such as those protecting investors, depositors or policy holders, and to protect the integrity and stability of the financial system. As pointed out by Agosin *et al.* (1995: 25), questions arise as to the effective power of small States when confronting powerful multinational financial holdings which, in addition, are their principal creditors.

Indeed, developing countries and transition economies are becoming incorporated into the global financial system, but the pattern is quite uneven. Some countries have better access to international financial markets than others. These latter, mostly the African countries, remain at the margin of private international finance and continue to rely on official development aid. The 1980s and the 1990s witnessed the debt problem and the Asian financial crises. They have impacted on capital flows to developing countries. Incorporation in financial markets is not exempt from speculation.

Part II
Regionalization in the Global Economy

9
Regionalization: Old Blends and New Incarnation

Globalization and regionalization are at first glance two opposing forces: globalization is characterized by openness of economies and a global market in which firms' strategies focus on efficient resources, whereas regionalization is characterized by preferential trading arrangements among countries and a regional network approach to resources, markets, and firms (Mucchielli *et al.*, 1998: xii). Regionalization would appear to erode potential globalization, and compete against world competition.

Weber and Zysman (1996: 172) envisioned three scenarios for the future. The first refers to a kind of managed multilateralism in which power is more evenly distributed among an alliance of the United States, Europe, and Japan. Regionalization is the second, which is similar to the scenario described by Thurow (1992: 65), and Rosenau (1996: 254) of encapsulated blocs with minimal extra-bloc transactions. The world economy is split into three largely autonomous trading regions with relatively low level of interdependence. They would work to limit any exposure to the others, and links would be managed internally, by agreements and not by the markets. The consequences would be extensive trade protectionism and, ultimately, the three independent trade blocs might well supplant the WTO. The third alternative is a regional rivalry. The world economy would be divided in three largely autonomous trading regions involved in a continuous competition.

Thus the legitimate question: does regionalization promote the ultimate goal of postwar global free trade or does it form a barrier to that regime? Does regionalization cause the multilateral trading system to relapse into rival blocs, based on North America, Europe, and East Asia, and as such fragment a globalized world economy, or does it foster the establishment of global strategies and policies and operate as building blocks to global strategies?

There is no clear evidence of a scenario of a world economy divided in three largely autonomous trading regions with relatively low levels of interdependence. Indeed, there is competition between the regions, and uneven distribution between them. However, there is also interconnectedness between regional economies, and some RIAs are looking for strategic alliances. In December 1994, the United States and 34 Latin American countries agreed at the Miami Summit to negotiate by 2005 a Free Trade Area of the Americas (FTAA), to be implemented over ten years. The Mercado Comum do Sur (MERCOSUR) has approximated the EU, as have NAFTA and ASEAN. None of the RIAs are similar to each other. Their aims, methods of functioning, and rationale are different.

The next two chapters contend that there are elements of fragmentation between the regions. Chapter nine is devoted to a comparison between the regions, and sheds light on the variance in regional arrangements. There is likely to be a wide range of factors that explain the variance of regional arrangements. Chapter ten explores the interregional trade flows, and finally the compatibility between the GATT trade regime and the RIAs. In some selected areas, RIAs complement multilateral arrangements.

What is regionalization?

Regionalization is not a novelty of our time. Great Britain proposed a union between England and Scotland in 1547–48. The 1703 Act of Union of England and Scotland established political as well as economic union. In France, Colbert planned in 1664 to unite all the provinces of the Kingdom of France into a customs union with internal free trade (Dessert, 1987).

The revival of interest in regionalization is due not least to its spectacular development, which has affected all continents. Virtually all members of the WTO belong to some sort of RIA. It is innovative in the diversity of its manifestations (see Table 9.1). Regional integration is multifaceted. Robert Hine (1992: 112) refers to regional integration as an association of countries that reduces intraregional barriers to trade in goods (and sometimes services, investment, and capital as well). There is a broader notion of regional integration than the removal of barriers to the free movement of factors of production. Integration refers also to the process of transferring benefits and loyal-

Table 9.1 Main features of some selected RIAs

Name, countries and regions	Member countries	Main feature
EU	Six founding, plus UK, Denmark, Ireland, Greece, Spain, Portugal, Austria, Sweden, Finland (ex EFTA countries)*	Political and Economic Union
ASEAN	Thailand, Indonesia, Malaysia, Philippines, Singapore, Brunei, Burma, Cambodia (postponed), Laos, and Vietnam	Free Trade Area
APEC (18)	Japan, NAFTA, Chile, NICs, ASEAN, China, Australia, New Zealand, Papua New Guinea	Free Trade Area
SAARC	India, Bangladesh, Pakistan, Sri Lanka, Nepal, Bhutan, Maldives, South Asian countries' regional co-operation	Free Trade Area
NAFTA	United States, Mexico, Canada	Free Trade Area
Southern Common Market (MERCOSUR)	Argentina, Brazil, Paraguay, Uruguay	Common Market
Andean Group	Bolivia, Colombia, Ecuador, Peru, Venezuela	Customs Union

Table 9.1 Main features of some selected RIAs *(continued)*

Name, countries and regions	Member countries	Main feature
Central American Common Market (CACM)	Costa Rica, El Salvador, Guatemala, Nicaragua	Common Market plus coordination of foreign policies
Caribbean Common Market (CARICOM)	Antigua and Barbuda, the Bahamas, Barbados, Belize, Dominica, Grenada, Guyana, Jamaica, Montserrat, Saint Kitts and Nevis, Saint Lucia, Saint Vincent and the Grenadines, Trinidad and Tobago	Common market
UEMOA	Benin, Burkina Faso, Côte d'Ivoire, Guinea-Bissau, Mali, Niger, Senegal, and Togo	Customs Union (aims to become a common market, with the support of the West African Monetary Union (UMOA))
ECOWAS	Benin, Burkina Faso, Cape Verde, Côte d'Ivoire, Gambia, Ghana, Guinea, Guinea-Bissau, Liberia, Mali, Mauritania, Niger, Nigeria, Senegal, Sierra Leone, Togo	Customs union
SADC	Angola, Botswana, Lesotho, Malawi, Mozambique, Namibia (joined in 1990), Swaziland, Tanzania, Zambia, Zimbabwe, and South Africa.	Customs union

* Future enlargement to Czech Republic, Hungary, Malta, Poland and Slovenia

ties from the pre-existing national state to some larger entities (Haas, 1958). Finally, expected gains from promoting regional integration are not only economic; countries can increase their bargaining power vis-à-vis third countries. This is referred as the process of *'externalization'* (Schmitter 1970: 161).

Regional integration entails some elements of complexity, stemming from an amalgamation between regional co-operation, regional integration, regionalization, and regionalism. In practice, the first two terms are interchangeable. However, they may be differentiated. The first, regional co-operation, aims at co-operating in certain areas of common interest, without the use of joint instruments. It is more limited in scope and depth. It can take place on a continuum stretching from limited projects to increased level of co-operation. Regional integration involves harmonization of policies in selected economic aspects of co-operation. It involves joint policy instruments.

To cloud matters further, regionalization and regionalism have to be added to this list. Regionalization could be considered as a process, regionalism as the final product. Lorenz (in Preusse, 1994: 153) distinguishes between 'regionalization' as 'focused on the rising intraregional interdependence' – the logical outcome of the integration process – and 'regionalism' as inward-oriented bloc-building. The former implies openness within and between regions, whereas the latter refers to one of the most significant developments in the world economy of the past decades. Thus, the term adopted here is regionalization.

A triad?

Re-activation of regional arrangements does not entail equity between regions. Three rival blocs or 'triads' seem to have emerged: many argue that current trend shows that far from being a system of regional free trade areas, regionalization has shifted to a system of large continental groupings with three regions on the core (Cable, 1996), namely a European bloc, including the next enlargement and Euro-Mediterranean bloc; a North American bloc, including Canada, the United States, and Mexico (NAFTA), or an extended free trade area (including all countries of the Americas and RIAs such as MERCOSUR, as envisioned by FTAA); and an Asia–Pacific bloc, including Japan and the Newly Industrialized Countries (NICs).

The United States/Canada and the European Union together represented more than 50 per cent of global GDP. Japan accounted for 17 per cent of global GDP, and Japan plus the East Asian NICs,

34 per cent of global GDP. In 1994, retained merchandise imports into the European Union and the United States accounted for almost 40 per cent of all retained merchandise imports in the world. Japan is the next biggest market (Borrus and Zysman, 1996: 37; Steinberg and Stokes, 1998: 6).

The three regions dominate high-technology industry and exports of technology-intensive goods. D'Andrea Tyson (1992: 25–6) recalls that computers and office equipment, communications and electronics, and aircraft and parts contributed to 68 per cent of total US exports. Between 1992 and 1994, EU exports of computer and information services doubled (WTO, 1998: 11). The distribution of exports of services by region reveals the overwhelming importance of the European Union which, according to the WTO Secretariat, accounts for 40 per cent of total world exports of services. It includes three out of the five largest exporters in the world (France, Italy and the United Kingdom). The United States accounts for 16 per cent of total world exports of services, while services accounted for 14.3 per cent of Japanese exports in 1999.

East Asia is the region that has shown the fastest growth rate of both exports and imports of services, over the past decade. Some of the 30 leading exporters of commercial services in the world are situated in Asia, namely Hong Kong, Singapore, the Republic of Korea, the People's Republic of China, Taiwan, Thailand, and the Philippines. Asia as a whole now represents 23 per cent of world exports of services.

In some current trends, there is a triadization playing out, particularly visible in the field of FDI. The triad dominates the picture in FDI, accounting for about 93 per cent and 91 per cent of FDI inflows into and outflows from developed countries in 1998 (UNCTAD, 1999b). The peak performance is mainly due to large-scale M&As between the United States and Europe.

Investigating the variance in regional arrangements

However, the existence of three economic poles does by no means impede global liberalization of international trade. Power is unevenly distributed among the three poles, and there are is variance between them. Regional integration encompasses very different experiences. Agreements are quite diverse; they range from free trade areas such as NAFTA or the Association of South East Asian Nations (ASEAN) to common markets such as MERCOSUR, or economic and political unions such as the EU in which there is free flows of goods, labor, services and capital, harmonized macroeconomic policy, including monetary policy, and political union in which member countries have ceded sovereignty to supranational institutions. Furthermore, RIAs differ in their scope of activity and in the number of issues covered by regional arrangements. Some agreements concern aspects other than the traditional goods sector, shifting from 'shallow integration', that focuses on trade restrictions like tariffs and quotas on manufactures and agriculture, to 'deep integration', covering governmental practices, like services and intellectual property, that are far more complex to handle, or investments and capital mobility integration (Lawrence, 1996: XVIII). In this case, we could speak of a *common market*. At the ultimate level, member countries would cede a larger part of their sovereignty in economic, monetary, or political areas. The setting-up of a supranational institution would bind community decisions for the member states.

Thus, regional arrangements are complex and multifaceted. Lindberg (1966: 345–66) has identified three central indicators that overarch individual cases into a more analytical framework. Following the lead of neofunctionalism, the first and second indicators are the scale of decision locus and the saliency of issue areas, which allow discovery of the intensity of the integration process and the commitments of the member states. The third indicator is the index of institutionalization. Lindberg draws a distinction between high institutionalization according to different dimensions: adaptability measured by the chronological age; complexity, measured in terms of sub-units as well as the functional variety of these sub-units; autonomy; and coherence.

Employment of these indicators allows for the observation of considerable variation in the regional arrangements. According to this framework, the European Union represents the archetype of regional arrangement. It is the most institutionalized, and has seen a record of remarkable successes and contrasting periods of hesitations, setbacks, and failures.

Scale of decision locus

The EU is a unique institutional setting, mixing supranational and intergovernmental organs and many distinct characteristics. As argue by Aggestam (1997: 83):

Unlike conventional international organizations, the European Union is a political structure set up by the Member States, whose objective is to go beyond merely inter-state arrangements typical of institutional activity at the international level, to strong and more effective institutions. Thus the EU bears a supranational character in that its central institutions can act on behalf of the Union.

The EU combines supranational institutions (the European Commission, European Parliament (EP), European Court of Justice (ECJ)) and intergovernmental institutions (European Council, Council of Ministers, European Political Co-operation). This combination is totally different from what can be observed in other RIAs. The community institutions such as the Commission, the EP and the ECJ are unique supranational entities, distinct from the member states. They press for the promotion of integration. They are independent bodies separate from the nation states. They provide impulses for further integration and communitarian policies.

The Commission is invested with policy initiative and agenda setting competencies (Pfetsch, 1995: 188). The Commission arbitrates conflicting interests, not only by benefiting from other institutions' weakness, but also by virtue of its own technical expertise. It has extensive competencies to make and revise policy. Furthermore, the Commission has close contacts with the national administration, prior to its policy proposals, and with interest groups to ensure the adoption of its proposals to the Council. The President of the Commission represents the Union vis-à-vis the outside world. The European Parliament participates in the decision-making process. It has evolved from an indirectly appointed institution to an institution legitimated by popular vote since 1979, and with ever more competencies. It is elected for five years and its 626 members mirror the size of the member countries. It has much less power than national parliaments, it cannot elect the executive, and has very few competencies to control governments by a vote of no-confidence. However it has increased its power: it has the budgetary authority, and has the right to increase expenditures. The ECJ is the guardian of the treaties of the community, with 16 judges from the member countries plus one further judge nominated in a rotating turn by one of the bigger countries.

The center of power remains in the Council of Ministers. It is, besides the European Parliament and the Commission, the legislative body and together with the European Council the main decision-making institution (Pfetsch, 1995: 192–3). However, its executive functions are constrained by the Commission, which initiates the law. The

Council can only decide after the Commission has presented a bill. The presidency rotates every six months. The Council of Ministers is assisted by the Committee of Permanent Representatives (COREPER), which plays a crucial role in the communications between the Council and the Commission. It helps to co-ordinate positions with the help of 180 working groups, and elaborates the proposals prepared by the Commission. European Political Co-operation (EPC) was promoted by General de Gaulle, and began in 1970 by acting as a conference of foreign ministers.

From its initiation in 1970 until its demise with the ratification of the Maastricht Treaty, EPC represented an attempt to harmonize the foreign policies of the Member States on an intergovernmental basis with each Member State exercising a veto over any common action (Whitman, 1999: 136). The successor to EPC, initiated by the Treaty of the European Union, is the Common Foreign and Security Policy (CFSP), introduced by Title C, Article J of the Treaty. The CFSP builds upon EPC by a systemic co-operation between Member States in the conduct of policy, and goes beyond EPC by the designation of 'joint action' areas (Whitman, 1997: 55).

The level of the institutional networks has been superposed by the growth of transnational and transgovernmental interactions (Wallace, 1994: 42). The EU is a system of managing intensive interdependence, and involves a lot of actors. There is a complex network of interactions between actors – governmental and nongovernmental – with multiple layers of internal negotiations within the Commission, between the Member States and the Council and within the Council, in its decision-making procedures. Agriculture provides an example. Agriculture was deeply entrenched across the Community, rooted in national ministries and in DG-6 of the Commission, but also drawing on a tight network of national organizations and on their European federations (COPA) and branching out into the agricultural committees of national parliaments and of the European parliament (Landau, 1998: 457).

The level of decision locus is much more modest in other regional arrangements than in the EU. Concerning regional arrangements in East Asia, the Heads of State and Government of the member countries – the highest authority in ASEAN – meets when necessary to give direction to ASEAN. It has met with little regularity: in 1976, in 1977, then in 1987 and 1992. The Ministers of foreign affairs and Ministers of economic affairs meet more regularly. At a lower level, the standing Committee consisting of the Minister of foreign affairs of the host country and ambassadors of the Member Countries carries out the work of the organization in between the ministerial meetings (UNCTAD, 1996b: 104). Meetings of other ministers are held when necessary. Up to 1996, five such meetings had been held in the fields of economy, labor, social welfare, education, and information. The permanent secretariat, established in Jakarta, forms the central co-ordinating body.

NAFTA presents a contrast with other regional arrangements. The institutional structure is more complex and consists of a number of independent bodies. However, NAFTA is an intergovernmental construction. The NAFTA Free Trade Commission (FTC) serves as the governing body of NAFTA. FTC members must be cabinet-level representatives of the three Member Countries. They are currently the US Trade Representative, Canada's Minister of Trade, and Mexico's Secretary of Trade and Industrial Development. The FTC's responsibilities include supervising the implementation of NAFTA, resolving disputes that may arise regarding NAFTA's implementation or application, supervising the work of NAFTA Secretariat comprising three National Sections and some 20 NAFTA committees and working groups, and establishing additional committees and working groups as needed (United States General Accounting Office, 1995: 15). The three Member Countries may envision the creation of a NAFTA co-ordinating Secretariat that would require additional staff and budget.

NAFTA encompasses two separate trilateral agreements on environment and labor, which each required a separate body. The North American Agreement on Labor Co-operation has two components – one trinational and one national. The trinational component is represented by the Commission for Labor Co-operation, which is comprised of a ministerial Council and a supporting Secretariat. The former members are the US Secretary of Labor, Canada's Minister of Human Resources Development, and Mexico's Secretary of Labor and Social Welfare. The Commission of Labor Co-operation which is located in Dallas, is invested with monitoring the labor accords and with fostering trilateral labor sector co-operation, with emphasis on health and safety, employment, productivity, and quality. The national component of NAALC consists of a federal government level in each country called the National Administrative Office.

The Commission for Environmental Co-operation, which is located in Montreal, is comprised of a three-member Council of cabinet-level or equivalent representatives from each country: the US Environmental Protection Agency Administrator, Mexico's Secretary of Social Development, and Canada's Minister of Environment; a Secretariat, and a Joint Public Advisory Committee. A Secretariat was created in

Montreal. However, unlike the EU, NAFTA bodies are composed of current government employees, and NAFTA has not created any supranational elite, except the North American Development Bank, which has hired staff of its own.

Institutionalization is less intense in NAFTA than in the EU. However, it is worthwhile noting that even if NAFTA has not yet led to the creation of supranational institutions, it has already unleashed a dynamic in which the activities of interest groups, involving farmers, consumers, environmentalists, labor, and business have crossed national boundaries. The different groups could have access to the information and keep a control over the process. NAFTA is on the agenda whatever the leading majority.

In MERCOSUR the decision-making rests with an inter-governmental Common Market Council, made up of the member countries' foreign and finance ministers – and in practice more often with the national presidents, at their twice-yearly meetings. Beneath the Council, the Common Market Group operates continuously, makes proposals, and sets up a working program. It may organize according to circumstances specialized sub-groups by a group of civil servants from a half-a-dozen ministries (Foreign and Economic Affairs, Industry, Foreign Trade, and/or Economics), and the central banks, in each country (Baptista, 1992: 577). It is assisted by a tiny secretariat in Montevideo, and a parliamentary commission, but there is no bureaucracy, no parliament, and a rather similar group of languages.

Saliency of issue areas in the EU

There has been a marked expansion of tasks covered by the EU, whereas the expansion is less marked in other regional arrangements. The European integration has been characterized by progressive broadening (adding more sectors and themes), and deepening of its scope of activity (moving towards harmonized and common policies). The EC had originally focused on trade policy, first abolishing tariffs and quotas on manufacturing and agriculture, then abolishing restrictions on trade such as health and environmental standards, to tackle more sensitive sectors such as services or intellectual property and to deal with issues such as investment and capital mobility. The issues covered by the EC have substantially broadened through the Single Market program of 1985, the Single European Act (SEA) of 1987, the Maastricht Treaty in 1992, and the Amsterdam Treaty in 1996.

Taylor has subdivided the integration process into different levels of intergovernmental co-operation (1990: 13–20). At the lower level, co-ordination involves the adjustment of government policies by a process of intensive consultation within member countries (consumer affairs, development, and public health). Each state retains powers and responsibility for executing the common task. Harmonization reflects the ability of an institution to identify and exploit existing compatibility between member countries (services, monetary integration, environment, education, research, and fiscal affairs). At the higher level, governments allow the management of an area of common interest on the basis of decisions taken either by majority voting or by committees of independent civil servants (trade in goods, trade in services, competition, cohesion and structural funds, and social). (Kennes 1995: 111).

The SEA passed in 1986 has completed the Common market initiated by the Treaty of Rome. It was no woolly declaration of worthy intent but an ambitious and vigorously pursued legislative timetable aimed at eliminating cross-frontier hindrances to trade. The principle of mutual recognition of national regulations and standards was applied as early as 1979, and rested on a Court of Justice decision concerning the Cassis de Dijon, according to which, a product manufactured and marketed in one Member State should be sold freely throughout the Community.

The SEA also extended the crusade to cover services and capital and, for this reason, included paragraphs calling for increased co-ordination in monetary policy (Griffiths 1995: 77). By early 1997, the Member States had adopted 94.3 per cent of all 1400 directives relevant to the Single Market. Of the four freedoms of movement promised by the Single Market – goods, services, capital, and persons – concerns remain only over competition policy (antitrust, merger policy, state aid, regulated industries), intellectual and industrial property, recognition of diplomas, and movement of persons.

The Economic and Monetary Union (EMU) should put the final touch to the Single European Market by reducing transaction costs associated with currency conversion, greater transparency within the Single Market, and increasing price competitiveness (WTO Trade Policy Review, 1997: 6). These consequences should propel intra- and extra-Community trade. The EMU is the result of a long process (see Table 9.2), initiated by the Werner's Report in the 1970s. The Report recommended a closer economic and monetary co-ordination, but could never be implemented. The EC embarked soon after in 1979 on the

Table 9.2   The EU's progress towards EMU

1970	Werner Report
1972	Basle Agreement: The Snake in the Tunnel Fix exchange rate: EC6 currencies within 2.25 per cent band (Snake) and in a 4.5 per cent band against the US dollar (Tunnel).
1973–8	European Monetary Co-operation Fund to assist the Snake. Many fluctuations among the Member Countries: France leaves in 1974, rejoins in 1975, leaves again in 1976. Germany leads 'mini-Snake' arrangement with Benelux, Denmark, Sweden, and Norway until 1978.
1978	European Currency Unit (ECU)
1979	European Monetary system (EMS) and exchange rate mechanism (ERM)
1983	Exchange rate union between Germany and the Netherlands
1986	Single European Act
1989	Delors Plan
1990	UK joins the ERM within 6 per cent band
1991	Maastricht Treaty
1992	Italy is suspended from the ERM
1994	Establishment of the European Monetary Institute, precursor of the European Central Bank. President is Alexandre Lamfalussy.
1995	Member Countries reckon that 1997 is unrealistic for the introduction of the single currency. They commit for an irreversible move by 1 January 1999. Euro will enter in force on 1 January 1999. Adoption of the economic convergence criteria, the Single Currency Stability Pact, and sanctions. Member Countries can run deficit to up to 3 per cent of GDP, although they should have balanced budget.
1996	Agreement on the introduction of euro on 1 January 1999. Spain and Italy commit to meet EMU convergence criteria. Revision on the exchange rate mechanism for 1999. Italy renters the ERM.
1997	Co-ordination on taxation. Agreement on the timetable and endorsement of the Single Currency Stability Pact. Members not making commitments for 1999 should do so by 2002.
1998	11 Member Countries commit to adopt single currency in 1999. UK opts out; Greece does not qualify. The European Central Bank is formally established.
1999	Intra-EU transactions will be automatically converted into the euro.
2000	Introduction of Euro banknotes and coins.

Source: Keesings

European Monetary System (EMS) and the exchange rate mechanism (ERM), which allowed the European currencies to achieve exchange stability and macroeconomic convergence despite the turbulent monetary conditions.

After Delors envisioned a three-stage approach to be completed in six years from 1993 to 1999, the EMU was finally introduced by the

Maastricht Treaty, and confirmed by the successive European Councils in Madrid (December 1995), Florence (June 1996), Dublin (December 1996), and Amsterdam (June 1997). In Madrid, the Heads of State or Government approved a reference scenario setting out the steps of the changeover.

The EMU experienced many set backs as only a few member countries were able to meet the convergence criteria: in 1995, Member Countries agreed on the convergence criteria:

● Inflation is to be no more than 1.5 per cent above the average of the three best performing Member States.

● Long term interest rates are to be no more than 2 per cent above the average of the three countries with the lowest inflation.

● Government deficit must not exceed 3 per cent of GDP.

● Public debt must not exceed 60 per cent of GDP.

Member Countries increasingly mobilized for meeting the economic convergence criteria: France made an effort to cut the budget deficit, and Germany adopted austerity measures. On 1 January 1999, Stage 3 of the EMU began with the irrevocable fixing of exchange rates among currencies of participating Member States and against the euro. Since then, capital markets have been booming: bond issues by European firms in the first three-quarters of 1999 have been running at roughly triple their rate in 1998 to $504 trillion (*The Economist*, 23 October 1999). By or around 1 January 2002, euro banknotes and coins will be introduced in the participating Member States. At the end of this stage, the euro will have completely replaced the national currencies and the changeover will be complete (WTO, 1998: 6–7).

The EMU entailed increasing political manoeuvrings between the EU Member Countries, especially between France and Germany, and is likely to raise increasing transatlantic friction (Dent, 1997: 91). There is a de facto multispeed monetary union. Sweden was not among the first countries to participate to the EMU, although it will be able to meet the convergence criteria. Denmark and the UK opted out; Greece did not qualify. In 1999, participation in the EMU gave way to a heated conflict within the UK. The evolution from a European Common Market to an Economic Community and to a European Union took over forty years, whereas some RIAs plan to do it in five years.

External relations

The EC has a wide and pyramidal network of agreements with external associates in Europe, the Middle East, and North Africa, taking the form of customs unions, free-trade areas, and non-reciprocal preferential trading arrangements (Landau, 1995: 468). It found itself by the beginning of the 1980s with a diverse mosaic of agreements. Some have brought only marginal benefits to countries whose commercial structures enter into competition with that of the European Union Member States. The Community has continued to consolidate its agreements. It has pursued the process of integration of the CEECs, and has negotiated a new generation of Association agreements with Mediterranean countries with the long-term objective of establishing a regional free-trade area by 2010. Negotiations with MERCOSUR, Chile, and South-East Asia have complemented the vast array of agreements. Further moves towards European integration at the end of the 1980s unleashed a chain of reactions, placing the division with EFTA countries on the European agenda, and expanding the borders of the European Economic Area (EEA).

Also remarkable has been the gradual enlargement of the EU. From a core of six countries, the EC has shifted slowly to nine, then 15 countries, and is likely to total 20 countries after the CEECs join. However, the process has not been easy, and the widening has transformed the deepening. Stretching the EU further east will necessarily reduce its present level of cohesion and integration. Previous enlargements were facilitated by tailor-made solutions, but these are more difficult to adopt in the present circumstances. Mutual adjustments have become increasingly more complex and more difficult in the EU of the early years of the twenty-first century. It is forced to consider extensive reforms which are deeply unpopular with voters and within the political leadership in the EU Member States. However, most of the reforms would have been necessary even without a further enlargement. Among them is the reform of the CAP, the Structural Funds and the Cohesion Fund.

Indeed, among the regional arrangements, the EU is the most sophisticated in terms of issues covered and openness as non-exclusive membership and trade are concerned.

Saliency of issue areas in NAFTA and ASEAN

NAFTA aims progressively to eliminate almost all US–Mexico tariffs over a 10-year period, with a small number of tariffs for trade-sensitive industries phased out over a 15-year period (see Graph 9.1). It creates different tariff phases or schedules: one for manufactured goods; a second for agricultural goods, and a third for textiles and clothing. Although the United States improved its attitude toward Mexican exports in the late 1980s, about 600 Mexican products faced 10–20 per cent US tariffs, and a few were subject to much higher tariffs. NTBs were still an obstacle for Mexican exports, particularly in iron and steel, textiles, clothing and agricultural products.

As regards agriculture, the average agricultural tariff in the United States is approximately 4 per cent, and eliminating these tariffs will not significantly affect the United States, whereas Mexico's average agricultural tariff is approximately 10 per cent (Interview Washington, August 1999). Mexico agreed to eliminate its most trade-restricting import policy in agriculture: the import licensing system for grains. In some cases, the licensing system was replaced by tariffs to be removed over a maximum of ten years. Canada negotiated exemptions from trade liberalization for the dairy and poultry industries. All agricultural commodities are eligible for NAFTA's general safeguard provisions in 11 highly import-sensitive commodities (among them cotton, dairy products, and peanuts) (US General Accounting Office, 1993: 56).

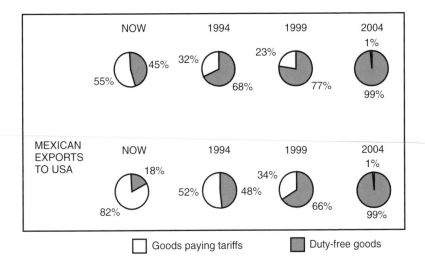

Graph 9.1   NAFTA's tariff elimination 1994–2004

NAFTA covers areas of deep integration. Telecommunications, banking and financial services in Mexico will open up. NAFTA upholds the principle of national treatment of goods, however it goes further than GATT in this regard, by stating that the national treatment requirements are binding on provincial, state, and local governments.

The US main objective for the NAFTA provisions for investment was to liberalize Mexican restrictions on investment and to lock in legal protections for investors (US General Accounting Office 1993: 19). Seven annexes list particular exceptions in respect of which each signatory plans to adhere to various provisions of the agreement. These exceptions must be made explicit (Rugman and Gerstrin, 1994: 53–4), and encompass national and MFN treatments, entry and establishment, ownership and control, and performance requirements (especially technology transfer and domestic sourcing).

Canada can limit foreign interests in the acquisition of state assets. Project approvals in the oil and gas industry are made conditional upon technology transfer, domestic research and development expenditure, and local presence (Rugman and Verbeke, 1994: 96). The United States has limited its exemption, but has retained its rights to review investments based on national security arguments, keeping foreign investors out of high technology consortia funded by the Pentagon. Mexico has clearly retained the largest list of exemptions both at the general and sectoral levels. Foreign involvement is not allowed in micro-industry enterprises (up to fifteen workers) or the oil industry. In all three countries, majority foreign ownership is still banned in telecommunications, civil airlines, the merchant navy, and the nuclear power, broadcasting, and fishing industries. The control of assets is restricted or even excluded in a variety of sectors including agriculture, entertainment, transportation, telecommunications, construction, petroleum products, auto parts, mining, and energy.

NAFTA also includes comprehensive provisions for the protection and enforcement of intellectual property, including copyrights, patents, and trade marks. However, at the insistence of Canada, NAFTA as CUFTA provides an exception to the general relaxation of trade barriers in the agreement for so-called 'cultural industries', including those heavily reliant on intellectual property rights, such as the movie and publishing industries. Cultural industries have long opposed Canada and the United States; the United States has a dominant position in Canadian audiovisuals (books, media, and film industries): 34 per cent of foreign books sold in Canada are American, as are 81 per cent of newspapers sold, and 85 per cent of movies shown (Donneur 1999:

39–40). The Canadian tax treatment of so-called 'split-run' periodicals (Excise Act) was found inconsistent with WTO obligations by the Dispute Settlement Body in 1997, and Canada had to withdraw the contested measure.[1]

Under the pressure of environmentalists like the Friends of the Earth, the Sierra Club, and Public Citizen, a supplemental North American Agreement on environmental co-operation (NAA) to NAFTA was concluded in 1992. Specific provisions are supplemented by a border plan in the areas of pollution prevention and abatement, inspector training, commitment to resources, and regulatory enforcement (Audley, 1997: 73–85). The agreement commits parties to fostering protection and improvement of the environment, but avoids creating trade distorting barriers.

In Latin America, MERCOSUR entails establishing an ambitious system for a free circulation of goods, services, and factors of production between the Member States, by reducing impediments to trade that guarantee openness and liberalization of trade, and eliminating subsidies. MERCOSUR aims at a customs union, based on the adoption of a common external tariff, the co-ordination of their macroeconomic and sectoral policies – external trade, agriculture, industrial, fiscal, monetary, transport and communications, and the harmonization of the Member Countries' legislation.

Concerning tariffs, Annex 1 to the Asuncion Treaty provides 'a program of progressive, linear and automatic customs rate reduction, which will benefit to the products'. The target of 75 per cent reduction was met by December 1992. A list of sensitive products was set up, supported by an exemptions list to be reduced by 20 per cent per year until it was completely eliminated by December 1995 (for Paraguay and Uruguay).

However, some objectives are more difficult to achieve, notably in the industrial location. In the auto sector, Argentina complained about unfair competition from Brazil, where most automotive production is located. Although both countries concluded a bilateral agreement, a dispute over cars erupted at the end of 1995. Brazil stepped back from the liberalization program by introducing a higher tariffs on cars than Argentina (*International Herald Tribune*, 23/24 March 1996).

Trade co-operation was low on ASEAN's agenda until it was reactivated by the Basic Agreement on Preferential Trading Arrangement (PTA) in 1977. The agreement provided adoption of measures to expand intra-ASEAN trade, which were subsequently improved in 1987 and in 1992, when the ASEAN Heads of Government agreed to establish an ASEAN Free Trade Area (AFTA) within 15 years, proposed by Thailand, and a customs union, proposed by Indonesia. A fast track covering 15 product groups was identified and a normal track should ensure liberalization of trade among the members.

APEC envisaged the removal of trade barriers by 2010 (or by 2020 for poorer members). However, the group had completed only a third of its tariff-cutting goals by the end of 1998 (*The Economist*, 18 September 1999). Furthermore, member countries backed away from a plan to cut their tariffs – on imports from within and outside the region – in 15 sectors, such as forestry and chemicals.

The index of institutionalization

The EU provides evidence of the high level of institutionalization, measured by the chronological age, complexity, number of sub-units as well as the functional variety of these sub-units. The EU is characterized by a formal institutional framework which consists of the community organs. This formal institutional framework has very specific competencies, responsibilities, and attributes (Pfetsch 1998: 300). However, this dense institutional structure is combined with a high degree of economic and social interaction. As argued by Hyde Price (1997: 22), formal and informal processes of integration have become very much intertwined. Many terms have been used to coin the multiple units of governmental and non-governmental agencies and the interactions between different levels of decision-making. Jönsson *et al.* (1998: 321) have spelt out some of them: multi-level polity; governance in a dynamic multi-level systems; multi-tiered systems of government.

The level of institutionalization is still very weak in the Asian region. Regional configuration of the Pacific region presents a patchwork of agreements. ASEAN co-exists with the Pacific Economic Co-operation Council (PEEC), the Pacific Rim Economic Council (PREC), the Pacific Conference on Trade Development (PCTD), and the Asia-Pacific Economic Co-operation (APEC).

The Association of South East Asia (ASEAN) started quite early in 1967 when Malaysia, the Philippines, and Thailand concluded a trade and navigation treaty. Some ten years later, after Indonesia and Singapore had joined, ASEAN held its first summit. ASEAN Preferential Trading Arrangement was formed in 1977. The integration process was subsequently improved in the 1990s. South Asian Preferential Trading Agreement was established in 1993 with the aim of forming a common

Market between Bangladesh, Bhutan, India, the Maldives, Nepal, Pakistan, and Sri Lanka.

The 1990s integration momentum in Asia was less the result of a genuine will to construct a regional area than a reaction by countries, moved by considerations of vulnerability, in the face of the dynamic of European integration and the emergence of NAFTA. Governments have multiplied efforts to enhance the area's attractiveness and competitiveness for promoting FDI. Indeed, the ASEAN countries have seen a significant increase in FDI since the early 1980s (see Chapter 7). The 1990s momentum was also propelled by political reasons. The objective was to ensure the stability of the region, and to enhance the bargaining power of its member states, by acting with a collective voice. ASEAN is driven by the dream of uniting Southern Asia and, even more important, by wanting to counter Chinese influence (*International Herald Tribune*, 2 June 1997). ASEAN found some legitimacy through balancing interests with influential foreign powers, such as the United States or the EU. ASEAN promoted a wide range of 'dialogue partner' relations, which started informally in 1972 with the EEC (UNCTAD, 1996b: 109). A selection of partners reflects trade trends. Australia, Canada, the EU, Japan, the United States, and New Zealand are the core members. Similar dialogue or graduated affiliation have been established with neighboring countries that include India, China, and Russia (Mols, 1996: 11).

APEC comprises the ASEAN countries and the United States, Japan, China, South Korea, Australia, New Zealand, Canada, Hong Kong, and Taiwan. Russia has applied for membership. Several elements combine to make the Pacific region into one of the regional areas that comply most faithfully with GATT rules: it is made up of countries that are firmly anchored to the international economic system by an earlier practice of trade liberalization. The safety clauses contained in the GATT agreements do not appear in APEC, which allows independent bilateral negotiations, insofar as they are not incompatible with the GATT (Aggarwal, 1994: 12–14). Despite recent controversies concerning its degree of economic liberalism, APEC operates in accordance with the principle that 'co-operation should consolidate the free trade system; it should not imply the creation of a regional bloc'.

Index of institutionalization in NAFTA and MERCOSUR

Geographic determinants have played a role in the NAFTA integration process. As far as population is concerned, 90 per cent of the Canadian population live within 100 miles from the border. Canada and the United States share a unique phone zone. Some states and provinces on both sides of the border have very similar economic structures: the territories by the Pacific with British Columbia in Canada and the States of Washington and Oregon in the US; the area around the Great lakes which has a high concentration of inhabitants and a widely established industry; and the prairies. The border between the United States and Mexico extends for almost 2,000 miles and run through four states: Texas, New Mexico, Arizona, and California.

The urbanized network along the borders of California, Arizona, New Mexico, and Texas cross-borders frontiers. Among the 14 sister or twin cities on the border, cities like El Paso, Ciudad Suarez, San Luis, San Diego, and Tijuana form a rather unified urban concentration. Many of the border issues such as air pollution or water supplies are transnational and transcend political boundaries. Many of the poorest counties in the United States are found at the border. Each year hundreds of thousands of illegal aliens enter the United States across the US–Mexico border.

Mexican industrial production is tied to the United States. The maquiladora (assembly plants that have preferential tax and tariff treatment) export-processing plants, located on Mexico's northern border, account for around a fifth of Mexico's overall industrial employment and 46.3 per cent of its total exports (US General Accounting Office, 1992: 8). Mexico's border region had a reported 1751 maquiladora plants with 651 580 workers. Some of them are shown in Table 9.3. At the end of 1991, before the NAFTA agreement was signed, the cumulative stock of US direct investment in Mexico was concentrated in maquiladoras (52.4 per cent) (US General Accounting Office, 1992: 7).

One factor behind the strong Canadian and Mexican interests in seeking a regional agreement with the United States was their high level of dependence on the US markets. Canada and Mexico are far more dependent on the United States than the latter is on them; in 1990, their exports to the United States represented 73.1 per cent and 75.5 per cent respectively of their total exports, compared with 28.3 per cent of American exports. Between 1987 and 1990 exports from the United States to Mexico more than doubled. Exports from Mexico to the United States grew even faster, giving Mexico a $1 billion surplus, and American exports grew more quickly than Mexico's giving the United States a $2 billion surplus in this now $65 billion two-way trade (Orme 1996: 17). As Weintraub (in Orme 1996: 42)

Table 9.3   The Maquiladora system

City, state	Number of maquiladoras	Number of employees
Tecato, Baja California	123	11 730
Mexicali, Baja California	179	50 368
Tijuana, Baja California	731	153 453
Nogales, Sonora	85	33 644
Ciudad Suarez, Chihuaha	254	216 945
Piedras Negras, Coahuila	44	15 687
Ciudad Acuna, Coahuila	57	33 426
Nuevo Laredo, Tamaulipas	54	21 533
Matamaros, Tamaulipas	118	58 734
Ciudad Reynosa, Tamaulipas	106	58 060
Total	1 751	651 580

Source: Mexican National institute for Statistics, Geography, and Information

noted, 'NAFTA is a way of formalizing a de facto integration that was already substantial'.

Besides geographic determinants, internal and external considerations played a role in initiating a regional arrangement between the United States, Canada, and Mexico. For the United States, the regional option was a viable one. There was the prospect that NAFTA would lock in liberalization reforms in Mexico, and thus would adequately contribute to stabilize one of the US's neighbors. As one official (interview, Washington, August 1999) noted 'we just could not ignore Mexico. We had to help stabilize our closest environment'. Reforms were linked to the migration problem that the United States was interested in solving. With around 50 per cent of the population under 18, solutions had to be found, and one of the most viable option was to create jobs and promote growth in Mexico. However, labor was the most sensitive issue. To conclude an agreement would provide the possibility of combining skilled workers with semi-skilled workers and cheap labor, producing a kind of production-sharing scheme between the two countries (Herzog, 1994: 6).

The US sought to negotiate a deal with Mexico that would set high standards (Cameron and Tomlin, 2000: 51). These standards were made necessary because the United States feared that Mexico would be a bridge to the US market. The automobile industry is a case in point. The objective of the American Big Three was to guarantee that Mexico did not become an export platform for Japanese or Korean producers.

NAFTA did not seek to adopt a common external tariff, to formulate rules of origins (Haggard, 1997: 27)

For the United States, a regional agreement nested also in more strategic concerns. NAFTA negotiations were launched when the Uruguay Round was stumbling into obstacles. The United States was frustrated with the slow pace of the negotiations, and thus was keen to send a message to its trading partners that unless sufficient results had been attained the United States was determined to opt for a regional solution to push on its rules.

American proposals in the NAFTA negotiations, such as strengthening intellectual property rights, restraining governments from imposing performance requirements on foreign-owned firms or the court to deal with disputes, were framed in part with an eye to the content of the GATT negotiations (Vernon, 1994: 38). The United States was clearly using NAFTA to place 'new issues' on the agenda. Mexico could also be used as a model for developing countries. Having reformed its economy, Mexico would agree to include services, protection of intellectual property, and reduction to obstacles to investments in the trade agreement with the United States. The agreement clearly linked trade and environment, which had always been blurred in the GATT negotiations, and included some labor standards.

On the other hand, NAFTA's critics forged a formidable coalition (Dryden, 1995: 386; Orme, 1996: 6). Opponents seemed to be popping out all over the political spectrum, from the trade unions, environmental groups, and even inside the administration. Contrary to other US Departments, the Department of Labor and the agency for the protection of the environment called for stronger rules for monitoring the agreement. Critics focused on the adverse effects on the environment along with downward pressure on real wages, especially wages of less skilled workers. One fierce opponent, Ralf Nader (1993: 6), focused on the large number of industrial companies moving from the United States to Mexico, where wages, pollution, and workplace safety standards were far lower. Nader listed many companies, including Ford, and Smith Corona, which discharged employees by moving their plants to Mexico, hemorrhaging US jobs to more 'efficient' foreign production. The impact of NAFTA on labor is difficult to assess. However, Mexico's economy is only 1/20. Per capita income is $27 000 in the United States, whereas it is roughly $3000 in Mexico thus 'the chance of Mexico having an impact is minimal' (interview, Washington, 27 August 1999).

For Mexico, NAFTA was part of a package of necessary economic reforms that were initiated in the 1980s. These were made necessary by the failure of the previous model of import-substitution industrialization, and the decline in oil prices in the 1980s. The terms of trade for fuel exporters deteriorated dramatically over a ten-year period (–17.0 between 1981 and 1991) (IMF, 1999: 168). Mexico was unable to pay its international debt obligations. Thus, Mexico was prepared to open up its economy. Import liberalization represented the first significant shift in economic strategy. Starting in 1985, tariffs and import permit requirements were reduced or eliminated. The Foreign Investment Law removed restrictions on foreign investment and foreign ownership for all industries, notably in petroleum exploration and refining (Teichman, 1994: 183).

NAFTA would allow Mexico to lock in the reforms undertaken, and increase their credibility. It was used by president Salinas to root out opposition to the new economic model that would have been 'sabotaged by the bureaucracy and opposed by the public had they not been seen as crucial to winning the NAFTA' (Cameron and Tomlin, 2000: 52). Raquel Fernandez (1997: 37) argues that RIA best contributes to solving the *time-inconsistency* problem of unilateral liberalization. The temptation to provide protection to some sectors, be they for income distributional reasons, for political economy concerns, or for terms-of-trade considerations, is likely to be large. Although a country would be willing to open up to foreign investment, it has the ability to withdraw its commitment, and 'confiscate' the favorable measures previously taken. It may also disregard regional partners by pursuing national goals. However, an RIA, by providing that the cost of exit from the RIA is high enough, could offer the best first choice for locking in liberalization measures. Whereas the GATT did not offer the same commitment device, WTO provides with stricter discipline.

Mexico would gain access to higher flows of investments that were needed to accelerate the modernization of the economy, to survive painful economic adjustments, and to develop skill-intensive industrial jobs. Because of concern over the political climate, transnational corporations have been reluctant to make massive investments in plants and equipment needed to take full advantage of cheaper costs in Mexico (Grinspun and Cameron, 1994: 241). NAFTA would make Mexico more appealing to American investors, and protect them against any future reversal of Mexican investment rules. NAFTA would lock in the rights of foreign investments to an international agreement that governments would find difficult to change. Investments increased from $15 billion in 1987 to $50 billion in 1992 (Orme, 1994: 132).

The prospective agreement between Mexico and the United States did not leave Canada with any alternative other than to enter into the negotiations in order to keep the gains from liberalization. Canada wanted to preserve trading access to the US market. Mexico's basic strategy encapsulated the same rationale (Herzog, 1994: 3). An FTA with the United States would avoid trade diversion from the CUFTA.

Regional agreements follow a commercial logic, that of negotiating agreements that can ensure reliable sources of supply and reduce the risk of the closure of export markets (Landau, 1999c: 23). The concern about the loss of market access was a major driver for the Canada–US FTA and NAFTA. The expansion of protectionism actions and the abuse of the administrative trade policy machinery in the United States raised some concerns in Canada. Winham (1986: 45) recalled that when Prime Minister Mulroney went to the House of Commons on September 25, 1985 to announce his intention to negotiate an agreement, a major justification was the need to reduce the risk to Canadian trade by establishing a dispute settlement procedure.

NAFTA is shot full of protectionism exemptions. Rules of origin are a case in point. The United States and Canada feared that many countries would try to take advantage of its cheap labor and proximity to the United States. Rules of origin are designed to preclude the circumvention of US tariff barriers by bringing in products through Mexico. NAFTA's content rules are stricter than those in the original US–Canadian free trade agreement. They are based on a set of fairly detailed rules mainly based upon changes in tariff classification. Products that are either produced in non-NAFTA countries or that are assembled or minimally produced in a NAFTA country do not satisfy the NAFTA origin requirement. For some sensitive products. like chemicals, machinery and equipment, and textiles, these rules are complemented by a value added requirement. In the automotive sector, which represents one quarter of the total trade among the three NAFTA countries, rules of origin require 56 per cent of local content, and then 62.5 per cent in four years. The threshold percentage of domestic content in the goods sector in NAFTA is between 60 and 62.5 per cent.

In textiles and clothing, rules of origin are even more complex and protectionist than for automobiles (Globerman, 1994: 5). The rules of origin are based on the principle of 'yarn forward': a product must be made of yarns of NAFTA material, or of textiles made of NAFTA yarn, and the products must be made of NAFTA fibers; however preferential treatment up to a quota level is extended for yarns, fabrics, and clothing that do not meet the rules of origin. NAFTA requires goods to be woven from North American fabric wholly obtained or produced in North America to qualify for the agreement's preferential tariff treatment. 'Wholly produced' means that the goods are produced in the NAFTA area and made up entirely of NAFTA-originating components. Goods containing imported materials from outside the area will be generally considered NAFTA originating if the foreign materials undergo processing or assembly in North America sufficient to result in a specified change in its tariff classification.

Anti-competitive barriers against many third-party products – from clothing to refined sugar to pickup trucks – are maintained, and in some ways strengthened, by NAFTA. During the protracted 15-year transition period, new duties will be applied to a host of politically sensitive farm products: juice, sugar, and peanuts on the US side, corn, beans, pork, and apples on the Mexican side. The US environmental regulations on Canadian and Mexican industries are also a case in point (Rugman and Soloway, 1998: 232). US regulations could have discriminatory effects against Canadian or Mexican firms compared to a domestic US firm. More than twenty environmentally related disputes have arisen under FTA and NAFTA over conservation (Tuna/ Dolphin, Lobsters, shrimps), packaging and labeling, and health and safety regulations.[2]

Finally, settlement procedures are clearly stated, and have been patterned on a joint committee Canada–USA. NAFTA elaborated dispute settlement procedures to deter non-compliance with regional procedures (Yarborough and Yarborough, 1997: 138). NAFTA Chapter 20 is quite comprehensive, and covers all disputes including interpenetration of NAFTA treaty obligations, alleged violations of the agreement, or nullification and impairment of benefits except dumping, countervailing duty, and investment cases. Yarborough and Yarborough (1997: 143–4) find similarities between NAFTA and dispute settlement procedures under the WTO; however, the dispute settlement procedure in NAFTA is a mechanism for governments to address trade problems, unlikely to end up in sanctions contrarily to the WTO dispute settlement procedure. Asymmetry prevails in the dispute settlement procedure.[3]

A combination of national security and commercial interest has served to push Mexico, Canada, and the United States towards a higher degree of economic integration (Randall, 1995: 39). Both Mexico and Canada have sought to establish productive relations with their neighbor, yet both have also sought to distance themselves from the United States. Mexico has sought to adopt policies in the Caribbean and Latin America, and to diversify its foreign policy and trade in order to diminish the weight of the USA (Rubio, 1996: 78). For Canada the approach has been similar though options in foreign policy include more commitment towards multilateralism.

MERCOSUR is the most visible regional arrangement in Latin America, and dates back to the 1960s. It was built around some prerequisites. The 'Cuenca del Plata' was traditionally an integrated region between Brazil and Argentina (Brigagão and Valle, 1995: 90) that culminated in a Treaty of Cooperation de la Cuenca del Plata in 1969 between Argentina, Brazil, Bolivia, Paraguay, and Uruguay.

At the bilateral level an Agreement of Technical Co-operation of Itaipu and Corpus was concluded in 1979, followed by additional agreements in the area of nuclear co-operation. Between 1986 and 1989, 24 protocols were signed between the two countries, promoting joint projects in nuclear and technical and scientific co-operation. In 1985, Argentina and Brazil signed the declaration of Iguacu, the Program of Integration and Economic Co-operation in 1986, and in 1988 a Treaty of Integration, Co-operation and Development, which set the stage for a common market between the two countries, with the gradual elimination of all tariff barriers and the harmonization of the macroeconomic policies.

After the adhesion of Paraguay and Uruguay, the Treaty of Asuncion was signed by four countries in 1991, creating the Southern Common Market. It has the ambitious aims to duplicate the main features of the EU, and to construct a common market with free circulation of goods, services, persons, and capital. It is open to all Latin American countries members of ALADI: Chile, Bolivia, Venezuela, and Colombia have already stated their interests. It adopted the criteria of democratic country required for the entrance into the EC.

Intraregional trade has increased: Brazilian exports to MERCOSUR's member countries have increased by 21.3 per cent. But most member countries have trade interests that go beyond MERCOSUR. Brazil's trade with its MERCOSUR partners represent only 15 per cent of its total trade, whereas Brazil represents 80 per cent of the MERCOSUR's GDP. In 1997, Brazil's main markets were to be found in the United States, Asia, or the EU, where Brazilian exports are more widely spread.

Following the 'Initiative for the America's', promoted by George Bush, MERCOSUR member countries concluded an agreement on trade and investment, known as the 'Rose garden Agreement' or Agreement 4+1, which is above all a forum for consultations in trade and investments matters. In 1994, the United States and thirty-four Latin American countries agreed to negotiate by 2005 a Free Trade Area of the Americas (FTAA), to be implemented over a further ten years. The United States envisioned a multilateral framework of negotiation, with MERCOSUR and the Andean Group as building blocs to be fitted together with NAFTA; it is still likely to be negotiation between NAFTA and an enlarged MERCOSUR. The United States are pressurizing for an agreement to comprehend, besides standards, unfair competition, safeguards, rules of origin, investments, customs procedures, intellectual property, and market-opening for services.

Simultaneously, Brazil launched the idea of a South American Free Trade Agreement (SAFTA), joining MERCOSUR, the Andean Group, and Chile in the framework of ALADI. The objective is to promote free trade in a period of 10 years. Brazil's main concern is to negotiate with the United States as an equal partner, and to try to convert the menu the United States would like to sell to MERCOSUR into a tailored-made agreement. For Brazil one could speak not of negotiation, but of membership to the North-American scheme.

In December 1995, MERCOSUR signed an Inter-regional Cooperation Agreement and a Declaration of Common Policies with the EU. Asymmetry characterizes the trade relations between the two blocs. The EU represents the first trading partner of MERCOSUR. EU exports to MERCOSUR increased to 147 per cent between 1990 and 1994, while MERCOSUR's exports to the EU decreased from 13.9 per cent between 1990 and 1993. The main problem of MERCOSUR/EU trade is the nature of the trade, which is mostly composed of agricultural and agrobusiness products, and which amount to 57 per cent of the total trade, with 30 per cent for soy beans. However, agriculture has been the main bone of contention in the EU/MERCOSUR relations, chiefly because of fears of France of competition from MERCOSUR's efficient agrobusinesses. The EU utilizes a wide range of instruments that impede Latin American agricultural products from having access to its market. About two-fifths of MERCOSUR's exports to the EU face customs barriers. Discussions on cutting tariffs would start only in 2001, and would run in parallel with the new round of global trade talks at the WTO (*The Economist*, 26 June 1999). For MERCOSUR, trade talks with the EU are important as they would allow MERCOSUR to play off the EU and the United States.

Some concluding remarks

RIAs present discrepancies. Some RIAs cover many issues, and have a high level of institutionalization and a complex decision-making process. The EU is a case in point. Institutionalization is quite dense in the EU. NAFTA covers many issues, has a fairly high level of institutionalization and a dispute settlement mechanism aiming to resolve problems arising from two developed countries' and one developing country's membership. However, NAFTA's institutions remain intergovernmental. On the other hand, the real thrust of the regional initiative was to harmonize the regulatory framework for investments and trade, and in this way NAFTA acted as an anchor for reforms, helping Mexico to gain credibility and to prepare better for competition at the global level.

Economic and political determinants have provided the underlying impetus for the Community integration process. The EU today is a pattern of formal and informal integration, as well as a political, economic, and social one (Wallace, 1990: 55). The growth of the Community-level institutions has been paralleled by the growth of a vast network of transnational and transgovernmental interaction. It would be difficult for either NAFTA or APEC, which have not attained the same level of institutionalization, to move far down the path toward managed regional integration without developing the same network (Wallace, 1994: 62). Moreover, the EU has moved from a core area of six countries, to nine, and then fifteen members, and has embarked on a new Eastward enlargement.

Enlargement will not be without problems for the EU. It will impact on economic and political structures, entail large budgetary costs, and contain the potential for 'dilution' of Community policies, to name only a few (Curzon and Landau, 1999: 14). But it is a matter of fact. Whether or not further members may accede in NAFTA is still unclear. NAFTA stated that candidates would have to fulfil special conditions, and follow serious macro economic policies and commitment to the GATT rules.

If the thesis of three blocs eroding globalization was true, it would mean that these blocs were equally strong, with some similarities. This chapter has evidenced that there is variance between the three blocs. Two questions remain to be asked. The first concerns the pattern of differentiated institutionalization. What are the factors that explain differences, which exist between the regional arrangements, between, say, the European Union and African RIAs? The second question concerns the degree of openness of regional arrangements. Are regional arrangements, which move to genuinely free trade among themselves, still compatible with trade liberalization and multilateralism? These will be the core issues of Chapter 10.

10
Regional Integration Arrangements: Trading Blocs or Building Blocs?

It is not easy to evaluate the impact of a regional agreement on trade liberalization. Such an evaluation is none the less necessary to assess the compatibility between regionalization and globalization. Some scenarios could be envisioned. The first refers to a world economy split into three largely autonomous trading regions with relatively low levels of interdependence (see Chapter 9). They would work to limit any exposure to the others, and links would be managed internally, by agreements and not by the markets. The consequences would be extensive trade protectionism and, ultimately, the three independent trade blocs might well supplant the WTO. There is another vision of interconnectedness between regional economies. One of the conditions for supporting this vision would be that the volume of imports by member countries from the rest of the world does not decline after the implementation of the agreement. Although the intensity of intraregional trade increases, so does the propensity of the RIAs to trade with the rest of the world. Thus, it is necessary to compare interregional and intraregional transactions. This chapter is devoted to this comparison, and analyses the issue of compatibility between regional integration and the WTO's Article XXIV and Article V of GATS.

What Viner's integration theory has to say

One of the most famous theories evaluating the impact of a regional agreement on trade liberalization is Jacob Viner's (1975), theory of trade creation and trade diversion, according to which the establishment of a preferential zone necessarily gives rise to a reorientation of trade flows. Trade creation resulting from tariff cuts within the region is desirable and beneficial for the member countries and for the world as a whole, and occurs when a member replaces goods produced domestically, at a relatively high cost, with goods imported from partner member countries at a relatively low cost. Conversely, classical economics claim that the trade diversion, which results from the imposition of an external tariff driving the member countries to concentrate on regional trade to the exclusion of trade outside the zone, can incur greater losses. Trade diversion occurs when low-cost goods imported from the outside world are replaced by higher-cost imports from other members.

Preferential trade agreements could be harmful to the multilateral trading system when they encourage member countries to import from other member countries and, in doing so, cause a decline in demand for imports from third countries. Viner's analysis has lost none of its cogency in the present context of a revival of regionalization. A regional agreement produces reaction directly linked to the trade benefits that it generates.

Intraregional and interregional trade

Between 1980 and 1997 intra-European trade has slightly decreased, contrary to the trend followed by APEC and NAFTA's intraregional exports, which have increased over the same period as shown in Table 10.1. Trade within Asia has grown faster than trade within NAFTA since 1980. By 1990, intra-Pacific Basin trade had risen to almost 69 per cent of the region's total trade, from about 58 per cent only ten years earlier. The major source of imports for each Asian economy is usually another Asian economy, most often Japan. Japan supplied on average about one-third of the Asian imports, notably in Korea, Taiwan, and Hong Kong, to which Japan supplied about 50 per cent of their total imports, in comparison with the United States, whose share amounted to 16–17 per cent of Asian imports in the same period.

In Latin America and Africa, intraregional exports increased after RIAs were re-activated. In Latin America, intraregional trade has more than doubled between 1980 and 1997, and accounted for 12 per cent of total trade (IMF, 1999: 114). Trade flows among member countries have benefited from re-activation of most of the RIAs in the 1990s. Intra-African trade shares are higher for the period 1990–97 than the shares for the previous period 1980–90. The gains are particularly impressive for SADC. Starting from scratch in 1980, the intraregional trade reached very high level in 1997. Some RIAs are lagging behind: UDEAC's share of intra-regional trade has stagnated or diminished. It

Table 10.1 Exports within blocs

Per cent of total exports	1980	1990	1997
High-income, low-income and middle income economies			•
APEC	57.9	68.5	71.9
EU	60.6	65.8	55.4
NAFTA	33.6	41.4	49.1
Latin America and the Caribbean			
Andean Group	3.8	3.8	10.1
CARICOM	5.3	8.1	13.8
MERCOSUR	11.6	8.9	25.4
Africa			
COMESA	5.8	6.2	8.3
ECOWAS	10.1	7.8	9.7
SADC	0.4	3.1	11.4
UEMOA	9.3	12.7	11.0
Asia			
ASEAN	16.9	18.7	22.2

Source: World Bank, World development indicators, 1999

represented 4 per cent of total trade in 1970, then fell to 2.8 per cent in 1986 to increase again in the 1990s, reaching the previous level. The share of intra-regional trade in the ECOWAS' total exports has increased from 3.9 per cent to 4.9 per cent, and this rising share was linked to external factors: the fall of oil prices. As a consequence, Nigerian and ECOWAS dollar exports declined by 47 per cent and 35 per cent respectively (Foroutan, 1992: 255).

What can be said about the extra-bloc transactions? Are they kept at their minimum? If this were the case it would substantiate the scenario of autonomous regional blocs with minimal trade links.

If intraregional trade has indeed increased, so has extra-regional trade as Table 10.2 shows. NAFTA, MERCOSUR, ASEAN, and the EU are cases in point, although in the latter case, after a steady increase over a decade, the EU's exports are now in decline. Results are more modest for other African or Latin American RIAs. Two decades down the road, exports are still lagging.

Assessing RIAs' trade patterns

Intra-EU exports have flourished with 55.4 per cent of total trade. However, the integration process has also generated considerable trade benefits for extra-EU trading partners. Extra-EU imports recorded

Table 10.2　Exports by blocs

Per cent of total exports	1980	1990	1997
High-income, low-income and middle-income economies			
APEC	33.7	38.9	47.4
EU	41.1	44.1	34.3
NAFTA	16.7	16.1	18.4
Latin America and the Caribbean			
Andean Group	1.7	1.0	0.9
CARICOM	0.6	0.2	0.1
MERCOSUR	1.9	1.3	1.5
Africa			
COMESA	0.6	0.4	0.4
ECOWAS	0.4	0.6	0.5
SADC	1.6	0.6	0.8
UEMOA	6.3	0.2	0.3
Asia			
ASEAN	3.9	4.2	6.3

Source: World Bank, World development indicators, 1999

significant growth – about a 50 per cent overall growth from 1985 until 1996 (WTO, 1998: 19). During the 1990s the EU was the world's largest international trader with 40 per cent of the world's total per annum, although the exports have slightly declined over the period 1990–97. During the period 1980–90 there was an increase in the share of intra-EU trade in manufactured goods, including processed agricultural goods from 60.6 to 65.8 per cent of exports as Graph 10.1 provides evidence. The corresponding increase for services in the same period was from 46.9 to 50 per cent for imports and 42.6 to 50.2 for exports (WTO, 1998: 18).

Trade patterns have remained relatively unchanged since 1994 as Tables 10.3. and 10.4 show. The EU's main imports originate from the United States, EFTA, and other OECD countries (13 and 7.2 per cent, respectively), and Japan (9.2 per cent). In 1998, the European Union absorbed 21.3 per cent of American exports – 45 per cent of which were in high technology goods – and exported 21.9 per cent to the United States (Eurostat, 1999: 42–3). Trade with the first 'wave' of applicant countries from East Central Europe – the Czech Republic, Estonia, Hungary, Poland, and Slovenia – has improved (Inotai, 1999: 83). Poland, the Czech Republic, Hungary, and Slovakia had a 2 per cent share of the EU's external imports in 1989, and 5.1 per cent in

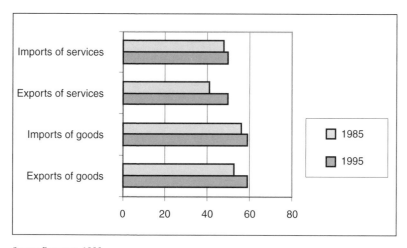

Source: Eurostat, 1999
Graph 10.1 Share of intra-EU trade in total trade, 1985 and 1995

1994 (adding Slovenia to these figures the share would be 6.5 per cent). They now account for 9.8 per cent of the EU total imports.

The four Central European countries exported less to the EU than Taiwan in 1989. In 1998, however, their exports bypassed the combined exports of the four Asian tigers (Singapore, Taiwan, Korea, and Hong Kong). They have gained market share against each of the non-EU member countries, Switzerland and Norway, with which trade has decreased. Switzerland had exported 3.6 times more to the EU than the four Central European countries in 1989. By 1995, Swiss exports were just 38 per cent higher than that of the five Central European countries. The East Asian region, led by Japan – the second trading partner in imports and third in exports – has also made noticeable advance in the EU's trade, EU exports to Asia increased in value by 15 per cent per year between 1993 and 1996. However, in the last years the EU has experienced a worsening of its trade balance with the East Asian region.

Regional affiliations follow a commercial logic, that of negotiating agreements that can ensure reliable sources of supply and reduce the risk of the closure of export markets: the United States is Latin America's biggest market, buying $57.6 billion from Latin America in 1991 (Orme, 1996: 249–50). But that is just two-fifths of the region's total exports. And Mexico, by far the region's biggest exporter, statistically skews this dependence. Over the past decade, the United States

Table 10.3   Patterns of EU trade, exports (in per cent)

	1994	1998
USA	19.8	21.9
Switzerland	8.9	7.8
Japan	5.6	4.3
Norway	3.2	3.4
NICs: Hong Kong. Singapore, Taiwan, Korea	8.4	6.8
CEECs	7.9	9.8

Table 10.4   Patterns of EU trade, imports (in per cent)

	1994	1998
USA	19.3	21.3
Japan	10.4	9.2
Switzerland	8.1	6.9
Norway	4.6	4.1
NICs	6.8	7.9
CEECs	5.1	7.3

Source: Eurostat, 1999

has absorbed well over 80 per cent of all manufactured exports from Mexico, as Table 10.5. shows.

With American sales accounting for a huge 75.5 per cent of its total exports, Mexico is in the same acute dependency league as Canada, which sends 84 per cent of its exports directly across the border, and receives from its neighbor 77 per cent of its imports. Dependency has deepened since the creation of NAFTA. In 1993, Canada's exports to

Table 10.5   Percentage share of Mexican exports to the United States

Exports of products	1985	1993
Manufactures	84	87
Food, materials & fuels	58	74
Total goods	65	83

Source: General Accounting Office, Washington, 1997

the United States accounted for 78 per cent of total trade, and imports to 74 per cent. The EU and Japan, respectively second and third trading partners, are far behind. In 1998, Canada's exports to both countries accounted respectively for 6 and 3 per cent of Canada's total exports (HTTP:/www.statcan.ca). Mexico's exports to the United States have also increased by 6 per cent between 1991 and 1999. The United States are far less dependent on their northern and southern neighbors, with Canada accounting for only 20 per cent of the US's total trade and Mexico for 9 per cent, as Graph 10.2 shows.

NAFTA has not modified the United States' trade flows, whereas it has had a strong impact on those of Canada and Mexico. The United States' trade flows with Canada have remained stable between 1992 and 1997, whereas trade has increased with Mexico in the same period. Trade has also diversified: the United States' main trading partners are now the EU and Japan. Asia is ahead from Latin America. From 1990 to 1997, imports from Asia have increased from 15.5 per cent to 19.2 per cent, and exports from 20.2 per cent to 24.4 per cent, whereas 7.5 per cent of EU trade is done with Asia and 9 per cent with the USA. Trade within NAFTA represents 49.1 per cent of its member countries' total trade, which is far behind the same figure for APEC or the EU intraregional trade (respectively 71.9 per cent and 55.6 per cent).

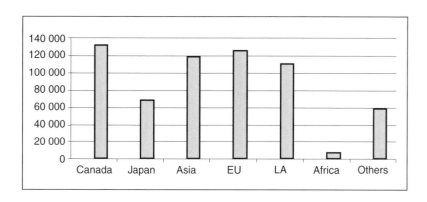

Source: World Bank, 1997
Graph 10.2 United States exports (1996) ($ million)

The EU is MERCOSUR's largest trading partner as Graph 10.3. shows. However, this masks significant variations among individual countries.

The United States is Brazil's first trading partner, while the EU comes second with 43 and 26 per cent respectively of Brazilian total trade.

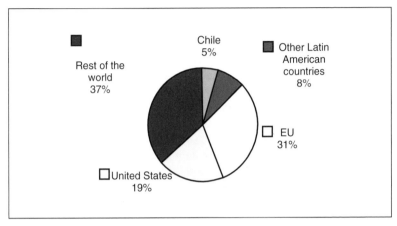

Graph 10.3   MERCOSUR's exports

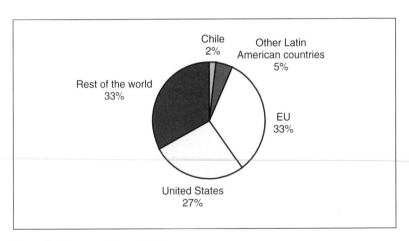

Source: *The Economist*, 26 June 1999
Graph 10.4   MERCOSUR's imports

By contrast, the strongest links of Argentina and Uruguay are with the European Union with 22 and 19 per cent respectively of their total trade, followed by the United States second with 14 and 9 per cent of these countries' total trade. Intraregional trade between Brazil and Argentina lags behind. Argentina accounted for only 11 per cent of Brazil's exports and 13 per cent of its imports in 1996. Argentina was much more dependent on Brazil, which accounted for 26 per cent of Argentina's total trade. By contrast, countries in the nearby Caribbean Basin typically send nearly half of their exports to the United States (Costa Rica 46 per cent, Guatemala 38 per cent, and Jamaica 36 per cent). Venezuela is an exception with its 55 per cent, due to its oil shipments.

Admittedly, this diversification is rarely conducive to an incorporation of the different South American regional components into NAFTA. While in Mexico NAFTA has consolidated the process of rapprochement that had already begun, its extension to include the Latin American countries would imply a far more stringent adaptation, which few of them are prepared to undertake (Rugman and Gerstrin, 1994: 573). However, their wait-and-see attitude toward NAFTA does not prevent them from cultivating privileged relations with Mexico or from seeking alternative solutions, such as a free trade area with the European Union and a rapprochement with the Pacific Rim.

Japanese trade with Asia has increased tremendously during the latter part of the 1980s. Japan's exports to the newly industrialized countries have increased from 32 per cent to 40.5 per cent over the period 1991–94. From 1992 onwards, Hong Kong and Taiwan have surpassed Korea as far as exports are concerned, whereas Korea is still leading in imports. The newly industrialized countries are consolidating their breakthrough on the international market, in the direction of neighboring Japan or the United States. For the majority of Asian countries, Japan and the USA are the major trading partners as Graph 10.5 shows. On the export side, the US is the largest partner, except for the market of primary products, in which Japan is the largest partner for Malaysia, Australia, and Indonesia. East Asian dependence on the US market remains quite strong: the major share of the region's exports goes to the US (21 per cent for Singapore, 36 per cent for Korea, 44 per cent for Hong Kong, and 48 per cent for Taiwan). On the imports side, the picture is the reverse, Japan being the largest importer in the East Asian countries, supplying the bulk of their manufactured goods imports.

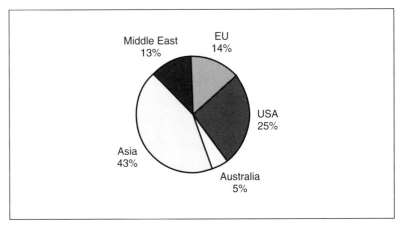

Source: World Bank 1999
Graph 10.5   Japan's imports 1997 (%)

The United States is Japan's second main outlet, although trade has remained stable over the period 1991–97. Japan's exports to the United States account for 28 per cent of Japan's total trade. Imports represent 22 per cent of its total trade. Japan's two peripheral neighbors, Australia and New Zealand, are also asserting themselves on the Asian market, at the expense of the Western markets, with which they used to conduct the bulk of their trade. The EU is Japan's third trading partner, although trade has slightly decreased since 1994, accounting for 13 per cent as for imports and 16 per cent as for exports.

Assessing the results

There is no clear-cut answer about the emergence of trade blocs centered on North America, Western Europe, and the Asia–Pacific region. A closer examination suggests that the creation of RIAs has induced increasing intra-trade flows. Nevertheless, the integration process has also generated considerable trade benefits from extra-trade flows. Therefore, there is no clear evidence of a scenario of a world economy divided in three largely autonomous trading regions with a relatively low level of interdependence. There is more contention of intercon-

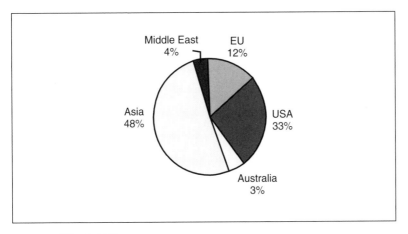

Source: World Bank, 1999.
Graph 10.6: Japan's exports, 1997 (%)

nectedness between regional economies. The volume of imports by RIA member countries from the rest of the world has not declined after the implementation of the agreement.

The EU has not turned into a fortress Europe as it was previously suggested, neither has it become the model for other regional schemes. Various elements tend to qualify the role of the regional schemes in the liberalization of trade. The EU is a case in point. It has adopted liberalization of trade barriers and controls, deregulation of markets and market operators, privatization of state-owned monopolies and other enterprises, measures against anti-competitive practices (see Chapter 9).

However, it is important not to underestimate the strength of national resistance, which further confirms the need to pursue multilateral solutions that might palliate the ambiguities of regional integration policies. As stated by Susan Stange (1998: 107):

the trade policies of Europe (like other RIAs) are an inconsistent mix of openness and protection. This reflects the conflicting interests of European Business, which sometimes wants trade barriers against foreign competition, especially from Asia, but at other times is all for a free and open market.

Preferential arrangements and RIAs: liberalization of services ahead of GATS?

So far we have focused on trade flows. Services are a domain in which preferential arrangements might contribute to the further liberalization of the multilateral trading system. Indeed, the Agreement on Services suffers from many flaws (Feketekuty, 1999; Mattoo and Low, 1999: 12). Some of them relate to the commitments undertaken by countries, that define minimum access guarantees which are less than the status quo in terms of access permitted to foreign services and/or foreign service suppliers; others refer to the overlapping modes of supply.

It may be easier to carry out liberalization of services on a regional than on a multilateral basis. In 1994, 11 RIAs involving 24 countries extended their provisions to services (Prieto and Stephenson, 1999: 4). Some are based on a 'positive list' or 'bottom-up' approach, where countries only open their service markets to foreign providers through commitments that are drafted in terms of specific sectors and regulatory measures (Prieto and Stephenson, 1999: 3). The MERCOSUR has opted for this 'bottom-up' type approach to extend liberalization to the area of trade in services. It provides for a gradual approach to liberalization based on the negotiation of specific sector commitments, which would progressively open members' services markets for a period of ten years.

A second approach is termed a 'negative list' or 'top-down' approach, whereby no specific commitments are established and all types of service transactions are considered to be free of restraint unless the contrary is indicated in lists of reservations and non-conforming measures. Many regional arrangements – 11, according to the Organization of American states – have adopted this approach. NAFTA has proceeded rapidly according to this 'top-down' approach, liberalizing across-the-board, except for some sectors that have been listed in the agreement. Financial services, for example, have been liberalized: US and Canadian firms have gained access to the restricted and protected Mexican financial markets. However, Mexico maintains restrictions on the ownership of banks, securities firms, or market share of the US and Canadian banks' subsidiaries and securities (US General Accounting Office, 1993: 45–7). Financial services within APEC have been fully liberalized, whereas some restrictions exist in distribution (wholesale and retail) and publishing. These exemptions are mostly related to share market of companies.

Various bilateral agreements have proceeded along these lines, such as the G-3 agreement, negotiated between Mexico, Colombia, and

Venezuela in January 1995, and the bilateral free trade agreements, concluded by Mexico with Bolivia and Costa Rica also in January 1995, with Nicaragua in December 1997, and with Chile in April 1998. Chile and Canada finalized a free trade agreement containing similar provisions on services in July 1997. These agreements relating to services form a complex set of overlapping understandings, co-operation agreements and treaties.

Certain service sectors have been excluded from the coverage of the sub-regional arrangements. Air transport has been excluded from all the sub-regional arrangements. NAFTA has exempted civil aviation, maritime shipping, basic telecommunications, Canada's cultural industries (film, video, broadcasting, cable, publishing, and sound recording), and Mexico's gas and oil drilling and retailing services. Cross-border financial services, telecommunications, land and water transportation, and social and professional services are excluded from the Canada/Chile free trade agreement.

Many RIAs are innovative, concerning several aspects of the services, and have a broader scope than the GATS. Government procurement is a case in point. NAFTA contains provisions on government procurement, whereas it is in the WTO, the Government Procurement Agreement (GPA) remains a voluntary instrument and procurement is not covered by the GATS[1] (Evenett and Hoekman, 1999: 4).

However, the majority of regional agreements containing provisions on services have not been notified to the WTO, in spite of the fact that this process has been going on for several years in certain cases and is, therefore, without multilateral oversight. The few regional agreements, notified to the WTO, and whose service provisions are being examined under the WTO Committee on Regional Trading Arrangements, have not yet been the object of any pronouncement as to their compatibility with multilateral discipline. Without a clarification of the WTO (Article V for services and Article XXIV for goods), the contribution of regional trading arrangements (or integration agreements) to multilateral trade liberalization will remain controversial and the link between the two imprecise and undefined.

GATT, WTO and regional integration

The GATT is no stranger to the ambiguity that characterizes relations between regional integration and the multilateral trading system. Established in 1947, the Agreement reflected the economic supremacy of the United States at the end of the war; but it also attests to a compromise with Britain, which managed to retain its preferential advantages within the Commonwealth. The GATT has never formally objected to regional agreements. To understand the reasons why the GATT acted in this manner, we should call to mind the characteristics of the international system at the time the agreement came into effect in 1947. The United States feared that the EEC could discriminate against it, and made several attempts to influence the development of trade provisions, and to ensure that the external tariff and agriculture policies would not adversely affect the interests of third countries, including its own interests (Landau, 1999c: 17). Yet the United States was willing to tolerate the discrimination and trade diversion effect because the European Economic Community could contribute to the stability of Europe in providing a political and economic counterweight to Soviet domination. The General Agreement on Tariffs and Trade was to examine the consistency of the common market with its fundamental principles; naturally, since the EEC was a strategic instrument supported by the US, the only possible conclusion was that the EC was GATT-consistent.

The conclusion of the GATT Uruguay Round of negotiations and the transformation of the GATT into the WTO have not put a stop to these arguments. Belous and Hartley (in Qureshi 1996: 153) spelt out the differences between the objectives pursued by a trade bloc and the GATT/WTO philosophy.

One of the main underlying principles of the GATT regulations is the most-favored-nation (MFN) clause, whereby the advantages granted to any one contracting party are to be extended to all other contracting parties. Free trade areas, customs unions, or preferential agreements

Table 10.6   GATT and RIA principles

GATT principles	*RIA principles*
1. Non-discrimination	1. Discrimination
2. MFN	2. Special preferences not granted to nations outside the bloc
3. Protection should be provided through tariffs	3. Protection could be provided through quantitative restrictions as well as tariffs
4. GATT/WTO is open to all who are willing to follow membership rules	4. The RIA could be an exclusive club

Source: Belous and Hartley, *Growth of regional trading blocs*, in Qureshi, 153

infringe this clause as they grant to their member countries concessions that are not necessarily extended to third countries.

Despite this fact, two articles allow for the contracting parties to depart from the MFN principle: Article XXIV and the Enabling Clause. Article XXIV of the GATT allows regional agreements to coexist with the General Agreement under certain conditions: regional arrangements must be established to facilitate trade, not to create barriers vis-à-vis non third countries (Article 4); customs duties and restrictive trade regulations must be eliminated on virtually all trade between the constituent territories in products originating in such territories (Article XXIV, 8b); the arrangements must not result in increased obstacles to trade with third countries, by producing a diversionary effect on trade; moreover, the member countries are required to supply information to the contracting parties (Article XXIV, 7a). The GATT is not opposed to regional agreements where '*customs duties are not higher or other trade regulations more restrictive than they were prior to the adoption of such agreements*' (paragraph 5a and 5b).

The Enabling Clause – Decision of Differential and More Favorable Treatment, Reciprocity and Fuller Participation of Developing Countries – resulted from the Tokyo Round of negotiations (1973–79), and included a number of provisions permitting GATT contracting parties to grant differential and more favorable treatment to developing countries. These provisions are less stringent for developing countries entering into regional or global preferential arrangements. Paragraph 2 (c) of the Enabling Clause allows developing countries to waive the provisions of Article I – non-discrimination. There are two central requirements laid down in Article XXIV which do not appear in the Enabling Clause: first, the substantial coverage of all trade between the participating countries; and second, elimination of tariffs on intra-area trade. As noted by Blackhurst (1997: 78), 'precisely because it lacks these two key requirements, the Enabling Clause offered a "soft option" for regional integration among developing countries.'

Some developing countries have preferred the 'soft option' of the Enabling Clause rather than notifying FTAs under Article XXIV. As noted by the WTO:

> the Enabling Clause does not contain any reference to Article XXIV, an omission which has left unclear whether the Enabling Clause applies in situations where that Article does not, or affects the terms of application of that Article. Indeed, views differ as to whether the Enabling Clause provides an appropriate basis for all regional

arrangements among developing countries or, as some governments maintain, was not intended to cover arrangements of major significance that, up to 1979, would have been handled under Article XXIV. (WTO, 1999)

Some tensions emerged when the MERCOSUR was notified under the Enabling Clause in 1991. After an examination process and an 18-month discussion between the MERCOSUR on one side, and the EU and the United States on the other, an agreement was set up. The MER-COSUR countries came to the view that Article XXIV was more appropriate, and they invoked one of the provisions pertaining to compensation to third countries.

Several factors contributed to re-address regional integration in the Uruguay Round of negotiations. One was the worldwide proliferation of regional agreements at the end of the 1980s. There were no less than 200 RIAs. Virtually all WTO Members belonged to a regional integration scheme, with the exception of Hong Kong and Korea. Around 60 per cent of world trade was realized under preferential arrangements. Provisions were either ambiguous or imprecise, thus open to political, economic or subjective interpretations. The concept of 'substantially all trade' was vague; or the principle of 'not on the whole higher or more restrictive' used to evaluate CET of a customs union difficult to apply. The GATT admitted that it might *'perhaps be expedient to revise the supervisory activities conducted by the working groups responsible for regional issues, so that their efforts are transparent and to the point'* (GATT, 1993: 13).

The reform of Article XXIV was considered in the Uruguay Round and an Understanding on its interpretation was agreed upon. The Understanding has clarified some of the points that have in the past given rise to difficulties – 'substantially all trade', or 'general incidence' – although it does not solve all the ambiguities.

Substantially all trade

The preamble to the Understanding strengthens the requirements that 'substantially all trade' be included in the elimination of barriers between members, by recognizing that the arrangement's contribution to the expansion of world trade will be increased if the removal of duties and other restrictions extends to all trade and diminished if any major sector of trade is excluded.

However, the statement is still a matter for debate, especially for those who think that substantially all trade translates into percentage.

What, then, is this percentage? The current trend is to set the limit at 90 per cent of all trade. Others reckon that substantial trade is not a matter of percentage. Some sectors are just off the table. Agriculture is a case in point. Some regional arrangements limit themselves to liberalize trade in industrial goods, yet some sectors are excluded from the arrangement. The preamble of the Understanding largely re-states the accepted arguments for regional trade arrangements, while leaving ground for further debate. The preamble does not point out whether other trade restrictions cover quantitative restrictions and, in this case, whether member countries should have common quotas.

General incidence

The Understanding clarifies Article XXIV: five requirement that the general incidence of a customs union's common duties and trade regulations be no higher than those existing before it was formed. The evaluation is to be made on a overall assessment of weighted average tariff rates and of duties collected. This assessment has in turn to be based[2] on detailed import statistics. The calculations are to be carried out by the WTO Secretariat.

The core of the issue was to allot the time and the compensation spent in reducing tariffs. The Understanding reasserts that the procedure established in the Article XXVIII of the GATT must begin before tariff concessions are modified by the formation of the customs unions. Negotiations must be to the mutual satisfaction of the parties involved. They must take due account of any tariff reduction by other members that affect the same product. If the compensation is not accepted, the customs union must go ahead with an increase or change in the concessions. Affected WTO Members then have the right to respond by withdrawing substantial equivalent concessions.

Transparency

The Understanding lays down the principle of transparency, and includes provisions for the examination of regional trade agreements. The Understanding establishes a ten-year maximum for the transition period for implementation of an agreement, although allowance is made for 'exceptional circumstances'. The provisions of this Agreement

> shall not prevent, as between the territories of contracting parties, the formation of a customs union or of a free-trade area or the adoption of an interim agreement necessary for the formation of a customs union or of a free-trade area; provided that: (a) with respect

to a customs union, or an interim agreement leading to a formation of a customs union, the duties and other regulations of commerce imposed at the institution of any such union or interim agreement in respect of trade with contracting parties not parties to such union or agreement *shall not on the whole be higher or more restrictive than the general incidence of the duties and regulations of commerce applicable in the constituent territories prior to the formation of such union or the adoption of such interim agreement, as the case may be.*

Article XXIV, 7a ensures that Members that form a free trade area or participate in a transitory agreement must notify without delay the contracting parties and provide all necessary information. The understanding strengthens the procedure by a decision that if an interim agreement does not contain the required plan and schedule, a WTO working group shall examine the agreement and shall make appropriate recommendations, and that the agreement shall not be brought into force unless the recommendations are accepted.

The Understanding makes clear that the examination of a regional agreement under Article XXIV does not exclude the right to invoke the WTO dispute settlement procedures on matters arising from the application of the article.

In 1996, the WTO Member Countries decided to set up a Committee on Regional Trade Arrangements, whose main tasks, according to its terms of reference, are to carry out a systemic analysis of implications of regional trade agreements on the multilateral trading system, and to develop procedures to facilitate and improve the examination process. This process has indeed accelerated: 100 regional arrangements have been notified to the GATT between 1948 and 1994. During the period 1990–94, 34 regional trading arrangements were notified to the GATT.

GATS and RIAs

The Uruguay Round of negotiations also resulted in a provision in the GATS (Article V) that is equivalent, for services, to the GATT Article XXIV and to the Enabling Clause. This provision reflects the fact that RIAs are concerned with aspects other than the traditional goods sector, and cover governmental practices, such as services. A large number of regional trading agreements that have been signed since 1990 contain provisions to liberalize trade in services.

Article V imposes conditions on economic integration agreements between signatories of the GATS: Such agreements must have 'substantial sectoral coverage' in terms of number of sectors, volume of trade affected, and modes of supply. They must not result in raising the overall level of barriers to trade in services, where specific commitments were made, beyond the level existing prior to the agreement. They must eliminate discriminatory measures and/or prohibit new discriminatory measures at the entry into force of the agreement or in a 'reasonable' time frame. However, some of the requirements under GATS are weaker than those under Article XXIV, concerning the 'substantial sectoral coverage' (GATS) compared with 'substantially all trade' (Article XXIV), the elimination of 'duties and other restrictive regulations of commerce' (Article XXIV) compared with 'the elimination of existing discriminatory measures and/or prohibition on new measures'. Finally, the time frame for implementation is stricter in Article XXIV than in GATS (Hoekman and Kostecki, 1995: 221–2).

As stated above, Article V of the WTO General Agreement on Trade in Services (GATS) is similar to Article XXIV; it permits countries to participate in regional trade arrangements that discriminate against the services or service providers of other countries. Thus Article V grants coverage for preferential treatment extended to trade in services in derogation of the MFN obligation of the GATS Article II. The exemption from the MFN obligation, however, must be based on certain requirements set out in the GATS. Such arrangements shall, inter alia, not create any new, and not raise existing barriers to trade in services in relation to other signatories, and shall in this respect be subject to multilateral discipline and surveillance. Moreover, substantial services sectors should be covered, and the other conditions should be met.

Article V suffers from the same flaws as the GATT Article XXIV (Stephenson, 1999: 3). This is because Article V is a compromise between those negotiators who felt it was important to use Article XXIV as a basis and others who felt that each economic integration agreement should be examined on a case-by-case basis with respect to services, independently of its content covering trade in goods (Croome, 1995: 314–15). There is considerable confusion and lack of clarity surrounding the interpretation of the conditions in the GATS Article V.

The lack of clarity lies in the meaning of the GATS Article V with regard to the concept of a substantial sectoral coverage. Should this be determined on a sector by sector basis, on a sub-sector by sub-sector basis? To recall, the schedules of commitments in the Article V of the GATS cover 12 sectors and 155 sub-sectors. Hence, does the requirement allow for the exclusion of one or more sub-sectors, or the exclusion of an entire sector?

The lack of clarity also exists with respect to the barriers that an economic integration agreement should be expected to eliminate. Barriers to trade in services are by their nature very different from barriers to trade in goods, as they consist of measures set out in domestic regulations. Such regulations may, for instance, prohibit foreign service suppliers in domestic industries, or they may be applied on a discriminatory basis to natural persons providing services, thus treating them less favorably than domestic producers (non-application of the national treatment principle). According to Mattoo (1999: 2):

> one of the ironies of the GATS is that among its weakest provisions are those dealing with domestic regulations, which have such an obviously powerful influence on international trade in services. The reason is not difficult to see: it is extremely difficult to develop effective multilateral disciplines in this area without seeming to encroach upon national sovereignty and unduly limiting regulatory freedom.

Liberalization of trade in services consists of the removal, or the reviewing of these domestic regulations by governments in the treatment granted to foreign as compared to domestic service providers. In turn, the removal or the review of regulations will lead to structural reform of service industries. Many ways could be devised: the conclusion of mutual recognition agreements that provide for the equivalence of foreign service providers with domestic service providers, or through the harmonization of national laws and/or regulatory practices. However, even in strongly integrationist Europe, despite a significant level of prior harmonization, the effect of Mutual Recognition Agreements may have been limited by the unwillingness of host country regulators to concede complete control (Nicolaïdis and Trachtman, 1999).

The question of domestic regulations poses a difficult problem for regional integration among developing countries. Many developing countries have very few, if any, regulations in some of their key service industries. This is in sharp contrast with the heavy, highly sophisticated, and projectionist regulatory systems existing in the developed countries. In NAFTA, most of the disputes between Mexico, Canada, and the United States, concern domestic regulations. The lack of regulations in many countries has been aggravated by the rapid privatization and deregulation processes and by the introduction of free market oriented policies, which has taken place in recent years in many developing countries.

In spite of the above-mentioned similarities, Article V of the GATS is distinct from Article XXIV of the GATT. Article V does not distinguish between Customs Unions and Free Trade Areas. It only mentions Economic Integration Arrangements. The need of a strong and viable GATS Article V is more pressing than ever, given the large number of regional trading agreements that have been signed or have been extended to the services area since 1990, most of which contain provisions to liberalize trade in services. Without a clarification of Article V for services, the contribution of regional integration agreements or preferential arrangements to multilateral trade liberalization will remain controversial and the link between the two imprecise and undefined (Stephenson, 1999: 5).

Concluding remarks

Regional Integration Arrangements have mushroomed in the last decades. Indeed, there is no clear evidence of a scenario of a world economy divided in three largely autonomous trading regions with relatively low level of interdependence. As far as trade is concerned, trade between blocs has steadily increased over the years, in the same way as trade within blocs. An assessment portrays failures in increasing intraregional trade in some RIAs.

However, there is an increasing awareness that greater economic co-operation and integration of markets into more viable blocs constitute instruments to gain more access to global markets at a time of globalization and stricter multilateral rules. Liberalizing trade or sectors of the economy among neighbors within an RIA would be the best way to help open up their protected national markets, and eventually meet the world market conditions. It would be far more difficult to meet those requirements unilaterally. Regional arrangements could increase competitiveness in the production of manufactured goods, and liberalize other key sectors, such as services.

In addition, regional integration increases the credibility of policies, in locking in macroeconomic policies and reforms undertaken by member countries. NAFTA is an illustrative example of the positive effect of regional integration. The fact that Mexico concluded a free trade area with Canada and the United States played an important role in providing additional credibility to policy reforms. The Europe

Agreements concluded between the EC and the CEECs provide further evidence of the credibility factor offered by regional agreements.

Credibility could also be demonstrated through the use of Article XXIV of the GATT in the notification of FTAs among developing countries to the WTO. Article XXIV would give evidence of the participating governments' serious commitment to genuine regional integration, thereby substantially increasing the credibility of the effort in the eyes of domestic and foreign investors. Article XXIV has been recas under the Uruguay Round. Some further clarifications will be needed, and the task of a systemic analysis of the implications of regional trade agreements on the multilateral trading system completed by the Committee on Regional Trade Arrangements is to clarify the compatibility between the WTO rules and the regional integration arrangements.

11
Conclusion

What is notable about globalization, as previous chapters have argued, is the convergence of all the nerves and nodes of globalization. Globalization has unleashed powerful forces which have generated a synchronized dynamism. That does not mean that social, political, economic, financial, and legal infrastructures were not there to support the process of globalization, but the consequences were unforeseen and have all acted in concert.

Those who want to see globalization as a stretching process, as a historical parallel to be drawn from previous ages, would only give a fragmented account of the story (Held et al. 1999: 437). Indeed, during the nineteenth century and during the first part of twentieth century, millions migrated, trade expanded, finance burgeoned. But contemporary globalization is made different by the interactive and multifaceted process playing out. Globalization is not the ultimate stage of capitalism, 'the single world marketplace in which capitalists make decisions according to their own socio-economic logic' (Cerny, 1999: 4). That does not mean that globalization does not encompass the neo-liberal credo, but globalization is also something else.

The flavor of globalization

It is not even the different components of globalization, trade, investment, institutional, and economic supports or capital flows which make the difference. It is their confluence at all levels that gives the flavor to globalization, and may also reduce the benefits for some players. All components of globalization are inextricably intertwined with each other; and supported by powerful social trends within the society, by players and institutions, and by regulatory structures. This multiplicity of linkages and interconnections generates a structural shift. Globalization is interestingly a dialectical process: trade, FDI, capital, and technologies are instruments of globalization; they are also its consequences. Indeed, this dialectical relation makes globalization more complex and more powerful.

Confluence is also witnessed in the distributional impact of globalization. Much of this book has been devoted to examining the cumulative character of the different domains of globalization and the impact of globalization on the configuration of the international system. Globalization is a multilayered process of structural differentiation rather than a homogenous one. Indeed, divisions between developed countries and developing countries were pre-existent to globalization. Important divisions have existed: in the 1960s between the oil-producing and non-oil producing countries; between those who adopted an import-substitution strategy and those who opted for export-orientation economies; in the 1980s and 1990s between low-income African countries and Latin American middle-income countries, or the Asian NICs; between commodity producers, and the rest. Over the period 1970–90, many lines of division have juxtaposed. Developing countries are not one homogeneous bloc, but a group with multi-layered divisions.

Creating new lines of division

Globalization has created new lines of division, which cut cross preexisting ones, and has increased polarization between the winners and the losers. Similar geographical and uneven patterns of global trade, investment, and capital have unfolded and reinforced each other. Globalization has deepened the stratification of the international system, criss-crossing old lines of division, and creating new ones among and within developed and developing countries. Indeed, globalization is not a homogenizing force (Held *et al.*, 1999: 441)

Increased trade flows, investment flows, and TNCs' activity have mostly benefited a cluster of developing countries composed by the East Asian countries and some very few others located in Latin America. African countries, bar a few, remain marginalized, and delinked from the cumulative process that characterizes globalization. If developing countries and transition economies are incorporating in the global financial system, the process has resulted in inequity. Some countries have better access to international financial markets than other, mostly the African countries. These remain at the margin of private international finance and continue to rely on official development aid.

Globalization has created new lines of division, congruent across all its components, as the arguments of previous chapters have pointedly emphasized, between a bundle of countries reaping the full benefits of open markets: some Latin American countries, such as Mexico, Chile, Brazil, or Argentina, the East Asian countries, and few catching-up countries. Most developing countries have not been able to exploit the benefits of the systemic changes. That is not to say that this pattern is inalienable. Catching up in a process of globalization is difficult. Countries are enmeshed in a network of regulating institutions. Globalization has had an institutional impact at the global and national level, and the international economy is more institutionalized now than some decades ago. Globalization may have resulted from business activities, but it was also produced by supportive organizations. Globalization has been supported by a multitude of regimes.

The creation of the WTO was consequential to the widening of the international trade agenda, and has helped to push liberalization further including in the areas of deep integration – services, intellectual property rights, investments, and competition – and to give a predictable environment favorable to business. Issues have a domino effect. Each one propels related issues on the agenda, which is continuously reconfigured under the pressure of globalization. Regulating institutions are an intrinsic part of the congruence of tendencies and components of globalization. In comparison, states have been less successful in the trade regime.

However, the success of the GATT/WTO in liberalizing the trading system should not be overstated. Restrictive trade practices have not disappeared. Tariff preferences have been preserved, protectionist practices are widely spread. Subsidies, state trading, discriminatory government procurements, monopolies, or antidumping actions have not been wiped out by the Uruguay Round of negotiations. Rules and regulations are becoming very attractive as means of border protection (Mahé and Ortalo-Magné, 1998: 2): so much so that Dan Esty (1998) called for 'greening' the GATT. If indeed, trade issues contrast with the obscure nature of financial issues, public debate about trade is still missing. Indeed, the process may infuriate the civil society.

There is still no formal role for NGOs at the WTO (Esty, 1998: 4; Marceau and Pedersen, 1999), and governments can still speak to each other, behind closed doors and away from indiscreet ears. Although economic negotiations have become politicized, they are often led in secrecy. If trade issues contrast with the obscure nature of financial issues, a public debate over trade is still missing. Are President Clinton's proposals that hearings by the WTO be open to the public, and all briefs by the parties be made publicly available, going to be implemented (WTO, 18 May 1998)? That would pave the way to a wider support from society.

International institutions are all actors in the same play. UNCTAD, which secured and mediated the developing countries' demands in the 1970s, has now been reincarnated in an organization preparing the developing countries for the challenge of globalization, and for the exigencies of the WTO international agenda. Globalization also benefits organizations in quest of a new role.

Developing countries are no longer protected by the safety net of special and differential treatment, and special provisions are restricted to periods of transition or technical co-operation. However, they have nothing to gain from maintaining their differential status, but everything to gain by playing a more stringent rules-based multilateral system In doing so, they will be heeded. The Uruguay Round has proven that getting something is possible when developing countries attempt to equalize power and overcome their power deficit, by negotiating on the same grounds than major powers, difficult as this could be.

Reorganizing the state

The increasing institutionalization of regulative functions encompasses the state. Globalization has exerted an impact on the state, between those who have accompanied, and reacted positively to the rising social and economic tensions consequential to globalization, and those lacking the basis for mobilizing the requested resources. Globalization requires strong domestic policy frameworks. The debate over the erosion of the states is misleading. The states are not eroded, because they regulate firms and markets, protect citizens against the market, and redistribute wealth.

Globalization is primarily about reorganization of the states rather than bypassing them. States are allies as well as competitors or opponents. They may fight to protect sectoral interests against the exigencies of worldwide production, or co-operate when needed. What remains true is that states are different, and perform differently their role as setter-up of the legal and institutional framework, of influencer of the way assets are utilized, and as entrepreneur. States are not uniformly equipped to face globalization, and some are more equipped than others. They dispose of institutions able to regulate the economic and political processes, and mediate distributional conflicts in the society. As Chapter 3 has argued, some countries have played an effective role in channeling the resources required to benefit from globalization. However, this role has not been without disruptive effects. In other parts of the world, the state lacks the basis of social consensus and rising social tensions will enhance their propensity to be more coercive. The debate over the erosion of the state or the loss of sovereignty diverts attention from the need to develop new strategies for transforming the state. States must endeavour to influence the rules of the game to make the outcome more equitable, and to ensure that the benefits are widely shared. This would include curbing the adverse effects of exclusion and providing social safety nets.

Globalization has an impact on the activities of governmental agencies and bureaucracy, and widens the field of bargaining games among players. Their power stems from their bargaining advantages (drawn from their expertise). Governments must first improve the quality of the public bureaucracy, the channels through which non-elite can make themselves heard and brought into the decision-making process, and devise new modes of co-ordination among these actors to maximize their skill and manage the complexity of the game.

There is a propensity of contemporary globalization to generate more conflicts at the national and global level. Globalization is not unanimously praised by the optimists. It is highly criticized by those who are excluded and the pessimists who denounce globalization's social impairment and increasing polarization between the winners and the losers, and the increased gap between those who are part of the new global work force and those who are left out.

Since 1995, 188 complaints have been brought before the WTO dispute settlement mechanism. Not all disputes originate from developed countries. Inspite of the costs entailed by such an exercize, some developing countries venture to complain against developed countries, and to denounce their unfair and disguised practices under the cover of environmentally friendly products, labeled products, or sanitary and phytosanitary measures.

At the national level, some players benefit from globalization more than others. For others – lagging regions, unskilled labor forces, women, or indigenous people – globalization leads to exclusion and exacerbates existing inequalities. Globalization has developed in the shadow of civil society, and now a vast array of citizens claim their fear of being left out, and their anger. Hence, the revenge sought by groups and citizens during global gatherings.

Uneven pattern of regionalization

Regionalization has generated the same disagreement as globalization. Yet it has been growing rapidly, and very unevenly. Debate is harsh between supporters of regionalization as an optimizing strategy to increase international competitiveness and to integrate member countries in the global economy. Conversely, detractors of regionalization emphasized the fragmentation effect of regionalization. Answers are not clear cut. RIAs may improve liberalization of trade by innovating and devising new instruments to be duplicated in multilateral agreements.

RIAs have excelled in addressing innovative topics, and have provided a model for the Uruguay Round of negotiations. A case in point is the European Union's treatment of trade in services (World Bank, 1997: 136). Another is the EU's treatment of investments, technical barriers, or government procurements. American proposals in the NAFTA negotiations, such as strengthening intellectual property rights, restraining governments from imposing performance requirements on foreign-owned firms, or addressing the competence of the courts to deal with trade disputes, were framed in part with an eye to the content of the GATT negotiations (Vernon, 1994: 38).

The United States has clearly used NAFTA to place 'new issues' on the international agenda. However, devising new instruments may not be favorable. NAFTA made changes by strengthening intellectual property rights, investment regime, and dispute settlement mechanisms. These were US responses to the asymmetry of relations within NAFTA between one major power, one middle power, and one developing country, and NAFTA is not free from protectionist policies. Rules of origin are a case in point, and were included in NAFTA before they were dealt with by the WTO.

Regional integration has a demonstration effect, increasing the probability that countries will move to similar actions, and devote themselves to similar endeavours. It has valuable domestic functions. Regional agreements lock in domestic reforms against potential political setbacks. For Mexico, NAFTA was part of a package of necessary economic reforms that were initiated in the 1980s, and was used by president Salinas to root out opposition to the new economic model.

Thus, regional integration and global liberalization 'simultaneously keep the bicycle moving' (Bergsten 1996: 7).

There is no clear evidence of a scenario of a world economy divided into three largely autonomous trading regions with relatively low level of interdependence. Nor is there evidence that intraregional trade has impeded interregional trade. Yet there is competition between the regions, and uneven distribution between them. RIAs present discrepancies. Some RIAs cover many issues, and have a high level of institutionalization and a complex decision-making process. The EU is a case in point. Institutionalization is quite dense in the EU. NAFTA covers many issues, has a fairly high level of institutionalization, and, has a dispute settlement mechanism aiming to resolve problems arising from two developed countries and one developing country's membership. However, NAFTA's institutions remain intergovernmental. On the other hand, the real thrust of the regional initiative was to harmonize the regulatory framework for investments and trade, and in this way NAFTA acted as an anchor for reforms, helping Mexico to gain credibility and to prepare better for competition at the global level. In Africa, the landscape is fragmented by overlapping and weak RIAs. Regional integration is somehow paradoxical in an environment of scarce resources.

Africa is marked by a proliferation of intergovernmental institutions for co-operation and integration with overlapping objectives and functions: the Common Market for Eastern and Southern Africa (COMESA); the Southern African Customs Union (SACU); and the South African Development Community (SADC) map out Southern Africa, while in West Africa, there were 40 or so intergovernmental organizations, including the Economic Community of West African States (ECOWAS), the Union économique et monétaire de l'Afrique de l'ouest (UEMOA), and the Mano River Union (MRU). In the Central African subregion, the ECCAS member countries of Cameroon, Central African Republic, Congo, and Gabon are members of the Economic Community of the Great Lakes Countries (ECGLC), and of the Union douanière des Etats de l'Afrique centrale (UDEAC). East Africa is also mobilizing: the East African Community is reviving, while Ethiopia, Eritrea, Sudan, Kenya, Uganda (two EAC member states) plus some others are launching a regional scheme, UDEAC.

Asia offers the same kaleidoscopic vision. Regional configuration of the Pacific region presents a patchwork of agreements. The ASEAN co-exists with the Pacific Economic Co-operation Council (PEEC), the

Pacific Rim Economic Council (PREC), the Pacific Conference on Trade Development (PCTD), and the Asia-Pacific Economic Co-operation (APEC). The Asian Free Trade Area (AFTA) spans countries of the ASEAN, and has agreed with Australia and New Zealand to set up a high-level force to establish a FTA by 2010.

Regionalization suffers the same flaws as globalization, by producing dividing lines between winners and losers, and by growing far from public scrutiny and indiscreet ears. Chiapas in Mexico have been left aside from the NAFTA process, and vociferously resent it. In Africa, RIAs are not concerned with a society that does not rely on regional integration for surviving and trading. RIAs have left out the burgeoning centres of civilian power that are located outside the State. They rather rely on ethnic kinship or interpersonal relationships, they have no connections with the state or any idea of the benefits they could draw from ECOWAS, UDEAC, and so on. They run their own trade, and provide their own services. This has tremendous consequences for the future of the continent. Indeed, elements of integration and fragmentation are at the core of globalization and regionalization.

Notes

Chapter 4   The Stratification of Global Trade

1 These 20 product groups were composed of medical and pharmaceutical products; paper and paperboard; international combutions piston engines and parts thereof; non-electric parts and accessories of machinery; automatic data processing machines and units thereof; parts and accessories of office machines and automatic data processing machines, telecommunications equipment and accessories for telecommunications and sound recording and reproducing apparatus and equipment; cathode tubes and valves; electrical machinery and apparatus; passenger motor cars; parts and accessories of motor vehicles; aircraft and associated equipment and parts thereof; furniture and parts thereof; outer garments, women's, girls' and infants' textile fabrics; other garments and other articles, knitted or crocheted; footwear; measuring, checking, analysing and controlling instruments and apparatus; baby carriages, toys, games and sporting goods; special transactions and commodities not classified.

Chapter 5   The GATT/WTO: Instrumentalizing Globalization

1 The Fuji Kodak case brought to the WTO dispute settlement mechanism casts light on the trade restrictive practices. The United States complained against the Japan's laws, regulations, and requirements affecting the distribution, offering for sale, and internal sale of imported consumer photographic film and paper. The US alleged that the Japanese Government treated imported film and paper less favorably through these measures, and that these measures nullified or impaired benefits that should flow for the tariff concessions that had been made on photographic films.

2 The panel had decreed that the US could not place embargos on imports of tuna products from Mexico simply because Mexican regulations on *the way tuna was produced* did not satisfy US regulations. (But the US could apply its regulations on *the quality or content* of the tuna imported.) This has become known as a 'product' versus 'process' issue (http///www.wto.org).

3 The WTO panel on the EU ban of the use of growth hormone fed beef was in favor of the United States, and found that EU had not met the SPS requirement of scientific evidence to justify the ban. The EU did not comply with the decision. However, the US improved control on hormone-free meat to settle the dispute (http://www.wto.org; Reuters, 9 March 2000).

4 The acceding Members are Albania, Algeria, Andorra, Armenia, Azerbaijan, Belarus, Bhutan, Cambodia, Cape Verde, People's Republic of China, Croatia, Estonia, Ethiopia, Former Yugoslav Republic of Macedonia, Georgia, Holy See (Vatican), Jordan, Kazakstan, Kyrgyz Republic, Lao People's Democratic

Republic, Latvia, Lithuania, Moldova, Nepal, Sultanate of Oman, Russian Federation, Samoa, Saudi Arabia, Seychelles, Sudan, Chinese Taipei, Tonga, Ukraine, Uzbekistan, Vanuatu, and Vietnam.

5 China must hold bilateral negotiations with any of the 13 WTO members that request them, and then consolidate the best market-opening agreements into a multilateral protocol. The EU wants its telecommunication companies to be allowed a controlling 51 per cent stake in Chinese firms, and its insurance companies to be allowed equity stakes of more than 50 per cent in joint ventures. The United States settled for only 49 per cent foreign ownership (*Financial Times*, 29 November 1999; *Far Eastern Economic Review*, 9 March 2000).

6 The EC restricted or prohibited imports of meat and meat products from the United States in 1986, on the basis that the use in livestock farming of certain substances may have a hormonal action. Both the United States and Canada brought a case to the WTO in 1996, claiming that the EC action was inconsistent with some GATT Articles. The Panel found that the EC ban on imports of meat and meat products was inconsistent with some of the SPS Agreement's articles.

7 Under that program, the Indonesian government designated 'PT Timor Putra national' as the only 'national car' manufacturing company eligible for exemption from customs duties and luxury taxes on condition that it achieve specified minimum local content rations. Furthermore, vehicles produced abroad by the Korean Kia Motors Corporation can be imported tariff-free as national cars so long as Indonesian workers participate in the foreign production of the vehicle and Korean companies purchase from Indonesia parts worth 25 per cent of the value of the vehicles to be imported thereunder (UNCTAD, 1997a: 57).

8 As a consequence, some developing countries claimed to be released from patent protection which increases prices of some strategic drugs, such as a HIV treatment drug.

9 See Venezuela and Brazil (US gasoline regulations that discriminated against complainants' gasoline).

Chapter 6 Foreign Direct Investment and the Global Economy: Why, How, and Where?

1 A distinction is usually made between three sources of FDI: equity capital, undistributed profits, and loans from parent companies to affiliates. The equity component is defined as 'investment that is made to acquire a lasting management interest (usually 10 per cent of voting stock) in an enterprise operating in a country other than that of the investor' (UNCTAD, 1999a: 116).

2 Privatization in Argentina began in 1990 when the government sold Aerolineas Argentinas for $260 million, and most of the major utilities followed – telephone, gas, oil, electricity and trains. TELECOM in Argentina was sold to a consortium of STET Italy and Telecom France. The Brazilian government has sold the Companhia Vale do Rio Doce, a mining and transport monopoly; Telebras, the telecoms monopoly worth a total of $45

billing; followed by Petrobras in 1998 (*The Economist*, 27 March 1999). Privatization accounted for 25 per cent of FDI inflows in 1998.

3 Vietnam is an illustrative example. For the first half of the 1990s, Vietnam was praised by FDI for its large market, and its well educated and hard working workforce. In 1993 and 1994, Vietnam adopted a legal framework for investments. After decades of communism, the country badly needed infrastructure and industrial production. By 1996, FDI had reached $8.3 billion a year, accounting for more than a third of Vietnam's GDP (*The Economist*, 8 January 2000). However, FDI came to an halt. In 1998, the FDI inflows were at the level of 1993 FDI. Government's commitment to FDI was more rhetoric than reality. *Doi moi* ('renewal') was accompanied by new rules, and companies were charged with a premium for every activity and imposed arbitrarily high tariff for imports.

4 Shell, the Anglo-Dutch firm that handles about half of Nigeria's oil production, spends $38 million a year to secure local good will.

Chapter 7   The Transnational Corporations: Channeling Disparities

1 Two main sources of information about TNCs are available: the first is the Fortune Global 500 list – the oldest list. It is unique in that it ranks firms by foreign assets and includes financial and non-financial corporations; the second is the UN Center for Transnational Corporations (UNCTC) publication in the World Investment Report, published by UNCTAD, which contains only non-financial corporations. But the data provided by UNCTAD are more comprehensive as they compile foreign assets, foreign sales and foreign employment, and reflect the TNCs involvement abroad by building an index of transnationality, a composite ratio of foreign assets/total assets, foreign sales/total sales, and foreign employment/total employment. Understandably, these two sources lead to surprising results. Whereas Seagram Company, the Canadian beverage and entertainment company, leads the UNCTAD list, it ranks 417th in the Fortune Global 500 list (Fortune, 1999: 24).

2 Daewoo, the Korean corporation, offered to restructure the state-owned automobile firm FSO in Poland. Daewoo proposed to inject a large amount of capital to transform FSO into a major platform for exports of passenger cars and car parts to the EU. The Daewoo offer gave the Polish government some leeway to negotiate with General Motors, which had initiated talks with the Polish government to take over FSO.

3 Until 1980, IBM insisted in doing everything by itself. Yet in 1981, its personal computer was developed in an alliance with Microsoft, Intel, and Lotus. It entered into an alliance with Siemens in Germany in the late 1980s to work on memory chips, and it is working with Apple, one of its fiercest competitors, to develop a new type of operating software (*The Economist*, 27 March 1993). One of the knowledge-based networks is the PC/TV link.

4 The German retailer Metro Holding, number 32 in the top 500 Fortune Global, is preparing a bid on Kingfisher, the British retailer, which had previously purchased Castorama Dubois (France). The American Wal-Mart,

number 4 of the 500 Fortune Global, had itself launched discussions with Metro Holding to penetrate the German market. Wal-Mart had previously acquired Asda, the British retailer. These countermoves were the result of a merger between Carrefour (the number 1 French retailer) and Promodès. In the telecoms sector, AT&T has acquired two cable companies: Tele-communications Inc.; and MediaOne Group. Microsoft has pursued a similar strategy through investments in cable companies in Europe and through a new alliance with AT&T. AOL acquired competitor Compuserve and then took over Netscape and established a joint venture with Microsystems to push forward electronic commerce. Microsystems had previously acquired Sun, a computer workstation manufacturer that had developed Java, a new software system that is able to work with every computer. The deal linked the biggest provider and a firm that invented a computer language.

5 DaimlerChrysler Aerospace (DASA), a German company resulting from a $41 billion merger between Daimler-Benz and Chrysler (United States), planned a merger with British Aerospace (BAe), but was soon to cry off, as a result of national considerations. The merger fell through because BAe preferred a $13 billion deal with GEC Marconi (United States). This blocked Marconi's potential merger with Thomson-CSF (French), but gave BAe a foothold in the American defence and aerospace markets after Marconi purchased Tracor, an American defence contractor. After the deal failed, DaimlerChrysler made an offer to Thompson-CSF and Lagardère Group's Matra (French), which could be effective only once the French government has privatized Aerospatiale and Thomson.

6 Vodafone AirTouch, a mobile phone company, draws its name from a previous merger between Vodafone Group and AirTouch Communications in 1999. Vodafone AirTouch raised a $155 billion offer for Mannesmann (Germany).

7 Pfizer's purchase of Warner-Lambert, an American rival, has formed the world's second-largest firm with a 6.7 per cent of the market. This deal ended some speculation about negotiations between Procter & Gamble and American Home Products and Warner-Lambert. Deals have multiplied since 1995 with the deal between Sweden's Pharmacia and America's Upjohn, and between Ciba-Geigy and Sandoz to form Novartis in 1996.

8 The latest was a bid from Pacific Century CyberWorks (PCCW) for Hong Kong's former telecoms monopoly, Cable & Wireless HKT, which was itself in talks to merge with Singapore's telecom company, Singtel. But the companies could not raise the finance for the bid, had to assemble a consortium, and relied on a Japanese mobile phone retailer, which is already a partner of PCCW. Moreover, PCCW has invested in Orange, a British mobile operator that was brought by Mannesmann before being the target of British Vodafone AirTouch (*The Economist*, 19 February 2000).

Chapter 9   Regionalization: Old Blends and New Incarnation

1 The application of favorable postage rates to certain Canadian periodicals was found justified by Article III 8(b) of GATT 1994.

2   California was recycling Ontario beer cans: Ontario imposed a 10 per cent can recycling tax. The USA claimed that it was discriminatory, as US beer is exported in aluminum cans while over 80 per cent of Canadian beer is sold in bottles.

3   In 1996, the United States introduced 22 cases against Canada, and the same number against Mexico, whereas Canada introduced 21 cases, and Mexico only 11. Since 1993, consultations with Canada have concerned beer, softwood lumber, wheat, music TV status, editions of magazines, and dairy and poultry products. Consultations with Mexico have concerned small package delivery services, standards, and telecommunications (WTO, 1996).

Chapter 10   Regional Integration Arrangements: Trading Blocs or Building Blocs?

1   The agreement is plurilateral. Membership of the GPA remains limited to the signatory countries: Canada, the member states of the European Union, Hong Kong, Israel, Japan, Korea, Norway, Singapore, Switzerland, and the United States.

2   This term 'general incidence' gave rise to some discussions. After joining the EU, Sweden, which did not impose any duties on semi-conductors, started to impose a 10–15 per cent duty. Korea and Japan, both important exporters, lost their shares of market. They complained that if the duties and other trade regulations were not globally higher, still on a sectoral basis, duty was calculated so as to inhibit imports.

Bibliography

Aggarwal, Vinod (1994) 'Comparing Regional Cooperation Efforts in the Asia–Pacific and North America', in A. Mack and J. Ravenhill (eds), *Pacific Cooperation: Building Economic and Security Regimes in the Asia Pacific Region*, Sydney: Allen & Unwin.

Aggestam, Lisbeth (1997) 'The European Union at the Crossroads: Sovereignty and Integration', in Alice Landau and Richard Whitman (eds), *Rethinking the European Union: Institutions, Interests and Identities*, Basingstoke: Macmillan Press – now Palgrave.

Agnew, John (1995) 'Democracy and Human Rights after the Cold War', in R. J. Johston, Peter J. Taylor and Michael J. Watts (eds), *Geographies of Global Change, Remapping the World in the Late Twentieth Century*, Oxford: Blackwell.

Agosin, Manuel R., Tussie, Diana, and Crespi, Gustavo (1995) 'Developing Countries and the Uruguay Round: An Evaluation and Issues for the Future', in *International Monetary and Financial Issues for the 1990s*, Vol. VI, UNCTAD, New York: United Nations.

Agosin, Manuel R. and Mayer, Riccardo (2000) *Foreign Investments in Developing Countries, Does it Crowd in Domestic Investment?* Discussion Paper No. 146. Geneva: UNCTAD.

De Almeida, Roberto Paulo (1994) 'O Brasil e o MERCOSUR em Face do NAFTA', *Boletim de integracao latino-americana*, 13, 15–23.

Audley, John J. (1997) *Green Politics and Global Trade: NAFTA and the Future of Environmental Politics*, Washington, D. C.: Georgetown University Press.

Axelrod, Robert and Robert Keohane (1985) 'Achieving Cooperation Under Anarchy: Strategies and Institutions', *World Politics*, 38, 226–54.

Babu, Ramesh (1998) 'The South Asian State in a Globalizing World', in Babu Ramesh, *Globalization and the South Asian States*, New Dehli: South Asian Publishers.

Bach, Daniel (1996) 'Crise des institutions et recherche de nouveaux modèles', in Réal Lavergne (ed.), *Intégration et coopération régionales en Afrique de l'Ouest*, Paris: Editions Karthala.

Bach, Daniel (1999) 'Revisiting a Paradigm', in Daniel Bach (ed.) Regionalisation in Africa: Integration and Disintegration, Oxford: James Currey.

Bach, Daniel and Helge Hveem (1998) *Regionalism, Regionalization and Globalization*, paper presented to the Third General Conference of ECPR in Vienna, September 12–16.

Bairoch, Paul (1996) 'Globalization Myths and Realities, One Century of external Trade and Foreign Investment', in Robert Boyer and Daniel Drache (eds), *States against Markets, the Limits of Globalization*, London: Routledge.

Bairoch, Paul and Kozul-Wright, Richard (1996) *Globalization Myths: Some Historical Reflections on Integration, Industrialization and Growth in the World Economy*, Discussion Paper No. 113. Geneva: UNCTAD.

Balasubramayam, V. N. and Greenaway, David (1995) 'Regional Integration Agreements and Foreign Direct Investment', in Kym Anderson and Richard Blackhurst (eds), *Regional integration and the Global Trading System*, New York: St. Martin's press – now Palgrave.

Bhagwati, Jagdish (1995) 'U.S. Trade Policy: The Infatuation with Free Trade Areas', in Jagdash Bhagwati and Anne O. Krueger (eds), *The Dangerous Drift to Preferential Trade Agreements*, Washington, D. C.: American Enterprise Institute Press.

Baptista, Luis Olavo (1992) 'The Asuncion Treaty establishing the Southern Common Market (MERCOSUR)', *International Business Law Journal*, 4(5), 567–88.

Barber, Benjamin (2000) 'Jihad vs. McWorld', in Frank J. Lechner and John Boli (eds), *The Globalization Reader*, Oxford: Blackwell Publishers.

Barry Jones, R. J. (1994) *Globalisation and Interdependence in the International Political Economy, Rhetoric and Reality*, London: Pinter Publishers.

Bell, Daniel (1999) *The Coming of Post-Industrial-Society*, New York: Basic Books.

Bergsten, Fred C. (1996) *Competitive Liberalization and Global Free Trade: A Vision for the Early 21st Century*, APEC Working Paper 96–15, Washington, D. C.: Institute for International Economics.

Bergsten, Fred C. (1997) *Open Regionalism*, APEC Working Paper 97–15. Washington, D. C.: Institute for International Economics.

Blackhurst, Richard (1997) 'Regionalism in a Rules-Based World Trading System' in *Regionalism and Development*, Brussels: The European Commission and World Bank Seminar.

Bordo, Michael D., Eichengreen, Barry and Irwin, Douglas A. (1999) *Is Globalization today really Different than Globalization a Hundred Years ago?*, National Bureau of Economic Research, Working Paper 7195. http://www.cid.harvard.edu

Borrus, Michael and Zysman, John (1996) 'Industrial Competitiveness and American National Security', in Wayne Sandoltz *et al.* (eds), *The Highest Stakes, The Economic Foundations of the Next Security System*, New York: Oxford University Press.

Boyer, Robert and Drache, Daniel (1996) 'Introduction', in Rober Boyer and Daniel Drache (eds), *States against Markets, The Limits of Globalization*. London: Routledge.

Brecher, Jeremy and Costello, Tim (1994) *Global Village or Global Pillage, Economic Reconstruction from the Bottom Up*, Boston, Mass.: South End Press.

Brigagão, Clovis and Valle, Marcello (1995) 'Argentina–Brasil: Modelo regional de confianza mutua para la seguridad nuclear', in *Integracion solidaria: América latina en la era de globalización*, Caracas: Universidad Simón Bolívar, Instituto de Altos estudioas de América latina.

Broadhurst, Arlen I. and Ledgerwood, Grant (1999) 'Environmental Diplomacy of States, Corporations and Non-governmental organizations: The Worldwide Web of Influence', *International Relations*, 14(3), 1–19.

Brownbridge, Martin (1998) *The Causes of Financial Distress in Local Banks in Africa and Implications for Prudential Policy*, UNCTAD Discussion Paper No. 132, Geneva: UNCTAD.

252 *Bibliography*

Bull, Hedley (1977) *The Anarchical Society*, London: Macmillan Press – now Palgrave.

Burtless, Gary, Lawrence, Robert, Litan, Robert and Shapiro, Robert (1998) *Globophobia: Confronting Fears about Open Trade*, Washington, D. C.: The Brookings Institute.

Cable, Vincent (1996) 'Globalisation: Can the State Strike Back?', *The World Today*, 52(5), 133–7.

Cameron, James, Werksman, Jacob, and Roderick, Peter (1996) 'Introduction', in James Cameron, Jacob Werksman and Peter Roderick (eds), *Improving Compliance with International Environmental Law*, Economic and Social Research Council, London: Earthscan.

Cameron, Maxwell and Tomlin, Brian (2000) 'Negotiating North American Free Trade', *Journal of International Negotiation* 5(1): 43–68.

Cerny, Philip G. (1999) 'Globalization and the Erosion of Democray', *European Journal of Political Research*, 36, 1–26.

Childers, Simon J. and Urquhart, Brian (1994) *Renewing the United Nations System*, Uppsala, Dag Hammarskojšld Foundation.

Clark, Ian (1997) *Globalization and Fragmentation, International Relations in the Twentieth Century*, Oxford: Oxford University Press.

Coker, Christopher (1993) 'The New World (Dis)order', in Armand Clesse, Richard Cooper, and Yoshikazu Sakamoto (eds), *The International System after the Collapse of the East–West Order*, Dordrecht: Martinus Nijhoff Publishers.

Cooper, Richard N. (1968) *The Economics of Interdependence: Economic Policy in the Atlantic Community*, New York: McGraw Hill.

Cox, Robert W. (1981) 'Social Forces, States and World Order beyond International Relations Theory', *Millenium Journal of International Studies*, 10(2): 126–55.

Cox, Robert W. (1982) 'Production and Hegemony: Toward a Political Economy of World Order', in Harold K. Jacobson and Dusan Sidjanski (eds), *The Emerging International Economic Order, Dynamic Processes, Constraints, and Opportunities*, Beverly Hills: Sage Publications.

Cox, Robert W. (1987) *Production, Power and World Debt: Social Forces in the Making of History*, New York: Columbia University Press.

Cox, Robert W. (1991) 'The Global Political Economy and Social Choice', in Robert W. Cox and Timothy J. Sinclair (eds), *Approaches to World Order*, Cambridge: Cambridge University Press.

Cox, Robert W. (1992) 'Towards a Post-Hegemonic Conceptualization of World Order: Reflections on the Relevancy of Ibn Khaldun', in Robert W. Cox and Timothy J. Sinclair (eds), *Approaches to World Order*, Cambridge: Cambridge University Press.

Cox, Robert W. (1996) 'A perspective on Globalization', in James H. Mittelman (ed.), *Globalization. Critical reflections*, Boulder, Col.: Lynne Rienner.

Croome, John (1995) *Reshaping the World Trading System, A History of the Uruguay Round*, Geneva: World Trade Organization.

Croome, John (1998) *The Present Outlook for Trade negotiations in the World Trade Organization*, http://www.wto.org

Csáki, György Sass and Magdolna, Szalavetz (1996) 'Reinforcing the Modernization Role of Foreign Direct Investment in Hungary', Working papers, Institute for World Economics, Budapest: Institute for World Economics.

Curzon-Price, Victoria and Landau, Alice (1999) 'Introduction: The Enlargement of the European Union: Dealing with Complexity', in Victoria Curzon-Price, Alice Landau and Richard Whitman (eds), *The Enlargement of the European Union, Issues and Strategies*, London: Routledge.

D'Andrea Tyson, Laura (1992) *Who's Bashing Whom? Trade Conflict in High Technology Industries*, Washington, D. C.: Institute for International Economics.

Daniels, P. W. and Lever W. F. (1996) *The Global Economy in Transition*, Harlow: Addison Wesley Longman Limited.

Das, Dilip (1990) *International Trade Policy : Developing Countries' Perspective*, London: Macmillan.

Demko, G. and Wood, W, *Reordering the World: Geopolitical Perspectives on the Twenty-First Century*, Boulder, Col.: Westview Press.

Dent, Christopher M. (1997) *The European Economy, The Global Context*, London: Routledge.

Dessert, Daniel (1987) *Fouquet*, Paris: Fayard.

Destler, Max (1992) *American Trade Politics*, Washington, D. C.: Institute for International Economics and Twentieth Century Fund.

Dicken, Paul (1992) *Global Shift: The Internationalization of Economic Activity*, London: Chapman.

Dicken, P. (1998) *Global Shift* (3rd edn), London: Chapman.

Dickerson, Kitty G. (1995) *Textiles and Apparel in the Global Economy*, Englewood Cliffs: Prentice Hall.

Doherty, Ann (1994) 'The Role of Nongovernmental Organizations in UNCED', in Bertram I. Spector, Gunnar Sjöstedt and William I. Zartman (eds), *Negotiating International Regimes: Lessons Learned from the United Nations Conference on Environment and Development (UNCED)*, London: Graham & Trotman/Martinus Nijhoff.

Donneur, André (1999) *La politique extérieure du Canada, 1997–(1998) priorité à l'Asie-Pacifique*, Montréal: Coop UQAM.

Drucker, Peter F. (1997) 'The Global Economy and the Nation State', *Foreign Affairs*, 76(5), 159–71.

Dryden, Steve (1995) *Trade Warriors, USTR and the American Crusade for Free Trade*, Oxford: Oxford University Press.

Dunn, J. 'The French Highway Lobby: a Case Study in State – Society Relations', *Comparative Politics*, 27: 75–95.

Dunning, John H. (1992) *Multinational Enterprises and the Global Economy*, London: Addison-Wesley.

Dunning, John H. (1993) *Globalization: The Challenge for National Economic Regimes*, Twenty-fourth Geary lecture, Dublin: The Economic and Social Research Institute.

Dunning, John H. (1997) 'Governments and the Macro-Organization of Economic Activity: A Historical and Spatial Perspective', in John H. Dunning (ed.), *Governments, Globalization and International Business*, Oxford: Oxford University Press.

Eaton, Curtis, Lipsey, Richard, and Safarian Edward (1994) 'The Theory of Multinational Plant Location in a Regional Trading Area', in Lorraine Eden (ed.), *Multinationals in North America*, Calgary: The University of Calgary Press.

Globalization of Industrial Activities 1994a. OECD world paper 2(48), Paris: OECD.

Economic Commission for Europe, *Statistical Survey of recent Trends in Foreign Investment in East European Countries*, Trade/R.624, Geneva: Economic and Social Council.

ECOWAS, *Annual Report 1991/199*, Executive Secretary Abass Bundu, Lagos: ECOWAS Secretariat.

Eichengreen, Barry, Rose, Andrew K., and Wyplosz, Charles (1996) *Contagious Currency Crises*, National Bureau of Economic Research, Working Paper No 5681, Cambridge: National Bureau of Economic Research.

Eichengreen, Barry and Mussa, Michael (1998) *Capital Account Liberalization, Theoretical and Practical Aspects*, IMF Occasional Paper No. 172. Washington, D. C.: International Monetary Fund.

Elliott, Kim (2000) 'Mismanaging Diversity: Worker Rights and US Trade Policy', *Journal of International Negotiation* 5(1): 97–127.

Elliott, Loraine, *The Global Politics of the Environment*, Basingstoke: Macmillan Press – now Palgrave.

Esty, Dan (1998) 'Why the World Trade Organization needs Environmental NGOs, International Centre for Trade and sustainable development', http//www.cid.harvard.edu.

European Community support for regional economic integration among developing countries (1995), Communication from the Commission, Brussels: Commission of the European Communities, COM (95) 219 final.

Evenett, Simon J. and Hoekman, Bernard (1999) *Government Procurement of Services: Assessing the Case for Multilateral Disciplines*, Paper delivered to the World Congress Services, Atlanta, November 1–3.

Faure, Guy Olivier (2000 forthcoming) 'Negotiation for Setting Joint Ventures in China', *Journal of International Negotiation*.

Feketekuty, Geza (1999) *Assessing the WTO general Agreement on Trade on Services and Improving the GATS Architecture*, Paper presented at the World Services Congress, Atlanta, November 1–3.

Felix, David (1994) 'International Capital Mobility and Third World Development: Compatible Marriage or Troubled Relationship', *Policy Sciences*, 3(1), 365–94.

Fernandez, Raquel (1997) 'Commitment, Signalling, and Insurance: An Analysis of Non-traditional Gains from RTAs', in *Regionalism and Development*, Brussels: European Commission and the World Bank.

Foroutan, Faezeh (1992) 'Regional Integration in subSaharan Africa: Past Experience and Future Prospects', in Jaime de Melo and Arvind Panagariya (eds), *New Dimensions of Regionalism*, Cambridge: Cambridge University Press.

Foucher, Michel (1996) *Les défis de la sécurité en Europe médiane*, Fondation pour les Etudes de défense, Paris: la Documentation française.

François, J. and McDonald B. (1996) 'The Multilateral Agenda: The Uruguay Round Implementation and Beyond', Staff Working Paper, Geneva: WTO.

Frankel, J. (1988) *International Relations in a Changing World*, Oxford: Oxford University Press.

Frankel, Jeffrey A., Stein, Ernesto, and Wei, Shang-Jin (1998) 'Continental Trading Blocs: Are They Natural or Supernatural', in Jeffrey A. Frankel (ed.), *The Regionalization of the World Economy*, Chicago: Chicago University Press.

Fransman, Martin (1985) 'Conceptualizing Technical Change in the Third World in the 1980s: An Interpretative Survey', *Journal of Development Studies*, 21(3), 572–652.

French, Hilary (1996) 'The Role of Non-State Actors', in: Jacob Werksman (ed.), *Greening International Institutions*, London: Earthscan Publications.

Fukuyama, Francis (1992) *The End of History and the Last Man*, New York: The Free Press.

Galal, Ahmed and Hoekman Bernard (eds), (1997) *Regional Partners in Global Markets: Limits and Possibilities of the Euro-Med Agreements*, London.

Ganesan, A. V. (1998) *Strategic Options Available to Developing Countries with Regard to a Multilateral Agreement on Investment*, Discussion Paper No. 134, Geneva: UNCTAD.

Garrett, Geoffrey (1998) *Partisan Politics in the Global Economy*, Cambridge: Cambridge University Press.

Gereffi, Gary (1996) 'The Elusive Last Lap in the Quest for Developed-Country Status', in James H. Mittelman (ed.) *Globalization. Critical Reflections*. Boulder: Lynne Rienner.

Gibbs, Murray and Mashayekhi, Mina (1998) *The Uruguay Round Negotiations on Investment: Lessons for the Future*, Geneva: United Nations.

Giddens, Anthony (1990) *The Consequences of Modernity*, Cambridge: Polity Press.

Giddens, Anthony (1994) *NowHere, Space, Time, and Modernity*, Berkeley: University of California Press.

Gilpin, Robert (1987) *The Political Economy of International Relations*, Princeton: Princeton University Press.

Globerman, Steven (1994) 'The Economics of NAFTA', in Alan M. Rugman (ed.), *Foreign Investment and NAFTA*, Columbia: University of South Carolina Press.

Gordenker, Leon and Weiss, Thomas G. (1995) 'Plurasing Global Governance: Analytical Approaches and Dimensions', *Third World Quarterly*, 16(5), 357–87.

Graham, Edward and Sauvé, Pierre (1998) 'Towards a Rules-Based Regime for Investment: Issues and Challenges', in Pierre Sauvé and Daniel Schwanen (eds), *Investment Rules for the Global Economy*, Ottawa: C. D. Howe Institute.

Griffiths, Richard (1995) 'The Dynamics and Stages of European Integration, 1945–1995', in *Regional Integration Process*, European Union/Southern Africa Development Community.

Grinspun, Ricardo and Cameron, Maxwell A. (1994) *The Political Economy of North American Free Trade*, New York: St Martin's Press.

Grundlach, Erich and Nunnenkamp, Peter (1998) 'Some Consequences of Globalization for Developing Countries', in John H. Dunning (ed.), *Globalization, Trade and Foreign Direct Investment*, Amsterdam: Elsevier.

Gupta, Indrani, Goldar, Bishwanath and Mitra, Arup (1998) 'The Case of India', in Simonetta Zarilli and Colette Kinnon (eds), *International Trade in Health Services: A Development Perspective*, Geneva: United Nations and World Health Organization.

Haarlov, Jens (1997) *Regional Co-operation and Integration within Industry and Trade in Southern Africa, General Approaches, SADCC and the World Bank*, Aldershot: Avebury.

Haas, Ernst (1958) *The Uniting of Europe*, Stanford: Stanford University Press.

Haas, Ernst and Rowe, Edward Thomas (1973) 'Regional Organizations in the United Nations. Is there Externalization?', *International Studies Quarterly*, 17(1), 3–54.

Haas, Peter (ed.) (1992) 'Knowledge, Power, and International Policy Coordination', *International Organization*, 46(1), 1–35.

Haggard, Stephen (1997) 'Regionalism in Asia and the Americas', pp. 20–49, in Edward Mansfield and Helen V. Milner (eds), *The Political Economy of Regionalism*, New York: Columbia University Press.

Ha-Joon, Chang (1996) *Globalization, Transnational Corporations and Economic Development: Can the Developing Countries Pursue Strategic Industrial Policy in a Globalising World Economy?*, Third World Network, Seminar on WTO and Developing Countries, Geneva, September 10–11.

Harayama, Yuko (1998) *Relationship between Stanford University and Silicon Valley industry*, Working Papers of Department of Political Economy, Geneva: University of Geneva.

Hart, Michael (1996) 'A Multilateral Agreement of Foreign Direct Investment: Why Now?', in Pierre Sauvé and Daniel Schwanen (eds), *Investment Rules for the Global Economy*, Ottawa: C. D. Howe Institute.

He, Xiahong (1998) 'From Trade Among Nations to Trade Within Firms Across National Borders', in Jean Louis Mucchielli, Peter Buckley, and Victor Cordell (eds), *Globalization and Regionalization: Strategies, Policies and Economic Environments*, New York: Haworth Press.

Heidelberg Confict Barometer (1999), htttp://www.hiik.de

Held, David (1995) *Democracy and the Global Order, From the Modern State to Cosmopolitan Governance*, London: Polity Press.

Held, David (1998) 'Democracy and New International Order' in Daniele Archibugi, David Held and Martin Köhler (eds) Stanford: Stanford University Press.

Held, David (1999) 'Democracy and Globalization', in Daniele Archibugi, David Held and Martin Köhler (eds), *Re-Imagining Political Community*, Cambridge: Polity Press.

Held, David, McGrew, Anthony, Goldblatt, David, and Perraton, Jonathan (1999) *Global Transformations, Politics, Economcs, Culture*, Cambridge: Polity Press.

Helleiner, Eric (1994a) 'The World of Money: The Political Economy of International Capital Mobility', *Policy Sciences*, 27(1), 295–8.

Helleiner, Eric (1994b) 'Freeing Money: Why States have been more willing to Liberalize Capital Controls than Trade Barriers', *Policy Sciences*, 27(1), 299–319.

Helleiner, Eric (1994c) *States and the Reemergence of Global Finance, from Bretton Woods to the 1990s*, Ithaca: Cornell University Press.

Helleiner, E. (1999) 'Sovereignty, territoriality, and the globalization of finance', in David Smith, Dorothy Solinger and Steven Topit (eds) *States and Sovereignty in the Global Economy*, London, Routledge.

Heilleiner, G. K. (1996) 'Why Small Countries Worry: Neglected Issues in Current Analyses of the Benefits and Costs for Small Countries of Integrating with Large Ones', *The World Economy*, 19(6), 759–79.

Herzog, Jesus Silva (1994) 'Introduction', in Victor Bulmer-Thomas, Nikkii Craske, and Monica Serrano (eds), *Mexico and the North American Free Trade Agreement, Who Will Benefit?*, New York: St Martin's Press–now Palgrave.

Hine, Robert C. (1992) 'Regionalism and the Integration of the World Economy', *Journal of Common Market Studies*, 30, (2), 115–23.

Hirst, Paul (1992) 'The Global Economy: Myths and Realities', *International Affairs*, 73(3), 409–27.

Hirst, Paul (1995) *Globalization in Question*, Political Economy Research Centre. University of Sheffield, Occasional Paper no. 11.

Hirst, Paul and Thompson, Graham (1996) *Globalization in Question, The International Economy and the Possibilities of Governance*, Cambridge: Polity Press.

Hobsbawn, E. J. (1968) *Industry and Empire, An Economic History of Britain since 1750*, London: Weidenfeld and Nicolson.

Hoekman, Bernard and Kostecki, Michel (1995) *The Political Economy of the World Trading System, From GATT to WTO*, Oxford: Oxford University Press.

Hoekman, Bernard and Saggi, Kamal (1999) 'Multilateral Disciplines for Investment-Related Policies?', http://www.cid.harvard.edu

Holland, Martin (1993) *The European Community Integration*, London: Pinter Publishers.

Holly, Brian P. (1996) 'Restructuring the Production System', in P. W. Daniels and W. F. Lever (eds), *The Global Economy in Transition*, Edinburgh: Addison Wesley Longman.

Holsti, Karl (1990) *Change in the International System: Essays on Theory and Practice of International Relations*, London: Edward Elgar Publishing.

Hufbauer, Gary, Lakdawalla, Darius, and Malani, Anup (1994) 'Determinants of Direct Foreign Investment and its Connection to Trade', in *UNCTAD Review*, Geneva: UNCTAD.

Hull, Hedley (1977) *The Anarchical Society*, Basingstoke: Macmillan Press – now Palgrave.

Hyde-Price, Adrian (1997) 'The New Pattern of International Relations in Europe', in Alice Landau and Richard Whitman (eds), *Rethinking the European Union, Institutions, Interests and Identities*, Basingstoke: Macmillan Press – now Palgrave.

Ikenberry, John (1993) 'Salvaging the G7', *Foreign Affairs* 72: 132–9.

Iklé, Fred (1964) *How Nations Negotiate*, New York: Harper and Row.

Imber, Mark (1996) 'The Environment and the United Nations', in John Vogler and Mark F. Imber (eds), *The Environment and International Relations*, London: Routledge.

IMF World Economic Outlook (1999), Washington, D.C.: IMF.

Inotai, Andras (1999) 'The Economy of Enlarged Europe: An Eastern and Central European States' Viewpoint', in Victoria Curzon Price, Alice Landau, and Richard Whitman (eds), *The Enlargement of the European Union: Strategies and Issues*.

International Trade Center (2000), *Africa's Export Success Stories*, Press Release No. 184, UNCTAD X, http://www.unctad-10.org

Investment, Trade, and U.S. Gains in the NAFTA, The Economic Impact of the North American Free Trade Agreement on the United States. A Review of the

Debate, The Stern Group, (1995) US Council of the Mexico–US Business Committee.

Jaspersen, Frederick (1992) 'Determinants of Private Investment in Developing Countries', in Peter Rashish (ed.), *Transatlantic and Global Economic Integration: The Role of Investment*, Washington, D.C.: The European Institute.

Jomo, K. S. (1996) *Lessons from Growth and Structural Change in the Second-Tier South East Asian Newly Industrialising Countries*, East Asian Development: Lessons for a new Global Environment, Study No. 4, UNCTAD, Geneva: United Nations.

Jönsson, Christer (1990) *Communication in International Bargaining*, London: Pinter.

Jönsson, Christer and Söderholm, Peter (1993) 'Cognitive Factors in Regime Dynamics', in Volker Rittberger (ed.), *Regime Theory and International Relations*, Oxford: Clarendon Press.

Jönsson, Christer and Söderholm, Peter (1995) 'IGO–NGO Relations and HIV/AIDS: Innovation or Stalemate?', *Third World Quaterly*, 16(3), 459–75.

Jönsson, Christer, Bjurulf, Bo, Elgström, Ole, Sonnerstedt, Anders, and Strömvik, Maria (1998) 'Negotiations in Networks in the European Union', *Journal of International Negotiation*, 3(3), 319–44.

Jordan, Robert S. (1982) 'Why a NIEO? The View from the Third World', in Harold K. Jacobson and Dusan Sidjanski (eds), *The Emerging International Economic Order, Dynamic Processes, Constraints, and Opportunities*, Beverly Hills: Sage Publications.

Kapstein, Ethan (1994) *Governing the Global Economy, International Finance and the State*, Cambrigde, Mass.: Harvard University Press.

Kassim, Hussein (1997) 'Air Transport and Globalization, a Sceptical View', in Alan Scott (ed.), *The Limits of Globalization, Cases and Arguments*, London. Routledge.

Keating, Michael (1992) 'Regional Autonomy in the Changing State Order: A Framework of Analysis', *Regional Politics & Policy*, 2(3): 45–61.

Kennedy, Paul (1989) *The Rise and Fall of Great Power, Economic Change and Military Conflict from 1500 to 2000*, London: Fontana Press.

Kennedy, Paul (1993) *Preparing for the Twenty-First Century*, New York: Random House.

Kennes, Walter (1995) 'Introduction to Common Policies, in the Development of European Institutions', in *Regional Integration Process*, Brussels: European Union/Southern Africa Development Community.

Keohane, Robert O. (1984) *After Hegemony, Co-operation and Discord in the World Political Economy*, Princeton: Princeton University Press.

Keohane, Robert O. and Nye, Joseph N. (1972) *Transnational Relations and World Politics*, Cambridge: Cambridge University Press.

Keohane, Robert O. and Nye, Joseph N. (1993) 'The End of the Cold War in Europe', in Robert O. Keohane, Joseph S. Nye, and Stanley Hoffmann (eds), *After the Cold War, International Institutions and State Strategies in Europe, 1989–1991*, Cambridge: Harvard University Press.

Kincaid, John (1994) 'Peoples, Persons, and Places in Flux: International Integration versus National Fragmentation', in Guy Laforest and Douglas Brown (eds), *Integration and Fragmentation, The Paradox of the Late Twentieth*

Century, Reflections Paper No. 12, Kingston: Institute of Intergovernmental Relations, Queen's University.

Kozul-Wright, Richard and Rayment, Paul (1995) *Walking on Two legs: Strengthening Democracy and Productive Entrepreneurship in the Transition Economies*, Discussion Papers, No. 101, Geneva: UNCTAD.

Krasner, Stephen (1983) 'Structural Causes and Regime Consequences: Regimes as intervening Variables', in Stephen Krasner (ed.), *International Regimes*, New York: Cornell University Press.

Krasner, Stephen (1999) 'Globalization and Sovereignty', in David Smith, Dorothy Solinger, and Steven Topit (eds) *States and Sovereignty in the Global Economy*, London: Routledge.

Krueger, Anne O. (1984) 'Trade Policies in Developing Countries', in Ronald W. Jones and Peter B. Kenen (eds), *Handbook of International Economics*, Amsterdam: North-Holland.

Krugman, Paul (1991) 'Is Bilateralism Bad? An International Trade and Trade Policy' in E. Helpman, A. Razin, J. De Mello, and A. Panagariya (eds), *New Dimensions in Regional Integration*, Cambridge: Cambridge University Press.

Krugman, Paul R. (1991), 'Increasing Returns and Economic Geography', *Journal of Political Economy*, 99(3), 483–99.

Laird, Sam (1996) 'Fostering Regional Integration', in *Regionalism and its Place in the Multilateral Trading System*, OECD: OECD Documents.

Laird, Sam (1999) *Multilateral Approaches to Market Access Negotiations*, WTO Staff Working papers. Geneva: WTO.

Lal Das, Bhagirath (1999) 'Strengthening the Developing Countries in the WTO', in *International Monetary and Financial Issues for the 1990s*, UNCTAD, New York: United Nations.

Landau, Alice (1990) *Les négociations économiques internationales: Stratégies et pouvoir*, Bruxelles: Editions Emile Bruylant.

Landau, Alice (1995a) 'Conceptualiser l'Union européenne, apports et limites des théories des relations internationales', *Revue suisse de Science politique*, (2–3), 255–82.

Landau, Alice (1995b) 'L'UE face à ses périphéries: de la nécessité d'une recomposition', *Revue internationale de poitique comparée*, 2(3), 467–83.

Landau, Alice (1995c) 'The External Dimensions and Geopolitical Determinants of European Construction' in European Union – Southern African Development Community Regional Integration Process. Bordeaux: CEAN/IEP.

Landau, Alice (1999a) 'From this Point Onwards', in Victoria Curzon Price, Alice Landau, and Richard Whitman (eds), *The Enlargement of the European Union: Strategies and Issues*, London: Routledge.

Landau, Alice (1999b) *Brazil: Training Needs in International Trade*, UNCTAD, unpublished manuscript.

Landau, Alice (1999c) 'Multilateralism and Regionalism in International Economic Relations', in Daniel Bach (ed.), *Regionalisation in Africa: Integration and Disintegration*, Oxford: James Carey.

Landau, Alice (2000) 'Analyzing International Economic Negotiations: Towards a synthesis of Approaches', *Journal of International Negotiation*, 5(1): 1–19.

Landes, David (1998) *The Wealth and Poverty of Nations, Why Some are so Rich and Some so Poor*, London: W. W. Norton & Company.

Langhammer, Rolf and Hiemenz, Ulrich (1990) *Regional Integration among Developing Countries, Opportunities, Obstacles, Options*, Kieler Studien, Nr 232. Tübingen: Institut für Weltwirtschaft an der Universität Kiel.

Lawrence, Robert Z. (1991) 'Emerging Regional Agreements: Building Blocs or Stumbling Blocs', in R. O'Brien (ed.), *Finance and the International Economy*, Oxford: Oxford University Press.

Lawrence, Robert Z. (1996) *Regionalism, Multilateralism, and Deeper Integration*, Washington, D.C.: The Brookings Institute.

Leebron, David W. (1997) 'Implementation of the Uruguay Round Results in the United States', in John H. Jackson and Alan O. Sykes (eds), *Implementing the Uruguay Round*, Oxford: Clarendon House.

Lever, William (1997) 'Market Enlargement: The Single European Market', in P. W. Daniels and W. F. Lever (eds), *The Global Economy in Transition*, Edinburgh: Addison Wesley Longman.

Lindberg, Leon (1966) 'The European Community as a Political System: Notes toward the Construction of a Model', *Journal of Common Market Studies*, 5(4), 344–87.

Lipsey, Richard G. (1997) 'Globalization and National Governemnts Policies: An Economist's View' pp. 73–113, in John H. Dunning (ed.), *Governments, Globalization and International Business*, Oxford: Oxford University Press.

Low, Patrick and Subramanian, Arvind (1995) 'TRIMs in the Uruguay Round: An Unfinished Business', Paper presented at the World Bank Conference on the Uruguay Round and Developing Economies, Geneva.

Low, Patrick, Olarreaga, Marcelo, and Suarez, Javier (1999) *Does Globalization cause a higher concentration of international trade and investment flows?*, WTO staff Working paper. Geneva: WTO.

Lubbers, R. F. M. and Koorevaar, I. G. (1999) *Governance in an Era of Globalization*, Paper for the Club of Rome Annual Meeting. http://www.globalize.org.

Lyakurwa, William, McKay, Andrew, Ng'eno, Nehemiah, and Kennes, Walter (1997) 'Regional Integration in SubSaharan Africa: A Review of Experiences and Issues', in: Ademola Oyejide, Ibrahim Elbadawi, and Paul Collier (eds), *Regional Integration and Trade Liberalization in subSaharan Africa, Framework, Issues and Methodological Perspectives*, Basingstoke: Macmillan Press.

Mace, Gordon (1981) 'Intégration régionale et modèles de développment: le cas du groupe andin', Thèse. Genève: Institut Universitaire des hautes études internationales; Québec/Bruxelles: Emile Bruylant

McGrew, Anthony and Lewis, Paul (1992) *Global Politics, Globalization and the Nation State*, Cambridge: Polity Press.

Machlup, F. (1977) *A History of Thought on Economic Integration*, London: Macmillan Press.

McMillan, Charles (1996) 'Shifting Technological Paradigms: From the U.S. to Japan', pp. 117–154 in Robert Boyer and Daniel Drache (eds), *States against Markets, The Limits of Globalization*, London: Routledge.

McMillan, John (1992) 'Does Regional Integration Foster open Trade? Economic Theory and GATT's Article XXIV', in Jaime De Melo and Arvind Panagariya (eds), *The New Regionalism in Trade Policy*, Washington, D.C.: The World Bank; London: Centre for Economic Policy Research.

Madeley, John (1996) *Trade and the Poor, The Impact of International Trade on Developing Countries*, London: Intermediate Technology Publications.

Madelin, Robert (1997) 'Benchmarking Best Practices', in Peter S. Rashish (ed.) *Transatlantic and Global Ecomonic Integration. The Role of Investment*, Washington, D.C.: The European Institute.

Mahé, L. P. and Ortalo-Magné, F. (1998) *International Co-Operation in the Regulation of Food Quality and Safety Attributes*, OECD workshop on Emerging trade issues in agriculture, COM/AGR/CA/TD/WS(98)102. Paris: OECD.

Maizels, Alfred (1999) *Economic Dependence on Commodities*, High level round table on trade and development direction for the twenty-first century, Bangkok: UNCTAD X.

Mansfield, Edward and Milner, Helen (1999) 'The New Wave of Regionalism', *International Organization* (53/3): 589–627.

Marceau, Gabrielle and Pedersen, Peter N. (1999) 'Is the WTO Open and Transparent? A Discussion of the Relationship of the WTO with Non-governmental Organisations and Civil Society's Claims for more Transparency and Public Participation', *Journal of World Trade*, 33(1), 5–49.

Markandya, Anil (1997) 'Eco-Labelling: An Introduction and Review', in Simonetta Zarilli, Veena Jha and René Vossenaar (eds), *Eco-Labelling and International Trade*, London: Routledge, in association with UNCTAD.

Matambalya, Francis A. S. T. (1995) *The Impact of Regionalisation Schemes on the Export and Economic Performance of Developing Countries, A Case Study of the Southern African Development Community (SADC)*, Südwind: Brandes & Apsel.

Mathews, Jessica T. (1997) 'Power Shift', *Foreign Affairs*, 76(1), 50–66.

Mattoo, A. (1997) 'National Treatment in the GATS: Corner-Stone or Pandora's Box?', *Journal of World Trade*, 31(1), 107–35.

Mattoo, Aaditya (1999) 'Developing Countries in the New Round of GATS Negotiations: From a Defensive to a Pro-Active Role', The WTO/World Bank Conference on Developing Countries in a Millennium Round, Geneva, September 20–21.

Mattoo, Aaditya and Low, Patrick (1999) *Is There a Better Way? Alternative Approaches to Liberalization Under the GATS*, Paper presented at the World Services Congress, Atlanta, November 1–3.

de Melo, Jaime, Panagariya, Arvind (1992), *The New Regionalism in Trade Policy*, London: Centre for Economic Policy Research; Washington, D.C.: the World Bank.

de Melo, Jaime and Panagariya, A. (1993) *New Dimensions in Regional Integration*, Cambridge: Cambridge University Press.

Mensah, Chris (1996) 'The United Nations Commission on Sustainable development', in Jacob Werksman (ed.), *Greening International Institutions*, London: Earthscan Publications.

Mergers and Acquisitions in Canada, (1998) Canadian Annual Directory, Ministry of Commerce.

Messner, Dirk (1997) *The Network Society, Economic Development and International Competitiveness as Problems of Social Governance*, London: Frank Cass.

Metcalfe, David (2000) 'The OECD Agreement to Criminalize Bribery. A Negotiation Analytic Perspective', *Journal of International Negotiation*. 5(1) 119–55.

Miall, Hugh, Ramsbotham, Oliver, and Woodhouse, Tom (1999) *Contemporary Conflict Resolution*, Cambridge: Polity Press.

Micossi, Stefano (1998) 'Confronting Domestic Policies. US–EU Regulatory Policy Cooperation', in Peter S. Rashish (ed.) *A New Approach for the Transatlantic Economic Partnership*. New York: The European Institute.

Minc, Alain (1993) *Le nouveau Moyen âge*, Paris: Gallimard.

Mitchell, Ronald B. (1996) 'Compliance Theory: An Overview', in James Cameron, Jacob Werksman and Peter Roderick (eds), *Improving Compliance with International Environmental Law*, Economic and Social Research Council. London: Earthscan.

Mitrany, David (1966) *A Working Peace System*, Chicago: Quadrangle Books.

Mittelman, James H. (ed.) (1996a) *Globalization. Critical Reflections*, Boulder: Lynne Rienner.

Mittelman, James H. (1996b) 'Rethinking the New Regionalism in the Context of Globalization', *Global Governance*, 3(4), 103–26.

Mittelman, James H. and Johnston, Robert (1999) 'The Globalization of Organized Crime, the Courtesan States, and the Corruption of Civil Society', *Global Governance*, 5, 103–26.

Mols, Manfred (1996) 'Regional Integration and the International System', in Shoji Nishijima and Peter Smith (eds), *Cooperation or Rivalry: Regional Integration in the Americas and the Pacific Rim*, Boulder: Westview Press.

Monnet, Jean (1976) *Mémoires*, Paris: Fayard.

Moran, Theodore H. (1974) *Multinational Corporations and the Politics of Dependence, Copper in Chile*, Princeton: Princeton University Press.

da Motta Veiga, Pedro, de Carvalho Jr, Mário C., Vilmar, Maria Lucia, Façanha and Heraldiva Mucchielli (1997) 'Eco-Labelling Schemes in The European Union and the Impact on Brazilian Exports', in Simonetta Zarilli, Veena Jha, and René Vossenaar (eds), *Eco-Labelling and International Trade*, London: Routledge, in association with UNCTAD.

Mucchielli, Jean-Louis, Buckley, Peter, and Cordell, Victor (1998) 'Globalization and Regionalization: Forces in Concert or in Conflict', in Jean-Louis Mucchielli, Peter Buckley, and Victor Cordell (1998) *Globalization and Regionalization: Strategies, Policies and Economic Environment*, New York: Haworth Press.

Mucchielli, Jean-Louis, Buckley, Peter and Cordell, Victor (1998) *Globalization and Regionalization: Strategies, Policies and Economic Environment*, New York: Haworth Press.

Muchlinski, Peter (1994) *Multinational Enterprises and the Law*, Oxford: Blackwell.

Nader, Ralf (1993) 'Free Trade and the Decline of Democracy', in Ralf Nader (ed.), *The Case Against 'Free Trade', GATT, NAFTA, and the Globalization of Corporate Power*, San Francisco: Earth Island Press.

Narula, Rajneesh (1999) 'Explaining the Growth of Strategic Alliances by European Firms', *Journal of Common Market Studies*, 37(4), 711–23.

Nicolaïdis, Kalypso and Trachtman, Joel P. (1999) 'From Policed Regulation to Managed Recognition: Mapping the Boundary in GATS', Paper delivered to the World Congress Services, Atlanta, November 1–3.

North American Free Trade Agreement (1992) *Assessment of Major Issues*, The United States General Accounting Office, Report to the Honorable Richard A. Gephardt, and Sander Levin, House of Representatives. GAO/GGD-92–131.

North American Free Trade Agreement (1993) *Impact and Implementation*, The United States General Accounting Office, Report to the Congress. Volume 2, GAO/GGD-92-137.

North American Free Trade Agreement (1997) *Assessment of Major Issues*, The United States General Accounting Office, Report to the Congress.

Nuttall, Simon (1990) 'The Commission: Protagonists of inter-Regional Cooperation', in Goffrey Edwards and Elfriede Regelsberger (eds), *Europe's Global Links, the European Community and Inter-Regional Cooperation*, London: Pinter Publishers.

O'Brien, Richard (1992) *Global Financial Integration: The End of Geography*, The Royal Institute of International Affairs, London: Pinter Publishers.

OECD (1994b) Globalization of Industrial Activities: A Case Study of the Clothing Industry. OECD working papers, No. 60, Paris: OECD.

OECD (1999a) *Policy Brief*, October, OECD Observer, Paris: OECD.

OECD (1999b) *Trade, Investment and Development: Reaping the Full Benefits of Open Markets*, Paris: OECD.

Ohmae, Kenichi (1995) *The End of the Nation State, the Rise of Regional Economies*, London: HarperCollins Publishers.

Orme Jr., William A. (1996) *Understanding NAFTA, Mexico, Free Trade and the New North America*, Austin: University of Texas Press.

Ostry, Sylvia and Nelson, Richard R. (1995) *Techno-Nationalism and Techno-Globalism, Conflict and Cooperation*, Washington, D.C.: The Brookings Institution.

Panagariya, Arvind (1996) 'The Free Trade of the Americas: Good for Latin America', *The World Economy*, 19(5), 485–515.

Panchamukhi, V. R. (1996) *WTO and Industrial Policies*, East Asian Development: Lessons for a new Global Environment, Study No. 7. UNCTAD. Geneva: United Nations.

Panitch, Leo (1996) 'Rethinking the Role of the State', in James H. Mittelman (ed.), *Globalization. Critical reflections*, Boulder: Lynne Rienner.

Passy, Florence (1999) 'Supranational Political Opportunities as a Channel of Globalization of Political Conflicts. The Case of the Rights of Indigenous Peoples', in Donatella della Porta, Hanspeter Kriesi, and Dieter Rucht (eds), *Social Movements in a Globalizing World*, Basingstoke: Macmillan Press.

Peet, R. (1984) *Manufacturing Industry and Economic Development in the SADCC Countries, Energy, Environment and Development in Africa*, Uppsala: The Scandinavian Institute of African Studies

Pellerin, Hélène (1996) 'Global Restructuring and International Migration: Consequences for the Globalization of Politics', in Eleonore Kofman and Gillian Youngs (eds), *Globalization Theory and Practice,*

Petrella, R. (1996) 'Globalization and Internationalization' in Robert Boyer and Daniel Drache (eds) *States against Markets: the limits of globalization*, London: Routledge.

Pfetsch, Frank (1995) 'The Development of European Institutions', in *Regional Integration Process, European Union/Southern Africa Development Community*, Bordeaux: CEAN.

Pfetsch, Frank (1998a) 'Negotiating the European Union. A Negotiation Network Approach', *Journal of International Negotiation*, 3(3), 293–317.

Pfetsch, Frank (1998b) 'Globalisation: A Threat or a Challenge for the State?', *Journal of International Relations and Development*, 1(1), 164–80.

Pfetsch, Frank and Landau, Alice (2000) 'Symmetry and Asymmetry in international Negotiations', *Journal of International Negotiation*. 5(1): 21–42.

Polyani, Karl (1944) *The Great Transformation*, New York: Rinehart & Company.

della Porta, Donatella and Kriesi, Hanspeter (1999) 'Social Movements in a Globalizing World', in Donatella della Porta, Hanspeter Kriesi and Dieter Rucht (eds), *Social Movements in a Globalizing World*, Basingstoke: Macmillan Press – now Palgrave.

Poulantzas, Nicos (1974) *Classes in Contemporary Capitalism*, London: NLB.

Preeg, Ernest H. (1970) *Traders and Diplomats*, Washington, D.C.: The Brookings Institute.

Preusse, Heinz G. (1994) 'Regional Integration in the Nineties, Stimulation or Threat to the Multilateral Trading System', *Journal of World Trade*, 28(4).

Prieto, Francisco Javier and Stephenson, Sherry (1999) *Multilateral and Regional Liberalization of Trade in Services*, Paper presented at the World Services Congress, Atlanta, November 1–3.

Qureshi, Asif H. (1996) *The World Trade Organisation, Implementing International Trade Norms*, Manchester: Manchester University Press.

Raghavan, Chakravarthi (1996) *The 'New Issues' and Developing Countries: Environment, Competition and Labour Standards*, Background Paper, Seminar of the WTO and developing countries. Geneva, September 10–11.

Randall, Stephen J. (1995) 'Managing Trilateralism: The United States, Mexico, and Canada in the Post-NAFTA Era', in Stephen J. Randall and Herman W. Konrad (eds), *NAFTA in Transition*, Calgary: Calgary University Press.

Rashish, Peter S. (1997) 'Conclusions from the Conference', in Peter S. Rashish (ed.), *Transatlantic and Global Ecomonic Integration. The Role of Investment*, Washington, D.C.: The European Institute.

Regional Experiences in the Economic Integration Process of Developing Countries, Geneva: UNCTAD, UNCTAD/ITCD/TSB/1.

Ricupero, Rubens (1996) 'Foreword' pp. xiii–xiv, in *Handbook of Economic Integration and Cooperation Groupings of Developing Countries, Regional and Sub-regional Economic Integration Groupings*, Volume I. New York: UNCTAD.

Ricupero, Rubens (1997) 'UNCTAD and Global Investment Cooperation', in Peter S. Rashish (ed.), *Transatlantic and Global Ecomonic Integration. The Role of Investment*, Washington, D.C.: The European Institute.

Risse-Kappen, Thomas (1995) 'Bringing Transnational Relations Back In: Introduction', in Thomas Risse-Kappen (ed.), *Bringing Transnational Relations Back In, Non-State Actors, Domestic Structures and international Institutions*, Cambridge: Cambridge University Press.

Robson, Peter (1993) 'The New Regionalism and Developing Countries', *Journal of Common Market Studies*, 31(3), 329–48.

Rodrik, Dani (1995) 'Developing Countries after the Uruguay Round', in *International Monetary and Financial Issues for the 1990s*, Geneva: United Nations.

Rodrik, Dani (1997) *Has Globalization Gone Too Far?*, Washington: Institute for International Economics.

Rodrik, Dani (1999) *The New Global Economy and Developing Countries: Making Openness Work*, Policy Essay No. 24. Washington, D.C.: John Hopkins University Press.

Rosenau, James N. (1990) *Turbulence in World Politics, A Theory of Change and Continuity*, Princeton: Princeton University Press.

Rosenau, James N. (1992) 'Governance, Order, and Change in World Politics', in James N. Rosenau and Ernst-Otto Czempiel (eds), *Governance Without Government: Order and Changes in World Politics*, Cambridge: Cambridge University Press.

Rosenau, James N. (1993) 'The New Global Order: Underpinning and Outcomes', in Armand Clesse, Richard Cooper, and Yoshikazu Sakamoto (eds), *The International System after the Collapse of the East-West Order*, Dordrecht: Martinus Nijhoff Publishers.

Rosenau, James N. (1996) 'The Dynamics of Globalization: Toward an Operational Formulation', *Security Dialogue*, 27(3), 247–62.

Rosenau, James N. (1997) *Along the Domestic-Foreign Frontier, Exploring Governance in a Turbulent World*, Cambridge: Cambridge University Press.

Rowthorn, Robert (1996) *East Asian Development: The Flying Geese Paradigm Reconsidered*, East Asian Development: Lessons for a new Global Environment, Study No. 8. UNCTAD. Geneva: United Nations.

Rowthorn, Robert and Kozul-Wright, Richard (1998) *Globalization and Economic Convergence: an Assessment*, Discussion Paper No. 131, Geneva: UNCTAD.

Rubio, Luis (1996) 'Mexico, NAFTA, and the Pacific Basin', in Shoji Nishijima and Peter Smith (eds), *Cooperation or Rivalry: Regional Integration in the Americas and the Pacific Rim*, Boulder: Westview Press.

Ruggie, John Gerard (1993) 'Territorialiy and Beyond: Problematizing Modernity in International Relations', *International Organization*, 47(1), 139–74.

Ruggie, John Gerard (1998) *Constructing the World Polity, Essays on International Institutionalization*, London: Routledge.

Rugman, Alan and Gerstrin, Michael (1994) 'NAFTA's Treatment of Foreign Investment', in Alan M. Rugman (ed.), *Foreign Investment and NAFTA*, Columbia: University of South Carolina Press.

Rugman, Alan and Soloway, Julie (1998) 'Corporate Strategies and NAFTA when Environmental Regulations are Barriers to Trade', in Alan M. Rugman (ed.), *Foreign Investment and NAFTA*, Columbia: University of South Carolina Press.

Rugman, Alan and Verbeke, Alain (1994) 'Foreign Direct Investment and NAFTA: A Conceptual Framework', in Alan M. Rugman (ed.), *Foreign Investment and NAFTA*, Columbia: University of South Carolina Press.

Ruigrok, W. and van Tulder, R. (1995) *The Logic of International Restructuring*, London: Routledge.

Sachs, Jeffrey (1996) 'Beyond Bretton Woods: A New Blueprint', in David M. Balam and Michael Veseth (eds), *Readings in International Political Economy*, Upper Saddle River: Prentice Hall.

Salvatore, Dominik (1998) 'Globalization and International Competitiveness', in John Dunning (ed.), *Globalization, Trade and Foreign Direct Investment*, Amsterdam: Elsevier.

Sassen, Saskia (1996) 'The Spatial Organization of Information Industries: Implications for the Role of the State', in James Mittelman (ed.), *Globalization. Critical Reflections*, Boulder: Lynne Rienner.

Sauvant, Karl (1998) 'Introduction', *Expert meeting on existing regional and multilateral investment agreements and their development dimensions*, Geneva: UNCTAD.

Schaeffer, Robert K. (1997) *Understanding Globalization, the Social Consequences of Political, Economic, and Environmental Change*, Lanham: Rowman & Littlefield Publishers.

Schatan, Claudia (1987) 'Out of the Crisis: Mexico', in Diana Tussie and David Glover (eds), *The Developing Countries in World Trade, Policies and Bargaining Strategies*, Boulder: Lynne Rienner Publishers.

Schmitter, Philippe (1969) 'Three Neo-Functional Hypotheses about International Integration', *International Organization*, 23(1), 161–6.

Schmitter, Philippe (1970) 'Central American Integration: Spill over, Spill around on Encapsulation', *Journal of Common Market Studies* 5(1), 1–48.

Schott, Jeffrey (1991) 'Trading Blocs and the World Trading System', *World Economy*, 14(1), 1–17.

Schwanen, Daniel (1996) 'Investment in the Global economy: Key Issues in Rulemaking', in Pierre Sauvé and Daniel Schwanen (eds), *Investment Rules for the Global Economy*, Ottawa: C. D. Howe Institute.

Seitz, John L. (1995) *Global Issues: An Introduction*, London: Blackwell Publishers.

Singh, Ajit (1996) *Savings, investment and the Corporation in the East Asian Miracle*, East Asian Development: Lessons for a new Global Environment, Study No. 9, UNCTAD. Geneva: United Nations

Soros, George (1999) *The Crisis of Global Capitalism, Open Society Endangered*, New York: PublicAffairs.

Spero, Jean Edelman (1981) *The Politics of International Economic Relations*, New York, St Martin's Press.

Srinivasan, T. N., Whalley, John, and Wooton, Ian (1995) 'Measuring the Effects of Regionalism on Trade and Welfare', in Kym Anderson and Richard Blackhurst, (eds), *Regional integration and the Global Trading System*. New York: Harvester Wheatsheaf

Stairs, Denis (1996) 'The Canadian Dilemma in North America', in Joyce Heobing, Sydney Weintraub, and Delal Baer (eds), *NAFTA and Sovereignty*, Washington, D.C.: The Center for Strategic and International Studies.

Steinberg, Richard (1998) 'Exploring the Prospects for Transatlantic Trade Policy Cooperation in Asia', in Richard H. Steinberg and Bruce Stokes (eds), *Partners or Competitors? The Prospects for US–European Cooperation on Asian Trade*, London: Rowman & Littlefield.

Stephenson, S. and Rieto, F. J. (1999) *Multilateral and Regional Liberalization of Trade and Services*, Paper delivered to the World Services Congress, Atlanta, November 1–3, 1999.

Stojstedt, Gunnar, Spector, Bertram, and Zartman, William (1994) 'The Dynamics of Regime-Building Negotiations', in Gunnar Sjostedt, Bertram Spector and William Zartman (eds), *Negotiating International Regimes, Lessons Learned From the United Nations Conference on Environment and Development (UNCED)*, PIN Project. London: Graham & Trotman.

Stopford, John M., and Strange, Susan, with Henley, John S. (1991) *Rival States, Rival Firms, Competition for World Market Shares*, Cambridge: Cambridge University Press.

Strange, Roger (1996) 'Trading Blocs, Trade Liberalization and Foreign Direct Investment', in George Chryssochoidis, Carla Millar and Jeremy Clegg (eds), *Internationalisation Strategies*, New York: St Martin's Press.

Strange, Susan (1986) 'Supranationals and the States', in John Hall (ed.), *States in History*, Oxford: Basil Blackwell.

Strange, Susan (1988) *States and Markets, An Introduction to International Political Economy*, London: Pinter Publishers.

Strange, Susan (1989) 'The Future of the American Empire' pp. 435–43, in Ernst Czempiel and James Rosenau (eds), *Approaches to World Politics for the 1990s*, Lexington: Lexington Books.

Strange, Susan (1995) 'The Limits of Politics', *Government and Opposition*, 30(3), 291–311.

Strange, Susan (1996) *The Retreat of the State: Diffusion of Power in the World Economy*, Cambridge: Cambridge University Press.

Strange, Susan (1997a) 'An International Political Economy Perspective', in John H. Dunning (ed.), *Governments, Globalization and International Business*, Oxford: Oxford University Press.

Strange, Susan (1997b) *Casino Capitalism*, Manchester: Manchester University Press.

Strange, Susan (1998) *Mad Money*, Manchester: Manchester University Press.

Tantraporn, Apiradi (1996) 'ASEAN Regional Economic Co-operation', in *Regionalism and its Place in the Multilateral Trading System*, OECD: OECD Documents.

Taylor, Paul (1990) 'A Conceptual Typology of International Organization', in John Groom and Paul Taylor (eds), *Frameworks for International Co-operation*, London: Pinter Publishers.

Teichman, Judith (1994) 'Dismantling the Mexican State and the Role of the Private Sector', in Ricardo Grinspun and Maxwell A. Cameron (eds), *The Political Economy of North American Free Trade*, New York: St. Martin's Press.

Ten Kate, Adriaan (1994) 'Is Mexico a Back Door to the U.S. Market or a Niche in the World's Largest Free Trade Area?', in Victor Bulmer-Homas, Nikkii Craske and Monica Serrano (eds), *Mexico and the North American Free Trade Agreement, Who Will Benefit?* New York: St Martin's Press.

The East Asian Miracle, Economic Growth and Public Policy 1993, World Bank Policy Research Report, Oxford: Oxford University Press.

Thomson, Janice and Krasner, Stephen (1989) 'Global Transactions and the Consolidation of Sovereignty', in James N. Rosenau and Ernst-Otto Czempiel (eds), *Global Changes and Theoretical Challenges*, Lexington: Lexington Books.

Thurow, Lester (1992) *Head to Head: the Economic Battle among Japan, Europe and America*, New York: Morrow.

Tilly, Charles (1992) *Coercion, Capital, and European States AD 990–1992*, Cambridge: Blackwell Publishers.

Tuathail, Gearoid O., Herod, Andrew, and Roberts, Susan M. (1998) 'Negotiating Unruly Problematics', in: Gearoid O. Tuathail, Andrew Herod, and Susan M. Roberts (eds), *An Unruly World? Globalization, Governance and Geography*, London: Routledge.

Tussie, Diana (1987) *The Less Developed Countries and the World Trading System, A Challenge to the GATT*, London: Pinter Publishers.

UNCTAD (1994a) Trade and Development Report, New York: United Nations.

UNCTAD (1994b) *The Outcome of the Uruguay Round: An Initial Assessment, Supporting Papers to the Trade and Development Report*, New York: United Nations.

UNCTAD (1995a) Trade and Development Report, New York: United Nations.

UNCTAD (1995b) *International Monetary and Financial Issues for the 1990s*, Vol. 6, New York: United Nations.

UNCTAD (1996a) Trade and Development Report, New York: United Nations.

UNCTAD (1996b) *East Asian Development: Lessons for a New Global Environment* Secretariat Report to the Conference on East Asian Development, Study No. 10. Geneva: United Nations.

UNCTAD (1996c) Handbook of Economic Integration and Cooperation Groupings of Developing Countries, Volume I. *Regional and Subregional Economic Integration Groupings* New York: United Nations.

UNCTAD (1997a) *Trade and Development Report: Globalization, Distribution and Growth*, New York: United Nations.

UNCTAD (1997b) *World Investment Report: Transnational Corporations, Market Structure and Competition Policy*, New York: United Nations.

UNCTAD (1998) *Trade and Development Report: Financial Instability and Growth in Africa*, New York: United Nations.

UNCTAD (1999a) *Trade and Development Report: Fragile Recovery and Risks, Trade Finance and Growth*, New York: United Nations.

UNCTAD (1999b) *World Investment Report: Foreign Direct Investment and the Challenge of Development*, New York: United Nations.

UNCTAD (1999c) *International Monetary and Financial Issues for the 1990s*, New York: United Nations.

UNCTAD/ICC (2000), *World's Largest Transnational Corporations*, Press release, Bangkok: UNCTAD X, TAD/INF/2839. http://www.unctad-10.org-

UNCTAD X (2000), *Beyond the Unification of Markets: A Global Community of Cooperation and Shared Knowledge for Security and Development*, Report of the Secretary-General, http://www.unctad-10.org-

UNCTAD, *Trade and development Direction for the 21st century: The Academic Perspective*, High level round table with eminent economists, http://www.unctad-10.org-

United Nations Development Program (1998) Human Development Report.

van der Pijl, Kees (1993) 'The Sovereignty of Capital Impaired, Social Forces and Codes of Conduct for Multinational Corporations', in Henk Overbeek (ed.), *Restructuring Hegemony in the Global Political Economy, The Rise of Transnational Neo-Liberalism in the 1980s*, London: Routledge.

van Tulder, R. and Junne, G. (1988) *European Multinationals in Core Technologies*, New York: John Wiley.

Vermulst, Edwin (1999) *Antidumping and Anti-Subsidy Concerns for Developing Countries in the Millennium Round: Key Areas for Reform*, http://www.cid.harvard.edu.

Vernon, Raymond (1977) *Storm over the Multinationals, the Real Issues*, Cambridge: Harvard University Press.

Vernon, Raymond (1994) 'Multinationals and Governments: Key Actors in the NAFTA', in Lorraine Eden (ed.) *Multinationals in North America*, Calgary: The University of Calgary Press.

Viner, Jacob (1975) *The Customs Union Issues*, New York: Carnegie Endowment in International Peace.

Wallace, William (1990) *The Transformation of Western Europe*, Royal Institute of International Affairs, London: Pinter Publishers.

Wallace, William (1994) *Regional Integration: The West European Experience*, Washington, D.C.: The Brookings Institute.

Wapner, Paul (1996) *Environmental Activism and World Civil Politics*, Albany: State University of New York Press.

Weber, Steve and Zysman, John (1996) 'The Risk that Mercantilism will Define the Next Security System', in Wayne Sandoltz *et al.* (eds), *The Highest Stakes, The Economic Foundations of the Next Security System*, New York: Oxford University Press.

Werksman, Jacob (1996) 'Introduction', in Jacob Werksman (ed.), *Greening International Institutions*, London: Earthscan Publications.

Whitley, Richard (1992) *Business Systems in East Asia, Firms, Markets, and Societies*, London: Sage Publications.

Whitman, Richard (1997) 'The International Identity of the European Union: Instruments as Identity', in Alice Landau and Richard Whitman (eds), *Rethinking the European Union: Institutions, Interests and Identities*, Basingstoke: Macmillan Press–now Palgrave.

Whitman, Richard (1999) 'The Common Foreign and Security Policy after Enlargment', in Victoria Curzon Price, Alice Landau, and Richard Whitman (eds), *The Enlargement of the European Union: Strategies and Issues*, London: Routledge.

Winham, Gilbert (1986) *Trading with Canada: the Canada–US Free Trade Agreement* New York: Priority Press Publications.

Wolvaardt, Gustaaf (1998) 'Opportunities and Challenges for Developing Countries in the Health Sector', in Simonetta Zarilli and Colette Kinnon (eds), *International Trade in Health Services: A Development Perspective*, Geneva: United Nations and World Health Organization.

World Bank (1997) *Global Economic Prospects and the Developing Countries*, Washington, D.C.: The World Bank.

World Bank (1997) *World Development Report: The State in a Changing World.* Washington, D.C.: The World Bank.

World Bank (2000) *Intra-Regional Trade in subSaharan Africa* (1991), Washington, D.C.: The World Bank.

WTO Annual Report (1997) (1998) (1999). Geneva: WTO.

WTO (1996) *Trade Policy Review, United States* Report by the WTO Secretariat. Geneva: WTO, WT/TPR/15/16.

WTO (1997b) *Trade Policy Review, European Union* Report by the WTO Secretariat. Geneva: WTO. WT/TPR/S/30.

WTO (1998) *Guide to the Uruguay Round Agreements*, regional trading arrangements, The WTO Secretariat, The Hague: Kluwer Law International.

Yarbrough, Beth V. and Yarbrough, Robert M. (1997) 'Dispute Settlement In International Trade: Regionalism and Procedural Coordination', in Edward

Mansfield and Helen V. Milner (eds), *The Political Economy of Regionalism*, New York: Columbia University Press.

Yergin, Daniel and Stanislaw, Joseph (2000) 'The Commanding Heights: The Battle Between Government and the Marketplace that is Remaking the Modern World', in Frank J. Lechner and John Boli (eds), *The Globalization Reader*, Oxford: Blackwell Publishers.

Youngs, Gillian (1996) 'Dangers of Discourse: The Case of Globalization', in Eleonore Kofman and Gillian Youngs (eds), *Globalization Theory and Practice*, London: Pinter Publishers.

Zacher, Mark W. (1992) 'The Decaying Pillars of the Westphalian Temple: Implications for International Order and Governance', in James N. Rosenau and Ernst-Otto Czempiel (eds), *Governance Without Government: Order and Changes in World Politics*, Cambridge: Cambridge University Press.

Index